John Corbet Anderson

A Short Chronicle Concerning the Parish of Croydon in the County of Surrey

John Corbet Anderson

A Short Chronicle Concerning the Parish of Croydon in the County of Surrey

ISBN/EAN: 9783337428488

Printed in Europe, USA, Canada, Australia, Japan

Cover: Foto ©Lupo / pixelio.de

More available books at **www.hansebooks.com**

A SHORT

CHRONICLE

CONCERNING THE

Parish of Croydon

IN THE COUNTY OF

SURREY

BY

J. CORBET ANDERSON

LONDON
REEVES & TURNER, 196, STRAND
1882

CONTENTS.

	PAGE
INTRODUCTORY	1
CHAPTER I.—GEOLOGY	3–6
" II.—PREHISTORIC CROYDON . . .	7–12
" III.—CROYDON IN THE TIME OF THE ROMANS	13–17
" IV.—SAXON CROYDON . . .	18–25
" V.—THE OLD CHURCH . . .	26–61
" VI.—PARISH REGISTER . .	62–67
" VII.—DOMESDAY BOOK . .	68–70
" VIII.—SITE OF CROYDON CHURCH AND PALACE	71–74
" IX.—THE ARCHIEPISCOPAL PALACE AT CROYDON	75–95
" X.—LORDS OF THE MANOR . .	96–144
" XI.—MANORIAL	145–168
" XII.—ANCIENT DESCRIPTION AND CHRONOLOGY	169–181
" XIII.—PAST TOPOGRAPHY	182–195
" XIV.—MISCELLANEOUS	196–226
" XV.—MODERN DEVELOPMENT . . .	227–244

INTRODUCTORY.

HAVING lived for many years amid the lovely scenery of Croydon, and inquired concerning the history of its Palace, Old Church, and Manors, besides having been an eye-witness of the numerous changes that have taken place here in recent times, it has occurred to me to write a short topographical and historical account of this parish, such a book as, without clashing with more learned and elaborate treatises, may serve to convey to the general reader some trustworthy information respecting the locality; and this I have endeavoured to accomplish in the following pages.

A Short Chronicle concerning the Parish of Croydon.

CHAPTER I.

GEOLOGY.

GEOLOGICALLY speaking, Croydon is situated at the edge of the London clay basin at its junction with the chalk. The cretaceous or chalk strata are well represented at the southern end of our parish. Chalk is of marine origin, and indicative of a rather deep sea and a warmer period than now obtains in England. The minute forms that constitute a large portion of the chalk belong to the lowest division of the animal kingdom, the Protozoa, which includes, besides them, the sponges, infusorial animalcules, and some other forms. Accumulations are now taking place in the depths of the Atlantic of the same species of Foraminifera as is washed out of the Croydon chalk, and associated with these are silicious parts of sponges and diatoms, that, hereafter, may become aggregated together, and form nodules or bands of flints, similar to those seen in the chalk of our parish. But that we are not still living in the cretaceous epoch is evident by the disappearance from the ocean of the huge Ammonite, and from the earth of the Pterodactyl, a gigantic winged lizard, as well as other now extinct reptiles. The chalk period was brought to its close by a change in the physical geography of these parts, through an elevation of the sea-bed probably, or it may have been by a shrinking of the sea; yet, whichever was the process, it preceded the commencement of what geologists term the Tertiary era.

Of the Tertiary series, the first are the Thanet sands, so called from the Isle of Thanet, where they attain their greatest thickness. These have but a limited extent near Croydon; they are seen, however, in the railway cutting near Combe Lane, and in the large pit beyond, at Duppa's Hill, and at Croham Hurst. As the fossils found in them indicate, these sands are also of marine origin. To these sea-beds succeed the Woolwich and Reading series, partly of fluviatile, estuarine and marine origin, showing a further change in the physical conditions of the district —evidence of land-surfaces down which rivers flowed, teeming with molluscous life, which have left traces of shell-beds at Park Hill, Duppa's Hill, East Croydon Station, and the Croydon Sewage and Gas Works, Waddon.* The Woolwich beds in question indicate sub-tropical conditions. Other geological revolutions following, this area became covered with a newer deposit of sand and pebbles, referred to the Oldhaven beds, those rounded pebbles so largely exposed on Addington and Duppa's Hill, and at Croham Hurst; the same being evidently due to some old coast line of chalk, from the flints of which they were derived, worn and rounded by a long-continued sea-wave attrition. Croham Hurst and Addington Hills, indeed, appear to have once formed small shingle-beached islands, peeping out from the ocean, a condition in which they seem to have remained for ages.

After the deposition of these sands, pebbles and estuarine beds, classed as the Lower Tertiaries, another physical and climatal change occurred, during which was deposited the

* "Lecture on the Geology of Croydon," &c. By J. Morris, F.G.S.

stratum known as the London clay, a thick and tenacious accumulation, extending over a considerable portion of the east and north sides of the parish. The muddy deposit referred to, seems to have been derived from the wear and tear of some old southern and western land, during a long period of time, in which, as in the preceding chalk period, a much warmer climate prevailed here than at present; as is evident from numerous remains of turtles and crocodiles found in the London clay. Of its Molluscan life, rich in genera, many are now restricted to tropical seas. In this deposit likewise are found remains of fishes, such as the shark and ray; nor are there wanting indications of land wading birds, and birds of prey; besides coniferæ, and the fruit of a peculiar palm, related to the Nipa, now flourishing in India.

With the London clay the Lower Eocene formations seen in the neighbourhood of Croydon terminate, and then a hiatus, apparently representing a long-continued period, intervenes between it and the deposit of the overlying gravel—an imperfection, or gap, involving the disappearance of the whole of the Miocene and Pliocene formations; and the magnitude of which may be inferred from this, that more than one-third of the land of Europe, it is conjectured, has been formed beneath the sea, and raised above it in the interval between the Eocene formation and the deposition of that superficial gravel which covers so large a portion of our parish. The geological record of this area consequently is imperfect: a succession of vast marine accumulations have been removed by a mighty denudation, either aqueous, sub-aerial, or otherwise. Like whole chapters torn out of a book, the loss of which can only be understood by referring to some more perfect copy, so the number and nature of these missing strata can only be ascertained by a careful collation with those sedimentary rocks wherein the history of the various strata constituting the surface of the earth is more continuous.

How far this evident interference with the succession of the crusts of the earth is due, either directly or indirectly, to that catastrophe known as the Noaic flood, we cannot say; yet, that was no very partial flood, as some pretend, which occurred when, in the sublime language of Scripture, "all the fountains of the great deep were broken up," and "all the high hills, that were under the whole heaven were covered." It must have been a far extending and mighty deluge indeed, when "all flesh died that moved upon the earth;" for man had lived long enough on the globe to have traversed over a wide area of its surface. Grotius called attention to the curious and numerous ancient testimonies of the flood; and Humboldt has remarked that similar traditions exist among all the nations of the earth. Like the relics of a vast shipwreck, these are highly interesting in the philosophical study of our species.

We will conclude this brief reference to the various circumstances under which, at successive periods, that portion of the earth included within the boundaries of Croydon appears to have been gradually adapted by the Great Creator for the residence of man, by recapitulating that, generally speaking, the crust of this parish exhibits primarily oceanic deposit. And if any confirmation were needed to prove that the ground on which Croydon now stands was formerly submerged by the sea, it will be found in the fact that a mass of petrified shells and oysters was found, about thirty feet down, when sinking a well at Shirley Vicarage; coupled with the circumstance that, when digging the well at the reservoir, on Park Hill, large oysters were found scattered through the sand. A petrified lobster and bed of oysters were also found at the north base of Duppa's Hill. Moreover, at a depth of 150 feet, they went through plenty of marine shells, and a great bed of oysters, when boring Aubyn's well, on the top of Norwood Hill.

CHAPTER II.

PREHISTORIC CROYDON.

IN writing a history of Croydon, the circumstance must not be overlooked that traces have been detected of an occupation by man of this neighbourhood in prehistoric times. Groping in the twilight of an uncertified past, geologists tell of a period when man shared the possession of Europe with the mammoth, the cave bear, the woolly-haired rhinoceros, and other now extinct animals; and, certain it is, human relics have been discovered in caves, and that, too, in England, strangely associated with bones of the hyæna and the elk. A fauna differing so widely from that now inhabiting our country would seem to imply climatal changes various and great. This they define as the Palæolithic, or older Stone Age; and then we come to a later Stone Age, called the Neolithic. The physical geography of North-western Europe seems to have settled into its present configuration ere the beautiful weapons and instruments made of flint and other kinds of stone of this later and more polished Stone Period, were fabricated. The untutored intelligence of the savage would naturally prompt him to adapt the hard stones he could so easily pick up to the piercing and cutting requirements of that fishing and hunting life which he led; and by chipping, or continuous rubbing, after long practice, the stone arrow and spear heads, cutting implements, saws, and perforated stone hammers found in ancient graves or barrows came to be formed. With these tools, rude although they seem to us, our primitive progenitors may have cut down trees, scooped them into canoes, or built huts, slain animals or enemies, and cut up their food.

Relics of the Neolithic or later Stone Age have been found at Croydon. Some time since a mutilated, but finely formed, white stone cutting implement was dug out of the gravel in this immediate neighbourhood; the accompanying sketch represents the interesting fragment.*

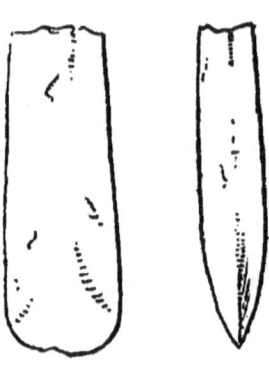

Overlapping into the Stone Age, in prehistoric times, in Western and in Northern Europe, the use of bronze appears to have preceded that of iron. The forms and ornamentation of the bronze instruments and weapons of what has been termed the Age of Bronze are singular, and very unlike those of the corresponding weapons and instruments in iron. It is a remarkable fact that wherever these bronze cutting instruments, gouges, or weapons are found, whether in the far west of Ireland, in Scotland, in Scandinavia, in Germany, or still further east in the Sclavonic countries, they are the same,—not merely similar in character, but identical. That these bronze weapons and implements were not derived from the Romans appears from this, that they are not discovered on Roman sites, and that they are frequently found in the south-west of Ireland and in Scandinavia, neither of which countries were occupied by the Romans; moreover, an analysis of the bronze of the Bronze Age and that used by the Romans shows that they materially differ. As it is certain that after the conquest of Britain by the Romans our forefathers became better

* The late Mr. West, of Wallington, found the stone celt referred to, when digging for the foundation of his cottages on Bandon Hill; it is now in the cabinet of Mr. Smee, of Wallington.

acquainted with iron,—a metal far more abundant, easier to work, and consequently one the use of which must soon have superseded that of bronze,—we are probably justified in assuming that the bronze celts which have been found in this neighbourhood were cast before the Christian era.

A number of articles in bronze were found in Wickham Park, and were deposited in the British Museum in the year 1855. A better lot of bronze celts, however, was discovered about the year 1866, as some men were digging out the earth preparatory to building one of the houses nearly opposite the Rectory, Beddington. The various forms of the articles comprised in the latter find, are exhibited in the annexed sketch.*

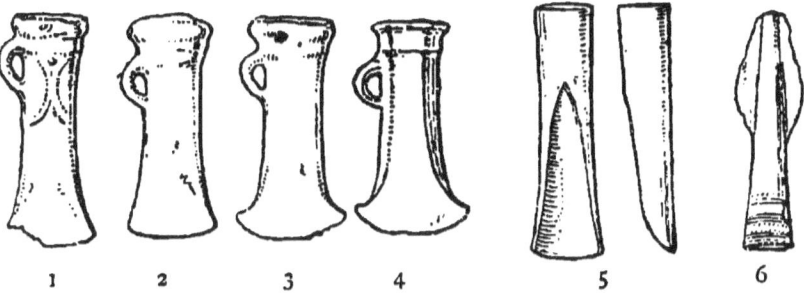

1   2   3   4   5   6

During that long period which preceded the landing of the Romans in Britain, the aspect of Croydon doubtless was very different to what it now is. Towards the south probably were, as there still are, tracts of heath and chalk lands, whose arid soils and iron-bound surface disqualified them for the production of trees other than those of a stunted growth; but mile upon mile eastward, and westward, and northward, stretched the primeval

* On the objects numbered 1, 2, 3, 5, and 6, the late J. Wickham Flower, F.G.S., wrote a Paper, which was printed by the Surrey Archæological Society. Figure 4, belonging to the same find, afterwards came into the possession of the author.

Coed, as yet uncleared by the axe. A remnant of this immense forest long afterwards was called Norwood. Through the lower parts of this leafy wilderness coursed unruly streams that, swollen in the rainy winter time, or flooded by the intermittent Bourne, ever and anon angrily would overflow every impediment that arrested their onward progress. Here a gigantic oak tree, struck by lightning, or succumbing to hoary age, falling athwart the stream, might arrest its progress, and cause it to overflow its channel, when the waters would wriggle out for themselves a new course through the valley, or swamp the neighbouring country. This must have caused meres and reedy stagnant pools to abound in the hollows of the undrained surface of ancient Croydon. Surrounding acres then, being covered by forest and reedy mere, it may easily be conceived that animals such as the wolf, the bear, the fox, the badger, and the wild cat sought and obtained an asylum in the gloomy recesses of those woods; and that the heron, bittern, snipe, and water-rail were busy among the rushes and flags of the ponds which, in our time, have become clean meadows.

The first inhabitant of this locality probably was the Kelt or Celt, and the science of language shews that Keltic or Celtic is the oldest of the Japhetic or Aryan family in Europe. Long after the aboriginal Celt had been driven from these parts, Cæsar wrote:—"The inhabitants of the interior of Britain are said by tradition to be the aborigines, but the coast is peopled by those who had passed over from Belgium [Belgic Gaul] for the purpose of plunder and making war." Among the various tribes peopling the south-eastern corner of Britain, when the second invasion of Britain by the Romans occurred, Ptolemy mentions the Cantii and Regni. From the Cantii the neighbouring country of Kent derives its name. Those districts to which, afterwards, the names Surrey and Sussex were applied, belonged to that kingdom of the Regni whose chief resided at Regnum (Chichester). The Belgæ had migrated westward into Hants, Wilts, and Somerset.

Vestiges of Celtic speech linger in one or two names of places in this neighbourhood; but more of this hereafter.

Our Celtic and early British ancestors enjoyed, perhaps, a higher degree of civilization than is generally supposed. They undoubtedly had also a religious belief of some description, and it is quite possible, and even probable, that the hideous rites of Baal and of Druidism have been practised, either on neighbouring heights, or amid the recesses of that great oak forest which formerly covered the larger portion of this parish. There is a name associated with one of the old manors of Croydon, the etymology of which has been traced to the Saxon *Hali* or *Halig*, holy; the terminal *ing* denotes originating from. Within the memory of living men the now curtailed estate known as Haling extended up to Duppa's Hill Terrace, but I am inclined to surmise that this sacred designation of Haling or Holy originally was applied to a district more extensive even than the boundary mentioned, and that it referred generally to all that elevated tract or tongue of land, the descent from which lands the pedestrian in Waddon on the one side, and on the other at the old churchyard. If this be a right conjecture, then we have in our midst a veritable high place, as well as a declivity sloping downwards towards a valley, where, in former ages, oak trees, thick set, entwining their gigantic limbs, may have caused shadowy recesses, like those amid which, as we read, the Druids practised their gloomy rites. The vale and base of hill alluded to formerly were plentifully watered by streams. Now running streams were also the objects of superstitious reverence with our heathen forefathers. Associations in connection with the various faiths of our forefathers seem to cluster round that neighbourhood. Close at hand lies Waddon, anciently spelt *Woddens*, a name clearly derived from Woden, the Saxon hero-god, whose idol may have been worshipped at one time on the spot. Underneath the hill stands the representative of that ancient Christian Temple, the origin of which is lost in a remote obscurity. There must be some reason for all these combining together just at this particular spot.

CHAPTER III.

CROYDON IN THE TIME OF THE ROMANS.

It may be inferred from certain military monuments they have left behind in the neighbourhood, that the Romans were no strangers to this district. Near to the south-eastern boundary of our parish may be seen the remains of a stupendous earthwork, which is traditionally associated with the conquest of Britain by the Romans, and called Cæsar's Camp. Not far off, but in an exactly opposite direction, is another earthwork, also named Cæsar's Camp. A straight line drawn from the former earthwork in Holwood Park to the other on Wimbledon Common, would pass through the centre of Croydon. Like the fragment of that circular earthwork on the hill known as War Coppice, at Caterham, these entrenched camps may originally have had a British origin, and were subsequently utilised by the Romans, and perhaps afterwards by the Saxons, in their various wars one with another, or against the Danes.

The Greek geographer Ptolemy, who lived in the first half of the second century, mentions $Νοιόμαγος$, which he places to the south of London, in the territory of the Regni. In the great Itinerary of the Roman empire that goes by the name of Antoninus, in the portion relating to Britain, Noviomagus is mentioned in the second Iter thus:—

Londinio	
Noviomago	M. p. x.
Vagniacis	M. p. xviii.
Durobrivis	M. p. ix.

The site of the Roman station, Noviomagus, has long been an undecided point with the learned. Some antiquaries have supposed it to have been situated in the vicinity of Holwood, where, independently of the earthwork just referred to, several undoubtedly Roman buildings and other remains have been found;* others, including Camden, Gale, Horsley, and Freeman, concur in placing the site of Noviomagus at Woodcote, near Croydon. The name Wallington, spelt in Domesday Book *Waletone*, implies, indeed, that somewhere hereabouts once stood a fortified or walled town.

At least one Roman road passed through the parish of Croydon. Like other roads made by the Romans in Britain, it is supposed to have traversed the country partly on the line of an original British trackway, the Ermyn Street. The Roman road to which we refer is to this day, in portions of the county, called the *Stane Street, Pebble Lane*, &c., on account of its superior construction of stone. From *Regnum*, Chichester, after crossing the Weald, it went underneath where now is Dorking Churchyard. It has been conjectured that this great causeway then ran *viâ* Woodcote to Broad Green, Croydon, where it is said to have been visible towards the close of last century,† and thence, through Streatham, to London. Coldharbour, of which there are numerous places so named in England in the vicinity of Roman roads, implies an exposed station for legionaries on the march; this tallies with the situation of a place on the south-west side of Duppa's Hill, known as Coldharbour. The etymology of Streatham is found in *Stráet-hám*, the *hám* or home on the street, that Roman *stratum* which once traversed our parish. Between *Durobrivis* (Rochester) and Noviomagus, a military highway also ran; so, if Noviomagus stood anywhere near Old Croydon, a second Roman *viâ*, a branch of the

* See in the *Archæologia*, vol. xxii. 1829.
† Paper read by Mr. Bray, in 1788; see vol. ix. *Archæologia*.

south-eastern Watling Street, must have cut through this district, and Croydon may have been pierced by a third Roman road, the road from *Anderida* (Pevensey) to *Londinium* (London).

On the verge of the parish of Croydon, in 1371, the remains of a Roman villa were brought to light at Beddington. Other evidences of a former occupation of this neighbourhood by the Romans may be seen in the circumstance that, not long since, the mutilated small Roman cup or vase here represented was taken out of the earth above the chalk pit on Croham Farm. It was found at the back of the skull of a skeleton, duly laid on the chalk; there was no coin. Vessels of this description are commonly found in Roman tombs and interments. They are generally supposed to have contained liquids, honey, and other things which were thought to be acceptable to the manes of the departed.

A large yellowish, red, coarse earthenware fragment of a neck and handles of an amphora was also recently dug up from a depth of about six feet, the last three being gravel, at the back of a cottage behind the water-works, Surrey Street.

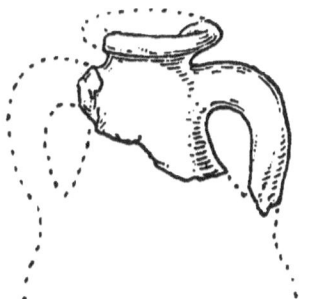

A Roman coinage, extending from the year B.C. 82 to the year A.D. 400, has, at various times, been picked up in our parish: of this we subjoin three specimens. The first of the coins represented on the next page is of an unknown type; it is a silver-plated piece of the Emperor Otho, and was found in a garden at the foot of Crown Hill; the head is in bold relief.

Otho was *Imperator* for three months only—namely, from the 15th of January, A.D. 69, the day on which the soldiery murdered Galba, till April 16th of the same year, when, after having been defeated by the generals of his rival Vitellius, with great deliberation Otho stabbed himself.*

OTHO.

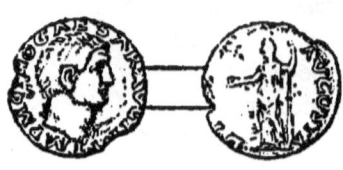

Obverse.—IMP. M. O[TH]O. CÆSAR AUG. TR. P. Head of Otho to the right.

Reverse.—[DIVA] AUGUSTA. A female figure standing to the left, holding patera and sceptre.

The next drawing represents a copper coin of Vespasian, Roman Emperor, A.D. 70–79, which was lately dug up when making the sewer in Church Road, just where this is joined by Sheldon Street.†

VESPASIAN.

Obverse.—IMP. CAESAR VESPASIAN AVG. COS. III. Head of Vespasian to the right radiate.

Reverse.—FORTVNAE REDVCI. S.C. Fortune robed, standing to the left; at her feet a globe.

As an able officer, Vespasian distinguished himself in the attack on Britain during the reign of Claudius, A.D. 43. When the Jewish war broke out in A.D. 66, Nero entrusted to Vespasian the conduct of the campaign.

---

* The coin referred to belongs to Mr. Chappell, of Surrey Street, Croydon.

† This coin is in the possession of the author.

The very perfect gold coin of the Emperor Hadrian,* here engraved, was dug up at the cemetery, Croydon, in 1873.

HADRIAN.

Obverse.—HADRIANUS AUG. COS. III. PP. Head of Hadrian to the right, bearded and laureate.

Reverse.—IOVI VICTORI. Jupiter seated to the left, holding sceptre and victory.

Hadrian thus addressed his departing spirit:

"Soul of mine, pretty one, flitting one,
Guest and partner of my clay,
Whither wilt thou hie away?"

He died on the 10th of July, A.D. 138.

* Now in the possession of the Rev. W. Wilks, M.A., Vicar of Shirley.

CHAPTER IV.

SAXON CROYDON.

THE great battle which, according to the "Saxon Chronicle," resulted in the establishment of Kent, the earliest founded kingdom of the Saxon Octarchy, was fought in A.D. 457, at Crecganford (Crayford), within fifteen miles of Croydon.

Of the history of this particular neighbourhood during that long period known as the Anglo-Saxon age, but a few scattered vestiges are left.

It has been previously mentioned that traces of Celtic speech linger in one or two names of places in this parish. In studying local etymology it will generally be found that the names of rivers and mountains are very ancient, those in our country not seldom originating in the language of those Celtic tribes which, ages ago, were driven from the soil. The language of the ancient Britons was substantially the Welsh. *Avon* is the Welsh, or old British, for *a river;* the Celtic *an*, denotes *water*, or a *stream*. From *an*, a stream, with the prefix V, or its relative *afon*, or *avon* contracted; and *el*, implying *little*, added; the Vandel, or, as it now is pronounced Wandle, the springs of which are in this parish, may derive its name. It would thus mean the *little* water or stream, in contrast with the *larger* river, Thames, into which it falls.

Parc is the Welsh for enclosure; and *the park* is a designation that generally indicates the oldest enclosure of a parish dating back to Celtic times. Of the Park—that is, Croydon Park—we have a reminiscence in the name Park Hill.

Combe is no other than the Cymric or Welsh *cwm*, modified afterwards by the Anglo-Saxons into *cumb*: it signifies a hollow in a hill, and is often found in the valleys of hilly parishes. In some instances the word is used alone, as in *Combe*; in others, it forms part of a compound word, as *Addiscombe*, anciently spelt *Adge-combe*, *Ege-combe*, and *Ads-combe*—the district lying at the edge or margin of the combe or valley.

Scar—*scaur*, in old British implies a steep hill; *bróc*, in Anglo-Saxon, means a brook or spring; which tallies with the situation of the old Scarbrook, formerly one of the sources of the Wandle.

It is not, however, to the Celt or Briton, but to the Teutonic invader that we are mainly indebted for the old nomenclature of these parts; and from this circumstance may be deduced the fact, that it is to the Saxons the reclamation and settlement of our soil is due. Of names of places in this parish having an Anglo-Saxon etymology, may be mentioned that of Ham, an estate or farm, situated at the eastern extremity of Croydon, towards Beckenham. *Ham*, in Anglo-Saxon, signifies a home or enclosure. The etymology of Selsdon is found in the Anglo-Saxon *sel* or *sele*, a seat or mansion; and *dún*, a hill or down. The name is spelt Selesdún in an Anglo-Saxon charter.* Selhurst derives from *Sel*, a dwelling, and the German *horst*, signifying a wood that yields food for cattle; it is the wood surrounding a dwelling-place. *Scyr* is the Anglo-Saxon for *a boundary* (whence Shire); and *leáz, a district*, a woody pasture; which corresponds with the part of our parish called Shirley, on the extreme border of Surrey.

The earliest mention of Croydon is in the joint will of Beorhtric and Ælfswyth, dated about the year 962.† In this Anglo-Saxon document the name is spelt Croȝbæne,

* "Codex Diplomaticus."
† *Ibid.* No. 492; Thorpe's "Registrum Roffense;" Lambarde's "Perambulation of Kent."

Crogdæne. Crog was, and still is, the Norse or Danish word for crooked, which is expressed in Anglo-Saxon by *crumb,* a totally different word. From the Danish come our *crook* and *crooked.* This term accurately describes the locality; it is a *crooked* or *winding valley,* in reference to the valley which runs in an oblique and serpentine course from Godstone to Croydon. The Anglo-Saxon *g* is equivalent to our *y;* and thus the name was pronounced in 962 exactly as it is now, with the substitution only, in the final syllable, of the letter *o* for the diphthong *æ,* a very common and venial corruption.* In any question relating to the meaning of names, the most ancient form of spelling them ought to have great weight. In the entry in Domesday book, relative to the manor, the Normans spelt its name *Croindene;* hence, Garrow supposed that the term originated in the union of two Saxon words, *crone, sheep,* and *dene, a valley*—sheep-valley. Ducarel considered that the name Croydon was derived from the old Norman-French word *cray* or *craire,* chalk, and the Saxon *dun* a hill; meaning a town near the chalk-hill;† but this surmise is open to the objection that, long ere the Norman language could have so prevailed, the place was known, as we have seen, almost by its present name.

NORWOOD.—Of the eminence which crowns the northern limits of our parish, no title in particular has descended to us although the hill in question always must have been a conspicuous landmark. But to the primeval *Coed,* the forest, amidst which it used to rear its head, our Anglo-Saxon forefathers gave the appellation Norðwood, Northwood, in order to distinguish it from that vast Southwood, the weald of Surrey, Sussex, and Kent. That the more northern forest formerly extended far beyond the limits assigned to a district now known as Norwood, is

* "Surrey Etymologies." By J. Wickham Flower, F.G.S.
† Ducarel's "Croydon," p. 73.

evident from numerous names suggestive of wood or forest found on maps of this part of the country, such as Forest Hill, Wood Side, Park Hill, the Hursts, &c. We may infer from thence that a very large proportion of the land in this neighbourhood formerly was sylvan. That in ancient times this was the swampy, murky, dreadful abode of the wolf, badger, boar, wild cat, and other noxious animals there is little doubt; yet, as the hand of man cleared and gradually overcame it, the delicious acorns it yielded might furnish a rich pasture for numerous herds of swine.

In the name Waddon we have, as before observed, apparently a trace of the old Anglo-Saxon worship of the god of war. Woden, or Odin, was the venerated hero-god of Saxon and of Scandinavian adoration. All the kings of both branches of the great Teutonic family, Germanic or Saxon, as well as Scandinavian or Northmen, without exception, contended that they sprang from that mysterious personage, Odin or Woden. We, the descendants of the Anglo-Saxons, still preserve a remembrance of the object of their fear in the name attached to the fourth day of the week, Wodnes dæg, Woden's day—Wednesday.

The origin of the name Beggar's Bush is uncertain, but its antiquity is shewn in the fact that it is found as *Beggares Thorn*, in a charter of the Anglo-Saxon King, Eadgar, dated in 975.*

In the middle of the month of June, in the year 1862, as the navvies were cutting the line that runs from West Croydon Station, through Selhurst and Thornton Heath, to Balham, within the Manor of Whitehorse, and not far from Collier's Water Lane, they found, at a depth of about two feet below the surface, what they called a stone coffin, without a lid. This coffin, or chest, crumbled under the picks and spades of these labourers, when, amid

---

* "Codex Diplomaticus," 687.

the *débris*, they discovered what seemed to be a mouldering bag full of something, for the possession of which there was a scramble among the navvies, and some of its contents were dispersed. But a brittle mass, matted together with clay and green oxide, was carried into the town of Croydon by the man who had first laid hands on it, and offered for sale at the shop of one of our High Street jewellers, where it was rejected as worthless; but eventually, as old silver, the lump was purchased at the rate of four shillings and sixpence an ounce. Upon a careful examination, the hoard, for such it turned out to be, was found to have originally consisted of about two hundred and fifty Anglo-Saxon coins, most of which were in fine preservation, together with a few small silver ingots, and a part of a torc, or neck ornament, also of silver, and two or three Cufic coins. The coins were of the sovereigns, Ethelward and Edmund, of East Anglia; Ethelred and Alfred, sole monarchs as they are termed; Burgred of Mercia (of which reign were about 200 of the mass); Louis the Debonnaire; and Charles le Chauve, or the Bald. There was also the half of a penny of Archbishop Ceolnoth, and a few oriental coins. From evidence supplied by the coins themselves, it seems almost certain that they were placed where they were found, in the year 874. In that year Burgred was driven from his dominions by the Danes, and took refuge in Rome. England was overrun by the invader, Alfred was powerless, and those who had treasure endeavoured to secure it by committing it to the earth.

The spot where this hoard was found, and all its surrounding neighbourhood, in ancient times probably was included within that great north forest of oaks, a portion of the site of which is now named Norwood. The treasure was secreted just at the foot of the hill; yet, as to who he may have been whose hand placed it in this spot, and why he came not back to take his wealth away, must for ever remain a mystery. Of these relics, not more than eight or nine scattered coins continue in the parish in which they were found.*

The coins from which the accompanying drawings were made formed part of the collection referred to.

ETHELWEARD.

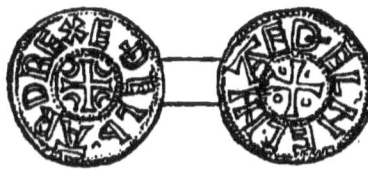

Obverse.—EDELWĀRD REX. (A cross, with crescent in each angle.)
Reverse.— ÆÐHELHELM. (Cross, with pellet in each angle.) Rare coin.

The above represents a very perfect silver penny of Ethelweard, one of those unknown East Anglian Kings, whose name only has been rescued from obscurity by the discovery of such pieces as this, his money : all the rest is shrouded in darkness.

EADMVND.

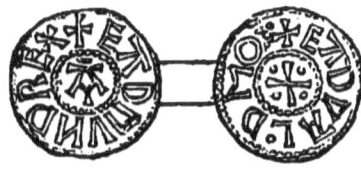

Obverse.— +EADMVND REX. (Monogram in field.)
Reverse.— +EADVAL · D MO :· (In centre, cross, with pellets in angles.)

Eadmund began to reign over the marsh-environed kingdom of East Anglia in the year 855 ; in 870 he was cruelly murdered by the Danes. Canonized, he is now commonly called St. Edmund. His coins are rather rare.

ÆLFRED.

Obverse.— +AELFRED . REX. (Bust to right.)
Reverse.—ELBERE.MON.ETA. (Moneyer's name.)

---

* The bulk of these coins have passed into the collection of John Evans, F.R.S., F.G.S., &c.

Within that bag which the navvies dug up at Whitehorse, were found no less than twelve varieties of the earliest coins of Alfred the Great. As the coinage of this King is very scarce, it is a circumstance worthy of note. Ælfred reigned from A.D. 871 to A.D. 901. From Ælfred the Great, whose image is so rudely impressed on this coin, Queen Victoria is lineally descended.

On Farthing Down, in the neighbouring manor of Coulsdon, are the remains, either of the burial place of some Anglo-Saxon chieftain, or of the cemetery of an Anglo-Saxon district. The tumuli referred to are situate upon a tract of down-land lying on the chalk. Sixteen of the graves were examined in the year 1871, and in every instance the skeletons were found extended at full length, with feet towards the east. From underneath one of the tumuli they exhumed the skeleton of a man of gigantic stature. Across his breast, and reaching from the right shoulder to the left knee, was a well preserved double-edged sword; on his right foot rested the umbo of a shield. In another grave was found, close to the head, the remains of a *situla*, or small bucket. A third grave contained a beautiful drinking cup. Lower down the same hill remains of an ancient earthwork can still be traced.

Vestiges of another Anglo-Saxon burial-ground were met with just on the border of this parish, at Beddington, not far to the south of the recently discovered Roman villa. But the cluster of tumuli on the brow of the hill towards Addington, mentioned by Lysons, appears to have been long since levelled by the plough.

About the year 1849, as the late Mr. Aris was digging the foundation of a house in Park Street, he discovered a leaden coffin. A Saxon coin, and also a bronze piece of money, were found by its side. Whether the bronze coin was of Roman mintage or not cannot now be determined; but, in all probability, it was either that coin of the Emperor Gratian, or the other defaced

Roman coin which Mr. Aris is known to have found on this site.* In 1871, from a depth of ten or twelve feet, another leaden coffin was dug up in the same locality; and near the spot where this second leaden coffin had been deposited, a coin of the Roman Emperor Valens was also turned up. Three hundred years ago a number of human remains were found as they were digging the foundations of Archbishop Whitgift's Hospital; the discovery of these remains puzzled Samuel Finch, who was Vicar of Croydon at the time when the Hospital was built.† A quantity of human bones have recently been found by the well, formerly at the corner of the Archbishop's Hospital, and many human remains have been dug up in George Street. When they dug the foundation of the "Victory," at the north-east end of Surrey Street, the labourers came on a very perfect human skeleton. Recently, they found in the middle of Surrey Street, a number of skulls and bones. At the rear of No. 22, High Street, a skull, and other human remains, were found not long since.

Putting together these various fragments of intelligence, it is difficult to avoid the conclusion that, in the centre of our town, in former ages, was a place of interment; but all documentary evidence, and every tradition connected with it, has been lost. It would seem that, at some very remote period, the gentle eminence along which the main street of Croydon now runs, was dotted over with interments, among which, perhaps, might have been seen early British carneddau, Roman sepulchral memorials, and Saxon barrows, in ages antecedent to the date when the old churchyard became the acknowledged last resting-place of the Christian inhabitants of this neighbourhood.

The old parish church of Croydon is a Saxon foundation.

---

* See " Croydon, Prehistoric and Roman," p. 69, and note on p. 71.
† Vide "Lambeth," MS. Lib., No. 275.

CHAPTER V.

THE OLD CHURCH.

GREAT as the alteration is which the hand of man has gradually wrought upon the aspect of our country, the change is not so vast as that revolution in society which the benign influences of Christianity have silently effected. For aught we know to the contrary, where now the praises of the Lamb are sung, in this õene or valley, once well watered by running streams,* amid the recesses of that primeval *Coed*, the forest, traces of which still linger in the neighbourhood of Croydon;—here, where the sacred oak tree formerly flourished, the cruel Druid may have fired his colossean image of wicker work, full of human victims sacrificed to appease the anger of his gods. Concerning so remote a period, little is known; but it is almost certain a population once dwelt hereabouts who knew not the true God, nor Jesus Christ whom He hath sent; this, to our far-off ancestors, was indeed a valley of the shadow of death, for as yet the Sun of Righteousness had not risen upon Britain.

Neither the time when, nor the circumstances under which, Croydon Church was originally founded are known. We may infer that there was a structure dedicated to the purpose of Christian worship at Croydon in the year 960, since to the will of Beorhtric and Ælfswyth, made about this date, is witness, "Elfsies, the Priest of Croydon"

---

* It has been already observed that running streams were the objects of superstitious reverence with our heathen forefathers.

Elꝼꞃɩeꞅ pꞃeoꞅꞇeꞅ on Cꞃoȝbæne ;* for it is not likely a person would be so designated unless a fabric of some kind was set apart for him to perform the ministerial office in. And the building in which Elfsies officiated might have been an old one, even in his day, as centuries had already passed by since Christianity had been brought to his pagan Anglo-Saxon countrymen; to say nothing of that earlier introduction into Britain of the glad tidings of salvation by Christ, which momentous intelligence appears to have first reached these shores when the Roman troops were overrunning the southern portion of the island, apparently about the time of the revolt of Boadicea, A.D. 60.†

Some missionary man, it may have been, who, with spirit stirred within him as he contemplated the ignorance and idolatry around, selecting a spot of land near a running brook,‡ and clearing it with axe, then out of the felled timber constructed here an oratory. Rude although it may have been, still this was a temple in which the living and true God might be worshipped. The humble house of prayer was reared just at the turn of the well-trodden path, leading to where, close by, stood a fane of the false god—the deity our pagan Teuton forefathers

---

* "Codex Diplomaticus." A copy of the Will referred to is printed in Lambarde's " Perambulation of Kent."

† Gildas. Tertullian, who wrote in the latter half of the second century says: "et Britannorum inaccessa Romanis loca, Christo vero subdita "; and those parts of Britain which were inaccessible to the Romans, are become subject to Christ. Tertul, "Adv. Judæ." c. 7 Augustine did not land upon the Isle of Thanet until long after, namely, in the year 597. In Ireland and in Scotland, in the fifth and sixth centuries (before Augustine landed), were Christian schools famous for their learning—viz., St. Finian, at Clonard near the Boyne, and the renowned seminary at the Isle of Hy, or Iona, in the Hebrides. Ven. Bede: Archbishop Usher.

‡ The river Wandle originally took its rise from various sources a little to the east and south of Croydon Church. Until recently, it coursed in two streamlets, one upon the north, and the other past the south side of the church.

fell down before, whose memory is still preserved in the name given to the fourth day of the week; for Woden, or Odin, dread, furious one, claimed to be lord of Woðnes-ðæg (Wednesday).* Under some such circumstances as these, it may have been that an eremite, or monk architect, put together the first Christian temple in Croydon.

Or, does the old parish church of Croydon owe its origin to that scheme of able Archbishop Theodor, when, planning the establishment in England of a parochial clergy,† and guided by an usage of his native Asia, with the sanction of King Æthelstan, he urged upon opulent proprietors the expediency of building and endowing churches upon their lands; by way of encouragement, offering them the right of patronage to the churches they might erect. Hence the origin of existing rights of patronage; and since some estates were large, whilst others were small, this accounts for the unequal size of parishes. If the Church here was founded under the latter circumstances, then we may presume that the marsh-environed, wattled stronghold of the opulent thegn who reared it, occupied the site adjoining the churchyard, where now stand the remains of the Archiepiscopal palace; for it is likely the Saxon noble would consult his own convenience and that of his household, and choose a spot whereon to erect his Church near his own residence.

Yet, wherever situate, or whatever may have been the

---

* The place now called Waddon, anciently *Woddens*, is not more than a quarter of a mile distant from Croydon Church.

† "The Anglo-Saxon Church, its History," &c. By Henry Soames, M.A., pp. 74, 75. Other writers, including Camden, state that "Honorius, Archbishop of Canterbury (a predecessor of Theodor), about the year 636, first began to separate parishes in England." Gough's "Brit.," vol. i. p. 189. Archbishop Theodor was solemnly enthroned at Canterbury, A.D. 668. The complete organization of the ecclesiastical power in England appears to have been effected by Theodor: "Isque primus erat in Archiepiscopis, cui omnis Anglorum ecclesia manus dare consentiret."—BEDA, *H. E.*, iv. 2.

antiquity or structural character of the fabric in which he officiated, certain it is we find that, about A.D. 960, Elfsies was the priest of Croydon.

The tenth century was one of the darkest in the intellectual night. In contrast to the apostolic simplicity of that band, who, in singleness of heart and holy fear, mingled with gladness, and relying upon their risen Lord, went forth from an upper room at Jerusalem to evangelize the world, the Church in the West now presented the spectacle of a vast and mysterious ecclesiastical polity which had gradually arisen out of the ruins of ancient pagan Rome. Scriptural religion had become undermined. The supremacy over all the kings and princes of the earth of "the servant of the servants of God," as the Pope, with ostentatious humility styled himself, was established; and a sacerdotal class, who deemed themselves invested with superior sanctity, separated from, and assumed absolute despotism over the laity.

The Anglo-Saxon Church and the English princes, however, never yielded a servile obedience to the See of Rome.

Yet vital religion everywhere was suffocated beneath the thick folds of superstition and ignorance. Literary appliances were scarce and costly, and the scant learning of the time was confined to the clergy. The pure Word of God was not then, as it now is, accessible to every reader, for although many of the churches were furnished with books, yet, as most of these were written in the Latin language, very few even of the clergy understood them. "Very few were they," says King Ælfred, "on this side the Humber (the most civilized part of England) who could understand their daily prayers in English, or translate any letter from the Latin. I think there were not many beyond the Humber; they were so few that I, indeed, cannot recollect *one single instance* on the south of the Thames, when I took the kingdom."* It is said that

* Alfred's Preface, p. 82—"Wise's Asser."

King Ælfred provided ancient England with a Bible in her native tongue.* Ælfred the Great died on the 26th day of October, in the year 900 or 901, and although Ælfred's plans for the improvement of the education of his people diminished the evil he complained of, yet succeeding turbulent times, incident upon a renewal of the Danish invasion, tended to thwart the enlightened measures of the Anglo-Saxon King.

The dogma of the infallibility of the Pope encounters a difficulty in the character of John XII., who was sovereign pontiff in the year 960, since there is no circumstance in history better attested than the fact that this Pope was solemnly deposed on account of murder, adultery, and other heinous crimes.

A.D. 960. This was the year in which St. Dunstan, as he is commonly called, having been appointed primate of the Anglo-Saxons, received the pallium from Pope John.† Returning to England, Dunstan signalized his advent to power by expelling the married secular clergy from their benefices, and obtruding into their places monks of the Benedictine rule. Yet, whether the Saxon priest of Croydon suffered from the new-fangled celibatic notions of his eccclesiastical superior, or otherwise, we have no means of determining.

According to the Anglo-Saxon Chronicle in—

> "AN. DCCCC.LXXV.
> Here ended
>   the joys of earth,
>   Eadgar of Angles King,
>   chose him another light,
>   beauteous and winsome,
>   and left this frail,
>   this barren life."

Or, as it is expressed in another version of the same, probably contemporary authority :—

---

* Spelm, "Vit. Ælf.," M. 167. The authority for this is an ancient "History of Ely."
† "Flor. Wig."

"A. 975. The 8th before the Ides of July.
Here Eadgar died,
ruler of Angles,
West-Saxons' joy,
and Mercians' protector.

* * *
* * *

Kings him widely
bowed to the King,
as was his due by kind.
No fleet was so daring
nor army so strong,
that 'mid the English nation
took from him aught,
the while that the noble king
ruled on his throne."

After all said, however, what more was it than a slip of land that acknowledged this whilom potent Anglo-Saxon, "Basileus" as lord, compared to the widespread extent of those dominions over which King Eadgar's descendant, our Sovereign Lady, sways her sceptre—an empire upon which the sun never sets! Great, indeed, has been the progress of the nation since Elfsies, the priest of Croydon, lived.

It was Eadgar who, in order to extirpate these ferocious animals from the country, commuted the tribute from Wales in 300 wolves' heads.

Scarce had King Eadgar departed, than the dread heathen, Vikingr of the North, in long gilt-prowed craft, with reafen ominously flouting at mast-head, bore down upon ill fated Saxon England, which, disunited and distracted, quickly succumbed to Suein. It was in the year 1014 that Suein added to his other titles that of "full King of England," and in the same year he died suddenly. The Danish army then elected Cnut, or Canute, Suein's son, to be his successor; and it is within the range of possibility that Elfsies may still have been doing duty as the aged priest of Croydon, when, in 1017, King Cnut commenced to rule over all England. The Dane swore to be just and benevolent, and touched the hands of the principal chiefs in token of his sincerity.

Although the son of an apostate, Cnut displayed great zeal for the Church. He discountenanced the eating of horse-flesh in honour of Odin. With the view to still further discourage the old Pagan creed, and stem that host of heathen superstitions which clung with the inveteracy of ancient association to the recent Danish converts, Cnut enacted laws against witchcraft and charms, the worship of stones, fountains, runes by ash and elm, and the incantations that do homage to the dead. We may take it for granted, therefore, that the rule of this Anglo-Danish monarch had a tendency to strengthen, rather than weaken, the hands of the Christian priest at Croydon.

But Cnut the Great, "Basileus," or Emperor of the Anglo-Saxons, Scots, Britons, Swedes, Danes, and Norwegians, passed away in 1035, when his empire, as had been the case with the empire of Charlemagne, fell to fragments. For another six years Saxon England groaned under the partial and oppressive imposts of Harold and Hardacnut; and then, not far from where Croydon Church stands, at Clapham, *Clapa-ham*, the *ham* or home of Clapa, the last-named intemperate ruffian fell down dead at the marriage feast of one of his nobles, as " he stood at his drink."* With Hardacnut expired the Scandinavian domination over England.

What a picture is here presented to us of the manners of that early period throughout which it is probable a succession of men, ignorant and grossly superstitious although they may have been, yet let us hope in sincerity, from the very spot where Croydon Church now stands, taught the Word of life—truly a light shining in a dark place!

It was in the year of our Lord 1041, that, amid every

---

* "Saxon Chron." An. 1041; another version recounts the circumstance under An. 1042, to which year R. Hoveden also assigns it. Clapham was formerly in the parish of Lambeth.

demonstration of Saxon affection, Edward the Confessor, as he is named, was crowned in Winchester Cathedral King of all England. The long and comparatively peaceful reign of the monk-king was distinguished by a church-building activity, and it is not unlikely that the fabric, if of timber, and still standing, in which Elfsies preached, was then pulled down, and a new church built at Croydon upon the model of those stone structures which Edward had so good an opportunity of examining during his protracted exile in Normandy.

The earliest direct notice of Croydon Church is in Domesday Book. An entry in that venerable record relates to the manor of Croydon : it contains the words " *ibi eccla*," signifying *here a church*. At the time of the survey there was, in the county of Surrey, one abbey, one monastery, one nascent convent, sixty-four churches, and three chapels. Our old parish church, therefore, is a Saxon foundation.

The fabric is dedicated to St. John the Baptist—a holy and remarkable character: his raiment was of camel's hair ; a leathern girdle was about his loins ; his meat was locusts and wild honey ; he drank neither wine nor strong drink.

If the first church erected in this county was reared in our parish, there would be a peculiar significance in the dedication of Croydon Church to the forerunner of Christ. Or does the dedicatory title of Croydon Church, contain an allusion to the particular circumstances of the site or locality upon which it was planted ; originally, in fact, an island, surrounded by running streams and a morass. That at the first introduction of Christianity to the Pagan Anglo-Saxons, before they had time to erect churches, it was not unusual openly to baptize the converts in rivers or streams, in a way similar to that practised by John the Baptist in the Jordan, appears from the relation of Venerable Bede. A very old man told Deda, Abbot of Parteney, that he himself, in the presence of Edwin, chief of the Angles, who lived on the north side of the River Humber (the North-Humbrians), had been baptized with a great many others in the Trent at noonday by Bishop Paulinus. Deda personally conveyed this information to Bede, by whom the interesting tradition has been handed down to us.*

The old parish church of St. John the Baptist at Croydon was burnt down on Saturday night, January 5th, 1867.

After the fire various curious revelations were made. The ground plan of a more ancient house of prayer, which had occupied the same site, could be distinctly traced. As each successive alteration had been made in the character of the structure, the old walls had been merely pierced, or taken down to the required level, but the ancient foundations had been religiously preserved. It is certain that, previously to the fire, the walls of Croydon Church had been thrice pierced for windows; and the presumption is, that this succession of lights exhibited a design in harmony with the general character which the fabric bore at the respective dates of their insertion, whether this occurred during the late Norman, Early English, Decorated, or Perpendicular periods.† It is an interesting fact that the walls of Croydon Church were found to be full of Norman, Early English, and Decorated fragments—débris of a former structure reverently used up. A sculptured history of our country may lie embedded in the walls of our old parish churches; stones wrought by Saxon and Norman hands—by men who lived in the stormy time of the Usurper, or who fought in the Welsh and Scottish wars of King Edward I.

It is conjectured that the work of rebuilding, or rather converting Croydon Church into what is technically known as a Perpendicular structure, was commenced by Arch-

* Ven. Bede, "Eccl. Hist. of Eng.," B. II, c.16.
† Indications of some of the ancient windows have been preserved in the north and south walls of our new Church.

bishop Courtenay from the circumstance of the arms of this prelate (*or*, three torteaux) having formerly been affixed to the north entrance; and to the same heraldic authority we are indebted, when we place the date of its completion in the days of Archbishop Chichelcy, whose arms (*argent*, a chevron, *gules*, between three cinquefoils of the last), were carved at the side of the western, or principal entrance. The Perpendicular style of architecture exhibited by the late structure attained its purest development towards the end of the 14th, and in the early part of the 15th century; exactly the period embraced by the archiepiscopates of the alleged re-constructors of the fabric.

If any confirmation were required to prove that the late building was only an alteration and enlargement of a church which for ages previously had stood upon the very same spot, it would be found in the circumstance that there is no ancient record of the consecration of Croydon Church. The rule of the Canon Law is never to consecrate a church unless it has been consumed by fire, desecrated, or built upon unconsecrated ground. It follows, therefore, that if this had been a new fabric, reared upon a fresh site, its consecration would have appeared in the register of the archbishop in whose time it was built.

In the year 1844, and again in 1857, specimens of rude mural decoration were found on the south wall of Croydon old Church.

The fire which deprived the inhabitants of Croydon of their parish church was occasioned by the over-heating of a flue-pipe. Such was the rapidity of the conflagration, that in little more than an hour a carcase of tower and skeleton outer walls were all that survived.

ADVOWSON, ETC.

The Church of St. John the Baptist, Croydon, is in the peculiar jurisdiction of the Archbishop of Canterbury;

and was formerly both a rectory and a vicarage. The original endowment of the vicarage cannot be discovered, but Henry de la Rye was presented to this vicarage in the year 1289 by Ægidius de Audenardo, the then rector. An ancient instrument, dated at Maidenston, 2nd of June, in the year 1348, in the time of Archbishop Stratford, whose register is lost, is preserved in that of Archbishop Courtenay, and contains an ordination made by Archbishop Stratford of what tithes were then to belong to the rectors and vicars of Croydon respectively.*

In the archives of the Bodleian Library is an ancient "Valor Beneficiorum," compiled in the twentieth year of King Edward I., which formerly belonged to Sir Henry Spelman. Of this, generally known as "Pope Nicholas's Taxation Roll," so much as relates to Surrey is printed in the Appendix to Aubrey's "Perambulation" of that county, in which, amongst other particulars, may be found

"Decanatus de Croyndon,

Ecclesia de Croyndon val. Lx. marc.
Vicaria ejusdem val. xv. marc."

In 1534, the vicarage was valued at 21*l.* 18*s.* 11½*d.*,† and in Ecton's "Thesaurus rerum Ecclesiasticarum" it is thus stated:—

Clear yearly value 45*l.* 0*s.* 0*d.*	Croydon V. (St. John Baptist) [Pecul] Pens. Prior. de Bermondsey cvis. viii*d.* Redd. Mansion ii*d.*	Yearly tenths, 2*l.* 3*s.* 10*d.*

In the "Liber Regis," the vicarage, discharged of the payment of first-fruits, is rated at 21*l.* 18*s.* 9*d.*

According to the Register of Archbishop Courtenay, an exchange was made of this advowson for the manor of Waddon, between that Archbishop and the Prior and Convent of St. Saviour's, Bermondsey. After the King's Licence and the Pope's Bull had been obtained, the matter

* The instrument itself is copied at length in the Appendix of Ducarel: see also Steinman's "History of Croydon," Appendix.
† "Reg. Winton." Fox, pl. 5.

was referred to Robert Braybrooke, Bishop of London, the sole judge delegated by the Pope for that purpose ; and he, having heard the pleas on all sides, in a solemn manner, in the Church of Croydon, by his sentence, dated January 16, 1390, brought the exchange to a satisfactory conclusion. It was also agreed by indenture (dated on the Monday in the first week of Lent, the fourteenth of King Richard II.) made between Archbishop Courtenay and the Prior and Convent of Bermondsey, that the collation and patronage of the vicarage of Croydon should remain in the Archbishop and his successors, and that in the event of a vacancy, the Archbishop, or his successors, should name two proper persons to the prior and convent, one of whom they should choose and present to the said vicarage, to be admitted and instituted vicar of this Church. Thus matters continued till the dissolution of the Convent of St. Saviour's* in 1538, when the great tithes, rectory manor, and chancel, as part of the posses-

* The following extract from Tanner's "Notitia Monastica" relates to the convent of Bermondsey :—
"*Cluniac Abbey.*—Aylwin Child, citizen of London, about the year 1082, began a new and fair church in Southwark, to the honour of our Holy Saviour, with design to place therein a convent of monks of the Cluniac order, who were procured from the priory *De Caritate*, in France, by means of Archbishop Lanfranc, A.D. 1089, about which time King William Rufus augmented the small estate which Aylwin had procured for these Religious with the grant of the manor of Bermondsey, and other revenues. This priory was made denison, 4 *Ric.* 2., erected into an abbey A.D. 1399, and was endowed, before the dissolution, with an yearly income worth 474*l*. 14*s*. 4*d*. ob. q. Dugd. 548*l*. 2*s*. 5*d*. ob. q. Speed. The site was granted 33 Hen. VIII., to Sir Richard or Robert Southwell."

The custom that prevailed before the Reformation, of suffering the great monastic establishments to absorb the advowsons of parishes, and leave only vicarages remaining, supplemented as this was, by the unprincipled manner in which the monastic houses themselves afterwards were broken up, and their acquired parochial endowments scattered, led to a confusion from which England suffers to the present day.

sions of that convent, fell to the Crown, and the advowson of the vicarage reverted to the See of Canterbury, where it remains.

In 1550, King Edward VI. granted the rectory to Thomas Walsingham, Esq., of Chislehurst, and Robert Moyse, Esq., of Banstead. In 1727 this estate belonged to James Walsingham, Esq., who by will, dated August 16th in that year, devised the same to his sister, Lady Elizabeth Osborne, for life, but made no ulterior bequest of it. He died in 1728, without issue, leaving three co-heirs—viz., Lady E. Osborne, Anthony Viscount Montague, and Mrs. Villiers. Lady Elizabeth left her third to Henry Boyle, Esq., who took the name of Walsingham, from whom it descended to the Hon. Robert Boyle Walsingham. He conveyed it in 1770 to Anthony Joseph Viscount Montague, descended from Barbara, a second sister of James Walsingham, who, inheriting his father's third, and purchasing that of Mrs. Villiers, died seised of the whole in 1787. The trustees under his will sold part of the tithes to Lord Gwydir and other land-owners, and conveyed the remainder to George Samuel Viscount Montague, who was drowned in Switzerland in 1793. He had conveyed his portion of the rectorial tithes to various land-owners, some buying the rectorial tithes of their own estates, and others (where proprietors declined) buying the rectorial tithes of the estates of other owners. Thus the rectorial tithes of this parish were widely distributed, and where they were bought by the owners of the estates on which they were charged, they became practically absorbed, and the estates free of great tithes. The last lot sold was the great tithes of the commons, a lot apparently of no value, and which was bought for a trifle by Mr. Robert Boxall. From small events, however, great ones often proceed, and this was the case here; for Mr. Boxall, finding that no corn, grain, hay, or wood existed on the commons, thought that if they were all enclosed, some titheable article might in time grow there, or, at any rate, that in an enclosure he might obtain an allotment for his prospective but then barren right. It was, therefore, Mr. Boxall who first stirred the important subject of the Croydon enclosure; and, when it took place, he had an allotment made to him in lieu of the rectorial tithes of all the commons of Croydon. Hence, every one now possessing land, formerly part of the commons, possesses land free from rectorial tithe rent charge. After these sales, the rectory itself consisted merely of the chancel of St. John's Church and the Manor House at North End, and these were sold to Mr. Robert Harris, father of the late surgeon, Mr. Francis Harris, and one of the magistrates of the Croydon Bench, who died in 1807. Mr. Harris's representatives sold the chancel and Manor House to the late Alexander Cauldcleugh, Esq., whose representatives sold the chancel after the fire in 1867 to trustees for the inhabitants of Croydon.

Under the same enclosure an allotment was made to the Vicar of Croydon, in lieu of the vicarial tithes of the commons of Norwood, so that any land in Norwood, formerly common, is now free from vicarial tithe rent charge; but the rest of the parish is subject to vicarial tithes.* Easter offerings are presented to the vicar throughout the parish.

A house was appropriated to the vicar in the reign of Edward III. This formerly stood on the south side of the old churchyard. Rebuilt by Archbishop Wake, at the instigation of his lady, in 1730,† this vicarage was pulled down in 1847, and the ground on which it had stood was added to the churchyard. The new vicarage was then erected about a quarter of a mile westward of the church.

---

* Under the Tithe Commutation Act of the year 1837, the vicarial tithes are now commuted into a rent charge.

† Mill's "Essay on Generosity."

On the 16th February, 1417, we find Archbishop Chicheley issuing a Commission, requiring John, Bishop of Sorron, to reconcile the parish church and churchyard of Croydon which had then been lately polluted by blood.* The cause and manner of this bloodshed remain a secret, and the country being at that time internally at peace, we are led to suppose that it arose from some popular affray.

Formerly there were two chauntries in this church, one dedicated to St. Mary, and the other to St. Nicholas. The first, dedicated to the Virgin Mary, was founded before 1402, by Sir Reginald de Cobham, Lord Cobham, of Sterborough Castle, Surrey. The incumbent was to pray for the repose of the souls of the said Sir Reginald, his wife Joan, his children, and of all faithful Christian people. The presentation of the chauntry priest the founder vested in twelve of the principal inhabitants of the town of Croydon. The total income of this chauntry, derivable from various tenements and lands in Croydon or elsewhere, was £16 1s. 2d. John Comporte was the last incumbent, who had a life pension of £6 13s. 4d. granted him at the dissolution of this chauntry in 1 Edward VI.

The other chauntry, dedicated to St. Nicholas, was founded for the repose of the soul of John Stafford, Bishop of Bath and Wells, and of William Oliver, Vicar of Croydon, before the year 1443, as in that year Bishop Stafford was translated to the See of Canterbury. The patronage of this chauntry seems to have been in the Weldon family, from their name being connected with several presentations. The total income of the chauntry was £14 14s. 6d., obtainable in a similar manner to that of St. Mary's. The last incumbent was Nicholas Sommer: he likewise had a grant of £6 13s. 4d. for life at the dissolution.†

* "Reg. Chicheley," fol. 331, a.
† Lists of the Incumbents of St. Mary's and St. Nicholas's

The following Bishops were consecrated at Croydon Church :—

1534, April 19, by Archbishop Cranmer, Thomas Goodrich, D.D., Bishop of Ely, and John Capon, *alias* Salcot, LL.D., late Abbot of Hyde, Bishop of Bangor. 1541, September 25, by the same Archbishop, John Wakeman, last Abbot of Tewkesbury and first Bishop of Gloucester. 1551, August 30, by the same Archbishop, John Scory, D.D., Bishop of Rochester, and Myles Coverdale, D.D., Bishop of Exeter.* 1591, August 29, by Archbishop Whitgift, Gervase Babington, D.D., Bishop of Llandaff. 1612, September 20, by Archbishop Abbot, assisted by John (King), Bishop of London, Richard (Neile), Bishop of Lichfield and Coventry, and John (Buckeridge), Bishop of Rochester, Miles Smith, D.D., Bishop of Gloucester.

Chauntries, and also the items of the endowments of these chauntries, are given in Ducarel, in Garrow, and in Steinman's Histories of Croydon.

* As the honoured instrument of greatly extending the knowledge of the Holy Scriptures, the name of Myles Coverdale will always be mentioned with veneration. The first *printed* English translation of the New Testament we owe to Tyndale, who afterwards was martyred. This rare book was printed in the year 1526. But to Myles Coverdale, subsequently consecrated Bishop of Exeter, in Croydon Church, the honour belongs of having been the translator of the first entire Bible printed in the English language. Upon the 4th of October, 1535, Myles Coverdale published his translation of the whole Bible. There is no evidence concerning the date at which he commenced this great work, and it is uncertain where it was printed. Coverdale was made Bishop of Exeter by Edward VI. Upon the change of religion in Queen Mary's reign, he was ejected from his See at Exeter, and thrown into prison; out of which he was released at the earnest request of the King of Denmark, and as a great favour permitted to go into banishment. Soon after Elizabeth's accession, he returned from exile. When Coverdale was old and poor, Grindal, Bishop of London, gave him the living of St. Magnus, at London Bridge. Here he preached for about two years, but not coming up to the terms of conformity then required, he relinquished his parish a little before his death. He died in 1569, being 81 years of age.

For upwards of eight hundred years the structure concerning which we write remained the only episcopal church at Croydon. But, owing to the vast increase in the population of the parish, the ancient status of St. John the Baptist has been modified by the division of the parish of Croydon into fifteen other ecclesiastical districts, and the erection therein of as many ecclesiastical edifices, all of which have been opened since the commencement of the year 1827.

By an order from the Secretary of State, the old churchyard was closed for interments on the 1st of August, 1861, a handsome cemetery having been provided for the town.

RECTORS AND VICARS.

Ælfsies was described as "the priest of Croydon," about A.D. 962.*

RECTORS.

The names of many of these have been lost; of those that have been discovered, the first which occurs is that of :—

ÆGIDIUS DE AUDENARDO, who was rector here in 1282 and 1295.†

JOHN MANSELL occurs as rector in 1309.

RICHARD AUNGERVILLE, "al' de Bury, cl' presentat. per regem ad eccl' de Croydon, archiepatu vac', 30th November, 1 Ed. III."‡ This was the learned author of the "Philobiblion." He was born at Bury St. Edmunds, in Suffolk, in the year 1287, and was educated at Oxford. In 1333, he was elevated by Edward III., whose tutor he had been, to the episcopal dignity, and in the succeeding year was appointed Treasurer, and afterwards Lord High Chancellor of England. He died at Auckland in 1345.

* "Codex Diplomaticus," ccccxcii.
† The authorities for this list of rectors and vicars are the Registers of the several Archbishops in whose time they were collated.
‡ "Pat." 1 Ed. III.

Better known as Richard of Bury, the delight of this eminent man was in books and learned men. To this passion he owed the honour of the personal acquaintance of Petrarch, which he acquired when he was on an embassy to Avignon. With Cicero, our former rector thought that to attach a library to his residence was to supply a soul to his household. Accordingly, Richard de Bury collected a library that was one of the wonders of the age.

The motives that induced Richard Aungerville to accumulate this vast literary collection do honour to his understanding and benevolent heart:—

"Moved," says Richard, "by Him who alone granteth and perfecteth a good will to man, I diligently enquired what among all the offices of piety would most please the Almighty, and most profit the church militant. Then before the eye of my mind there came a flock of chosen scholars, in whom God the Artificer, and Nature his handmaiden, had planted the roots of the best manners and sciences, but whom penury so oppressed that these fruitful germs were dried up, since, in consequence of want, they were watered by no dew in the uncultivated soil of youth, so that their virtue lay hidden and buried, and the crop withered away, and the corn degenerated into tares, and those who might have grown up into strong columns of the Church by the capacity of their genius were obliged to renounce the pursuit of learning. . . . . What can the pious man behold more deplorable? What can more excite his compassion? . . . . The result of my meditation was pity for this obscure race of men, who might render such service to the Church, and a resolution to assist them, not only with means for their subsistence, but also with books for their studies."*

It was in the library, formed by Richard de Bury, that Bradwardine "The Profound" obtained the materials that enabled him to produce his immortal work "Concerning the Cause of God against Pelagius."

JOHN DE TONNEFORD was rector of Croydon in 1348,

WILLIAM DE LEGHTON in 1351.

WILLIAM DE WITTLESEYE, collated to this rectory by his uncle, Archbishop Islip, 12th April, 1352. He after-

* "Philobiblion," Prolog.

wards became a Doctor of Canon Law at Oxford, and was preferred, by his uncle, to the office of Vicar-General, then to the Deanery of Arches, the Archdeaconry of Huntingdon, the Bishoprics of Rochester and Worcester, and at last became Archbishop of Canterbury.

ADAM DE HONTON, LL.D., who was admitted to it 3rd May, 1359. He was consecrated Bishop of St. David's in 1361, and appointed Chancellor of England in 1377. He built St. Mary's College, near his Cathedral, which he endowed with £100 *per annum*.

ADAM DE ROBELYN was rector in 1363.

WILLIAM BOURBRIGG in 1363.

JOHN QUERNBY was rector in 1364.

JOHN GODEWYKE, admitted 29th March, 1365.

JOHN GODEWYKE, LL.D., presented, on the 6th November, 1370, to this rectory by Edward III., who became patron by reason of the temporalities of the vacant Archbishopric being in his hands. He was the last rector of this church, being rector here when the church was appropriated to the Convent of St. Saviour's, Bermondsey, in 1390; whereupon he resigned.

VICARS.

The names of those that have been discovered are as follows:—

HENRY DE LA RYE became vicar of this church at the presentation of Ægidius de Audenardo, rector of the same, 4th August, 1289.

THOMAS DE SEVENOKE is mentioned as vicar in 1309.

THOMAS DE MAYDENESTAN was presented May, 1309.

JOHN DE HORSTEDE, 1348.

JOHN DE STANSFELDE was appointed Dean of Croydon, by a commission from Archbishop Islip, dated at Lambeth, 11th February, 1349.

RICHARD ATTE LICH', presented 7th June, 1356.

JOHN DE HAMYLDON, 1361.

ROBERT OKELE, 1373.

JOHN LANE, LL.D., occurs as vicar in 1376; upon whose resignation

JOHN BROWN was presented, 1st September, 1387.

WILLIAM DAPER was vicar in 1402.

RICHARD BONDON, presented 14th August, 1402, by the convent and prior of St. Saviour's, Bermondsey.

JOHN SCARBURGH, presented by the same patrons in 1405.

JOHN ALDENHAM, *alias* CAUSTON, presented by the same patrons, 1408.

WILLIAM OLIVER became vicar about 1420. This vicar is supposed to have given some lands to the chauntry of St. Nicholas, that the priest there might pray for the repose of his soul.

JOHN LANGTON.

HENRY CARPENTER, LL.B., 1467.

WILLIAM SHALDOO, 1487.

ROWLAND PHILLIPS, D.D., collated June 4th, 1497, by Archbishop Morton, with the unanimous consent of the prior and convent of St. Saviour's, Bermondsey. Of this celebrated man we subjoin the following notices:—

Preaching at St. Paul's against printing, then lately introduced into England, this vicar uttered the following remarkable words:—"*We (the Catholics) must root out printing, or printing will root out us.*"*

"And even as there was much ado amongst them of the Common House, about their agreement to the subsidie, so was there as harde holde for a while amongst them of the clergie in the Convocation House; namelye, Richard, Byshoppe of Winchester, and John, Byshoppe of Rochester, held sore against it; but most of al, Sir Rowlande Phillips, Vicar of Croydon, and one of the Canons of Paules, being reputed a *notable preacher* in those dayes, spake most against that payment. But the cardinall taking him aside, so handled the matter with him, that he came no more into the house, willingly absenting himselfe,

* Fox.

to his great infamie and losse of that estimation which men had of his innocencie. Thus, the Bellweather giving over his holde, the others yielded, and so was granted the halfe of all their spirituall revenues for one year, to be paid in five yeares following, that the burden might y̅ᵉ more easily be borne."*

"He (Ruthall, Bishop of Durham) paid his last debt to nature at Durham Palace, near London, on Wednesday, the fourth of Feb., in fifteen hundred twenty and two, and was buried in the Chapel of S. John Baptist, joyning to the Abbey Church of S. Peter, in Westminster; at which time Dr. Rowl. Phillips, Vicar of Croydon, *a great and a renowned Clerk*, preached an excellent sermon."†

In 1531, John Hewes, a draper of London, was made to abjure, for saying that he heard the Vicar of Croydon [Phillips] preach openly, "That there is as much baudry kept by going in pilgrimage to Wilsedon or Mouswel, as in the stews beside," &c.‡ Phillips attended the funeral of Abbot Islip, at Westminster, in 1532, and preached his funeral sermon.§

PETER BUROWGH, M.A., collated by Archbishop Cranmer, 9th May, 1538.

JOHN GYBBES, S.T.B., collated by the same Archbishop, 12th April, 1542. He enjoyed it but about eight years, being deprived for refusing to pay his tithes to the King, and was succeeded by

DAVID KEMP, in 1550.

WILLIAM COOKE, 1553.

RICHARD FINCH, collated by Archbishop Parker, 23rd April, 1560.

SAMUEL FYNCHE, collated by Archbishop Grindal, 26th May, 1581.

---

* Holinshed's "Chron.," p. 1524.
† Wood's "Ath. Ox.," vol. ii. p. 723.
‡ "Fox," vol. ii. p. 592.
§ Widmore's "Hist. of West. Abbey," Appendix 10.

SAMUEL FYNCHE, at the presentation of the King, by lapse, 28th February, 1603.

HENRY RIGGE, M.A., collated by Archbishop Abbot, 20th September, 1616.

SAMUEL BERNARD, S.T.B., collated 10th August, 1624. He was displaced by the committee for plundered ministers in February, 1643, "for errors in doctrine, superstition in practice, and malignancy."*

THOMAS BUCKNER, D.D.,† who was succeeded by

SAMUEL OTES, M.A., who died in 1645.

FRANCIS PECK.

EDWARD CORBETT, M.A., *cir.* 1648.

JONATHAN WESTWOOD, appointed by Sir William Brereton, Bart., who was become possessed of the Archiepiscopal Palace at Croydon, and was ordered £50 a year for the use of such minister as he should provide to serve the Cure of the Church of Croydon. Westwood was in the receipt of this stipend from the 31st May, 1654, to the 9th June, 1657.

WILLIAM CLEWER, D.D., collated by Archbishop Juxon, in 1660,‡ who deserves to be recorded only as a disgrace to his profession. His singular love of litigation, and his criminal and disgraceful conduct, eventually caused his ejectment from this benefice, in 1684.§ It was, probably, after his deprivation, that he was *tried at the Old Bailey, and burnt in the hand for stealing a silver cup.* In Smith's "Lives of Highwaymen,"|| where this fact is

* Walker's "List of Ejected Clergy," p. 210.

† "Samuel Barnard being displaced in 1643, Thomas Buckner, D.D., was appointed, but died in 1644." Rawlinson's MS. Notes on Aubrey.

‡ "Parish Reg." This vicar's name is generally spelt *Cleiver*, but it is an error; his signature appears frequently in the Parish Register, and invariably *Clewer*.

§ "Reg. Sancroft," fol. 404, *b.* See also Case of the Inhabitants of Croydon, printed in 1673: appendix to Steinman's "Hist. of Croydon."

|| Vol. i. p. 257.

mentioned, the following anecdote is also to be found:—
"O'Bryan, meeting with Dr. Cleiver, the parson of Croydon, coming along the road from Acton, he demanded his money; but the Reverend Doctor having not a farthing about him, O'Bryan was for taking his gown. At this our divine was much dissatisfied, but, perceiving the enemy would plunder him, quoth he, 'Pray, sir, let me have a chance for my gown;' so pulling a pack of cards out of his pocket, he farther said, 'We'll have, if you please, one game of all-fours for it, and if you win it, take it and wear it.' This challenge was readily accepted by the foot-pad, but being more cunning than his antagonist at slipping and palming the cards, he won the game, and the doctor went contentedly home without his canonicals."

HENRY HUGHES, M.A., collated by Archbishop Sancroft, 26th June, 1684.

JOHN CÆSAR, M.A., collated 18th January, 1688.

ANDREW TREBECK, B.D., collated by Archbishop Wake, 28th April, 1720.

NATHANIEL COLLIER, M.A., 29th Nov. 1727.

JOHN VADE, M.A., collated by Archbishop Herring, in January, 1755.

EAST APTHORP, D.D., collated by Archbishop Secker, June, 1765. He was the author of "Letters on the Prevalence of Christianity."

JOHN IRELAND, D.D., collated by Archbishop Moore, 15th July, 1793. Dr. Ireland was the author of "Five Discourses, containing Certain Arguments for and against the Reception of Christianity by the Ancient Jews and Greeks," 1796. He became Dean of Westminster.

JOHN CUTTS LOCKWOOD, M.A., collated by Archbishop Sutton, 30th March, 1816.

HENRY LINDSAY, M.A., collated by Archbishop Howley, 4th November, 1830. He was author of "Practical Lectures on the Historical Books of the Old Testament."

JOHN GEORGE HODGSON, M.A., collated by Archbishop Howley, January, 1846. He was vicar here when the church was destroyed by fire, and in his time it was rebuilt. Upon his resignation, the

Rt. Revd Edward Wyndham Tufnell, D.D., formerly fellow of Wadham College, Oxford, and Bishop of Brisbane, Queensland, was collated by Archbishop Tait, Septr. 1879.

Monuments and Epitaphs.

In Croydon Old Church were various interesting monuments,* but, with one or two exceptions, these either perished or were terribly mutilated by the fire. The tomb least injured was the oldest in the church; it still remains on the south wall and is presumed to commemorate Thomas Warham, Esq., who, dying at Haling in 1478, ordered his body to be buried in the Chapel of St. Nicholas, before the image of our Lady of Pite.

The oldest inscription in the church was on a brass plate, beneath the indents of a cross, &c.

> Hic jacet Egidius Seymor, qui obiit xxij die
> Decembr. a. dni mccclxxxx cui'aie. ppiciet. ds.

In the north-east corner of St. Mary's Chancel was an altar tomb to the memory of Elye Davy. His figure, which was on a brass plate, had been torn away; underneath was the following inscription :—

> Orate pro anima Elye Davy, nuper Civis & Merceri
> London, qui obiit iiij die mens' Decembris, Anno Dni
> Mill'imo ccclv. cujus anime propicietur Deus. Amen.

Elye Davy founded the almshouse in Croydon called after his name.

---

* We shall here notice only those more important monuments which appear to demand a particular description. Lists of the Epitaphs in Croydon Church are to be found, up to the year 1718 in Aubrey, to 1783 in Ducarel, and to 1834 in Steinman. In the year 1855, and again in 1857, the author published a description of the Monuments and a list of Epitaphs in Croydon Church; which publications were accompanied by a series of careful drawings from the now-destroyed national monuments of Croydon Old Church: he made the drawings referred to during the years 1853-4, thirteen years before the destruction of the monuments.

Continuing to notice the inscriptions according to their chronological sequence, in the corner of the mid-chancel, on the ground, was the figure of a priest incised in brass, with the accompanying lines underneath. This brass was recovered after the fire.

> Silvester Gabriel cujus lapis hic tegit ossa,
> Vera sacerdotum gloria nuper erat,
> Legis nemo Sacre Divina volumina verbis
> Clarius, aut vita sanctius explicuit.
> Cominus ergo Deo, modo felix, eminus almis
> Qem, pius in scriptis viderat ante, videt.
> Anno dni Millimo v,xv., iiij. die Octobr vita est funct.

Near was a brass which, judging from the armorial bearings, was intended to commemorate one of the family of Herone.

Against the north wall of St. Mary's Chancel stood a large tomb of freestone, with an ascent of three steps. On the tomb were represented, in alto relievo, the figures of a man in armour, kneeling before a desk, attended by his five sons, and of a woman in the same manner, attended by her eight daughters.

Over the heads of the women were these initials :—

> K. A. M. S. E. A. M. E. M.

Between the figures :—

> Anno Domini, 1568.

Over the heads of the men :—

> H. W. T. I. P. N.

At the bottom of the tomb was this inscription :—

> Tumulus Nicholai Herone, Equitis, sepulti primo die Septem.

In the middle chancel, upon the north side, within separate recessed arches, and flanked and divided by a Corinthian column, were the painted effigies of a man and woman kneeling before desks. Above the entablature were three shields of arms.

Over the man was this inscription :—

   Obiit 21 Jana 1573, aet. suæ 69.

Under the man were these lines :—

   Heare lieth bvried the corps
   Of Maister Henrie Mill,
   Citezen and grocer of
   London famovs cittie,
  Alderman and somtyme shreve,
   A man of prvdent skill,
   Charitable to the poore
   And alwaies fvll of pittie,
 Whose sovle wee hope dothe rest in
  Blise, wheare ioy dothe stil abovnde
  Thovghe bodie his fvll depe do lie
   In earthe here vnder grovnde

Over the woman :—

   Obiit 2 Aug. 1585, æt. suæ (*left blank*).

Under the woman :—

   Elizabeth Mill his lovinge wyf
   Lyeth also bvried heare,
  Whoe sixtene children did him beare
   The blessing of the Lorde,
 Eight of them sonnes, and the other 8
   Weare davghters, this is cleare
  A witnes svre of mvtvall love,
   And signe of greate accorde,
  Whose sole amonge the patryarks,
   In faithfvll Abrams brest,
  Thovghe bodie hirs be wrapt in clay
   We hope in ioy dothe rest.

At the south side of the Communion Table, against the wall, on a sarcophagus within an arched recess, the entablature of which was supported by Corinthian columns, lay the painted effigies of a churchman in his scarlet robes. Surmounting the entablature were three shields of arms, viz., centre shield, the arms of the see of Canterbury, impaling quarterly *or.* and *az.*, a cross quartered *erm.* and *or.*, between four pea-hens, the first and fourth *az.*, and the second and third *ar.;* dexter shield, the arms of the see of York; sinister shield, the arms of the see of London, both impaling the same. On either side of the sarcophagus, beneath the columns, Grindal's arms were repeated. Beneath his effigies were these verses :—

>Grindall' doctus, prudens, gravitate verendus,
>Justus, munificus, sub cruce fortis erat.
>Post crucis ærumnas Christi gregis Anglia fecit
>Signiferum, Christus cœlica regna dedit.
>In Memoria æterna erit justus.—Psal. cxii.

At the top of the monument :—

>Beati mortui qui in Dno moriuntur :—
>Requiescunt enim à laboribus suis.
>Et opera illorum sequuntur illos.
>Apoc. 14.

Under the above were the two following verses, in juxtaposition :—

Præsulis eximii ter postquam est auctus honore,	Mortua marmoreo conduntur membra sepulchro,
Pervigiliq greges rexit moderamine sacros :	Sed mens sancta viget Fama perennis erit,
Confectum senio durisq laboribus ecce	Nam studia et Musæ, quas magnis censibus auxit,
Transtulit in placidam Mors exoptata quietem.	Grindali nomen tempus in omne ferent.

Immediately above the effigies was this inscription :—

Edmund' Grindall' Cumbriensis, Theol : Dr, Eruditione, Prudentia, et Gravitate clarus, Constantia, Justitia, et Pietate insignis, civibus et peregrinis charus : ab exilio (quod Evangelii causa subiit) reversus ad summum dignitatis fastigium (quasi decursu honorum) sub R. Elizabetha evectus, Ecclesiam Londinen. primum, deinde Eborac. demu. Cantuarien. rexit. Et cum jam hic nihil restaret, quo altius ascenderet e corporis vinculis liber ac beatus ad cœlum evolavit 6° Julii an. Dni. 1583. Ætatis suæ 63. Hic, præter multa pietatis officia quæ vivus præstitit, moribundus maxima. bonorum suorum partem piis usibus consecravit. In Parœcia Divæ Beghæ (ubi natus est) Scholam Grammatic. splendide extrui et opimo censu ditari curavit. Magdalenensi cœtui Cantabr. (in quo puer primum Academiæ ubera suxit) discipulum adjecit, Collegio Christi (ubi adultus liris. incubuit) gratum Μνημόσυνον reliquit; Aulæ Pembrochianæ (cujus olim Socius, postea Præfectus, extitit) Ærarium et Bibliothecam auxit, Græcoq. Prælectori, uni Socio, ac duobus Discipulis, ampla stipendia assignavit. Collegium Reginæ Oxon. (in quod Cumbrienses potissimum cooptantur) nummis, libris, et magnis proventibus locupletavit. Civitati Cantuar. (cui moriens præfuit) centu. libras, in hoc, ut pauperes honestis artificiis exercerentur, perpetuo servandas, atq. impendendas dedit. Residuum bonoru. Pietatis operibus dicavit. Sic vivens moriensq. Eccliæ, Patriæ et bonis literis profuit.

The following is an extract from the Archbishop's will and testament:—" First I bequeath my soul into the hands of my Heavenlie Father, Humbly beseeching Him to receive the same into His gracious mercies, for His Christ's sake; and my body I will to be buried in the quere of the Parish Church of Croydon, without any solempne herse or funeral pompe."

He was buried, according to his desire, in the Chancel of Croydon Church, and over his remains the curious and costly monument, referred to, was erected to his memory. His effigies lying at length, displayed deceased with his hands in the posture of prayer. The face bore a resemblance to the painting of him at Lambeth Palace. The eyes had a kind of white in the pupil, to denote his blindness. He had a long black beard, forked and curling, and was vested in his doctor's robes. The fire that destroyed Croydon Church, irreparably injured this interesting national monument; it crumbled to pieces soon afterwards.

On the south wall of the church, on a brass plate:—

> Here under lieth Buried the bodie of Franc
> Tirrell, sometime Citizen and Grocer of London.
> He was a good Benefactor to the poore of
> divers Hospitalls, Prisons, and Pishes of London,
> and to the continuall relief of the poore
> Fremen of the Grocers. He gave to this Pishe

200*l*. to build a newe Market house,* and 40*l*. t° beautifie this Church, and to make a new Saintes Bell.† He died in September 1609.

In the south-east corner of St. Nicholas's Chancel was a monument bearing the recumbent effigies of a churchman in his robes, with his hands in the act of prayer. The arms on the tomb were : centre shield, the arms of the See of Canterbury, impaling *arg.* on a cross fleury *sa.* 5 bezants ; dexter shield, the arms of the See of Worcester ; sinister shield, the arms of the Deanery of Lincoln, both impaling the same. On the sarcophagus were the arms of the See of Lincoln, the colleges of Trinity, Pembroke, and Peter-house. At the top of the monument was the following inscription :—

Post tenebras spero Lucem.

Above the figure :—

> Whitgifta Eborum Grimsbeia ad littora nomen
> Whitgifta emisit. Fœlix hoc nomine Grimsbei
> Hinc natus: non natus ad hanc mox mittitur hospes
> Londinum: inde novam te, Cantabrigia, matrem
> Insequitur, supraq. fidem suavi ubere crescit :
> Petro fit socius : Pembro : Triadiq magister :
> Fitq. Pater matri, Cathedræq. Professor utriq.
> E. Cathedra Lincolna suum petit esse Decanum :
> Mox Wigorn petit esse suum : fit Episcopus illic :
> Propræses Patriæ quo nunquam acceptior alter.
> Post annos plus sex summum petit Anglia patrem ;
> Plusquam bis denos fuit Archiepiscopus annos,
> Charior Elisæ dubium est, an Regi Jacobo :
> Consul utriq. fuit. Sis tu Croidonia testis
> Pauperibus quam charus erat, queis nobile struxit

---

* When the old market house was pulled down in 1807, the following inscription was discovered :—

"This Markett Hovse was buylt at the coste and charges of Franck Tirrell, citezen and Grocer of London, who was borne in this towne, and departed this worlde in Sept. 1609."

† One John de Aldermaston, who was buried in this Church in 1403, left, by will, twenty sheep, for the purchase of a new saints' bell.—*Vide* " Reg. Arundel," fol. 212, *b*.

Hospitium, puerisq. scholam, dotemq. reliquit.
Cœlibis hæc vitæ soboles quæ nata per annos
Septuaginta duos nullo enumerabitur ævo.
Invidia hæc cernens moritur, Patientia vincens
Ad summum evecto æternum dat lumen honori.

A little lower, the two following verses, in juxtaposition :—

Magna Senatoris sunt nomina, pondera & æqua
Nominibus, quem non utraq. juncta premunt?
Præsulis accedat si summi nomen ad ista
Pondera quis ferat, aut perferat illa diu?

Pax vivo grata est, mens recti conscia pacem
Fert animo, hæc mortem non metuisse dedit.
Mors requiem membris, animæ cœlestia donant
Gaudia; sic potuit vincere qui patitur.

Beneath the figure :—

Gratia non miror, si sit divina Johannis
Qui jacet hic, solus credito gratus erat.
Nec magis immerito Whitgiftus dicitur idem;
Candor in eloquio, pectore candor erat.
Candida pauperibus posuit loca, candida Musis;
E terris moriens candida dona tulit.

This is the celebrated Archbishop Whitgift's monument; it also suffered much from the fire. The inscriptions are said to have been composed by Dr. Benjamin Charior, one of the Archbishop's chaplains.

Compared to Warham's tomb, Whitgift's monument was a poor work of art.

To the east wall of the same south Chancel aisle was affixed a small monument, bearing under a recessed arch the effigies of a man in a gown, kneeling before a desk. Over his head was this inscription :—

Ossa Michaelis sunt hic sita
Murgatroidi. Da, pia posteritas,
verequiete cubent.

Michael Murgatroid was secretary to Archbishop Whitgift.

On a black marble ledger, on the ground, at the entrance of the north aisle, from the west:—

> Here lieth the body of
> Marmaduke Wyvell, Esq.,
> and one of ye King's Majie^{ts} Pentioners,
> second Sonne to Sr Marmaduke Wyvell,
> of Cunstable-Burton, in Yorksheire, Knight and Barronet,
> who dyed ye xxth of August, 1623, aged 58.
> Juxta hic jacet
> In spem certam resurgendy (*sic orig.*) Depositum
> Corpus Marmaduci Wyvell, Armigeri,
> Filii secundo—geniti Dni Marmaduci
> Wyvell, de Cunstable-Burton, in Agro
> Eboracensi, Equitis & Baronetti.
> Ibidemque reconduntur Corpora Mar-
> maduci et Judithæ filiæ ejusdem
> Marmaduci Wyvell, supra nominati:
> Beati sunt pulveres,
> Quibus promittitur a Christo
> Resurrectio ad gloriam in Regno suo:
> Adveniat cito ora tu etiam Lector,
> Obiit 2 die Mar^{ij} 1678, ætut suæ 69.

Not far from Archbishop Whitgift's tomb, on a ledger:—

> M.S.
> To the memory of ye worthy
> Lady Elizabeth Gresham,
> Late wife of Sir William
> Gresham, Knight, who, after
> She had lived 72 yeares,
> Unspotted in her conversation,
> Charitable to the poore,
> Sincere in Religion, Re-
> signed up her soule into the
> hands of her Creator, upon y^e
> 9th day of December, 1632,
> & Lieth here interred in
> hope of a glorious
> Resurrection.
> For a Memoriall of which
> Singular virtues her deare &
> only Daughter, E. G., hath
> consecrated this marble as a
> Duty she could
> Performe.

In the nave, on the ground, on a rough marble, with arms :—

> Here lieth interred the body of the truly pious and
> singularly accomplish'd Lady Dame Ruth Scudamore,*
> daughter to Griffith Hamden, of Hamden, in the county
> of Bucks, Esq.; first married to Edw. Oglethorpe, Esq.,
> sonn & heir to Owen Oglethorpe, in the county of
> Oxford, knight, and by him had 2 daughters;
> after to Sr Philip Scudamore,
> of Burnham, in the county of Bucks, K^t; and lastly to
> Henry Leigh, Esqr, sonn and heir to Sr Edw. Leigh,
> of Rushall, in the county of Stafford, K^t,
> by him had one son, named Samuel, now living.
> She dyed at Croydon, March 28, 1649,
> being the 73rd year of her age.

Also, in the nave, on a brass plate, with arms :—

> Here lyeth buried the body of Nicholas Hatcher,
> of Croydon, in the county of Surry, Gentleman, who was
> Captaine of a Troop of Horse, under his
> Most Sacred Majestie King Charles the First,
> and Yeoman-Usher in Ordinary to his Majestie
> King Charles the Second.
> Who departed this life the 29th of September, in the year
> of our Lord God 1673, aged 69 years.

In the Chancel of St. Nicholas, against the south wall, was a splendid monument to the memory of Archbishop Sheldon, representing the recumbent effigy of the Prelate, in his archiepiscopal robes and mitre. His left hand sustained his head, and in his right was a crosier. There was great individuality in the physiognomy of the Prelate, which, together with the mitre, was very nicely sculptured. Round the sarcophagus portion of the monument, executed in bold relief, were the remains of an allegorical kind of subject, in which winged hour-glasses, bits of coffin, bones, worms, and dirt commingle. The composition of this relief was excellent; the gradual manner in which it increased from the sides to the centre, skil-

---

* Lady Scudamore was aunt to the patriot, Hampden.

fully rendered, whilst the critical accuracy of the anatomical knowledge displayed was indeed surprising.

On the tablet above the statue of the Archbishop was the following inscription :—

> Hic jacet
> Gilbertus Sheldon,
> Antiquâ Sheldoniorum familiâ.
> In Agro Staffordiensi natus,
> Oxonii
> bonis literis enutritus,
> S, S^{ae} Theologiæ Doctor insignis;
> Coll. Omnium Animarum Custos prudens et fidelis,
> Academiæ Cancellarius Munificentissimus,
> Regii Oratorii Clericus,
> Car. I^{mo} B: Martyri Charissimus;
> sub Serenissimo R. Carollo II^{do},
> MDCLX, magno illo Instaurationis anno,
> Sacelli Palatini Decanus,
> Londinensis Episcopus;
> MDCLXII, in secretioris Concilii ordinem
> cooptatus;
> MDCLXIII, ad dignitatis ARCHIEPISCOPALIS apicem
> evectus.
> VIR
> Omnibus Negotiis Par, omnibus Titulis Superior,
> In Rebus adversis Magnus, in prosperis Bonus,
> Utriusque Fortunæ Dominus;
> Pauperum Parens,
> Literatorum Patronus,
> Ecclesiæ Stator.
> De tanto Viro
> Pauca dicere non expedit, Multa non opus est;
> Norunt Præsentes, Posteri vix credent:
> Octogenarius
> Animam Piam et Cœlo Maturam
> Deo reddidit
> v Id. ix B^{ris}
> MDCLXXVII.

Surmounting the tablet, on which the foregoing was inscribed, were cherubim supporting a shield of arms—viz., the arms of the See of Canterbury impaling *arg.* on a chev. *gu.*, three sheldrakes of the first; on a canton of the second, a rose of the last; with motto, " Fortiter et Suaviter."

Before the tomb of Warham, on a ledger :—

>Here lieth the body of
>Sir Joseph Sheldon, K^t,
>some time Ld Mayor of London,
>the eldest son of Ralph Sheldon, Esqr,
>who was the elder brother of Gilbert Sheldon,
>Ld Archbishop of Canterbury.
>He left issue two daughters, Elizabeth & Ann,
>and died Augst ye 16°, 1681,
>in the 51st year of his age.

On a handsome veined marble monument, in the north gallery, adorned with arms; the monument was broken to bits :—

>Sacred to the memory of John Parker, Esq.,
>formerly of London,
>who died the 6th of March, 1706, aged 46 years, and is here interred.
>
>Also of
>Elizabeth, his relict, who died the 10th of August, 1730,
>aged 70 years.
>This pair, whilst they lived together, were
>A pattern for conjugal behaviour;
>He a careful indulgent husband,
>She a tender engaging wife;
>He active in business, punctual to his word,
>Kind to his family, generous to his friend,
>But charitable to all;
>Possest of every social virtue.
>During her widowhood,
>She carefully & virtuously
>Educated five children,
>Who survived her:
>She was an excellent economist,
>Modest without affectation,
>Religious without superstition;
>And in every action behaved
>With uncommon candour and steadiness.

In St. Nicholas's Chancel, on the ground, adjoining the east wall, on a black marble ledger :—

> Depositum
> Gulielmi Wake
> Archiepiscopi Cantuariensis,
> Qui obiit XXIV Januarii, Anno Dom. MDCCXXXVI.
> Ætatis suæ LXXIX.
>
> Et
> Etheldredæ uxoris ejus,
> Quæ obiit XI Aprilis MDCCXXXV,
> Ætatis suæ LXII.

Archbishop Wake died at Lambeth Palace: he was interred here in a private manner.

On a neat, white marble tablet, affixed to the wall, nearly opposite the last, now destroyed :—

> Beneath are deposited the remains of the most reverend
> John Potter, D.D., Archbishop of Canterbury,
> who died October X. MDCCXLVII,
> in the LXXIVth year of his age.

On the ground, adjoining the east wall of the same Chancel, on a black marble ledger :—

> Here lyeth the body of
> The most reverend D[r] Thomas Herring,
> Archbishop of Canterbury,
> Who died March, 13, 1757, aged 64.

On the wall at the south-east end of the Nave was an elegant column of white marble, supporting a funereal urn, designed by Glover, the author of "Leonidas;" it was erected to the memory of Philippa Bourdieu.

On the eastern wall of St. Mary's Chancel was a beautiful monument by Flaxman, representing an angel bearing up a female.

It was in front of this last-named tomb that, on September 19th, 1815, John Singleton Copley, the distinguished artist, father of the still more celebrated Lord Lyndhurst, was buried.

Beneath where Flaxman's monument was fixed, lies Lewis Nockalls Cottingham, the architect, who died on the 13th of October, 1847.

Of epitaphs in the old church-yard, one at least is deserving of notice. It is on a vault near the north entrance :—

> Mr. William Burnet, Born January 29, 1685;
> died October 29th, 1760.
>
> What is man?
> To-day he's drest in gold and silver bright,
> Wrapt in a shroud before to-morrow night;
> To-day he's feasting on delicious food,
> To-morrow, nothing eats can do him good;
> To-day he's nice, and scorns to feed on crumbs,
> In a few days, himself a dish for worms;
> To-day he's honour'd, and in great esteem,
> To-morrow, not a beggar values him;
> To-day he rises from a velvet bed,
> To-morrow, lies in one that's made of lead;
> To-day, his house, though large, he thinks too small,
> To-morrow, can command no house at all;
> To-day, has twenty servants at his gate,
> To-morrow scarcely one will deign to wait;
> To-day, perfum'd and sweet as is the rose,
> To-morrow, stinks in every body's nose;
> To-day, he's grand, majestic, all delight,
> Ghastly and pale before to-morrow night.
> Now, when you've wrote and said whate'er you can,
> This is the best that you can say of man!

CHAPTER VI.

PARISH REGISTER.

MANY parish registers, and amongst the number that of Croydon, commence in 1538, when Cromwell, Vicar-General, issued an order for parish registers to be kept throughout the kingdom.

The following averages of Baptisms and Burials, gleaned from this Parish Register by Ducarel and Lysons, enable us to judge respecting the comparative state of the population of Croydon, during the periods embraced by the dates mentioned.

	Average of Baptisms.	Average of Burials.
1580—1589	67	43
1730—1750	$116\frac{3}{4}$	$137\frac{1}{2}$
1760—1780	127	129
1780—1789	$150\frac{1}{2}$	130

From these documents we learn, that the number of persons who fell victims to the plague at Croydon,

From July 20, 1603, to April 16, 1604, was	158
In the year 1625	76
Ditto 1626	24
Ditto 1631	74
From July 27, 1665, to March 22, 1666	141

In a note it is stated that "from the 11th to the 18th of August, 1603,—3054 persons died of the Plague in London and the liberties thereof, and that many died in the highways, neare about the citie," and that, "from the 25th of August to the first of September, 3385 persons died."

The following instances of longevity are recorded :—

"Alice Miles, 100 annos nata, was buried Mar. 6,

1633—4." "Margaret Ford, aged 105 years, was buried Feb. 2, 1714—5." "John Baydon, aged 101 years, buried Dec. 12, 1717." "Elizabeth Giles, widow, aged 100, was buried Aug. 17, 1729." "Elizabeth Wilson, from the Black Horse, aged 101, was buried March 17, 1771."

The following miscellaneous items are arranged according to their respective dates:—

On June 10, 1552, "Alexander Barckley, sepult." This was Barkley, the poet.

1563. "Mr. Wyllm Heron, justyce, was buryed the x day of January."

—"Nicolas Voode, the son of the good wyfe of the grewond [Greyhound], was buryed the xxixth day of January."

1568. "Syr Nicolas Heron, Knight, deceassed the fyrst day of September, and was buryed the ix day of the same month."

1578. "This Candlemas was the great snowe."

—"Lady Mary Heron [widow of Sir Nicholas] was buryed the xx day of Apryll, and her funerall was made the xxiiij day of Apryll."

1579. "Richard Gornarde, the son of Bryan Gornarde, was chrystened the viiij day of Marche." This was Sir Richard Gurney, the celebrated Lord Mayor of London.

1583. "Edmunde Grindall, L. Archbushop of Canterburie, deceased the vj day of Julye, and was buryed the fyrste day of Auguste, anno dni. 1583, and anno regni Elizabethae 25."

1584. "Bonaventure Ryder, travelynge between Wonswthe and Croydon, was found dead in Waddon mill, upon the xxx day of Julye, and was buried the iiij day of August abovesayd."

1585. "Memoranda.—That on the xxvth day of Julye word was broght to the towne of Croydon, that there lay one dead in a close nye Pollarde hill, who was putrified and stanck in most horrible manner; wherefor none cold be gotten by the officers to bringe hym; whereupon he lay there tyll the tuesday at nyghte after, beinge the xxviith day, at which tyme the Vicar [Samuel Fynche *primus*] hired one Robert Woodwarde, and they two went unto hym, and found hym lyeng on his backe, wth his legs pulld up to hym & his knees lying wide, his right hand lying on his right legge, & his left crosse his stomacke, the skin of his face & the hear [of] his hed beaten of wth the weather no pportyon in the lineaments of his body to be proaved, they ware so putryfied, a rnt. rottn canvas dublet, & his hose ragged, a blacke felt hat wth a cypres bande, and two laces tyed at thende of the band. Woodward digged the grave hard by hym where he lay, and they two pulled hym in, wth each of them a long foke."

—" Roger Pryce leaninge on a calyver charged wth hayle shotte on his left side, his matche in the same hande, the peece discharged soddenlye & kylled hyme presently, savinge as much tyme as wherein he prayed the standers by to pray to God for hym, & soe fallinge downe, desiered God hartely to forgive hym all hys synnes, and soe dyed the xxvith day of Julye. And was buried the xxvijth."

1589. "Elizabeth, the daughter of John Kynge & Clemence wyfe of Samuell Ffynche [*primus*] vycar by the space of vij yeares, mother of V children at severall byrthes, of the age of xxj yeares; deceased the xvijth day of November, and was buryed the xviijth, anno dni. 1589."

1596." Memoranda, that wheras Samuell Ffynche, Vicar of Croydon, lycensed Clemence Kynge, the wyfe of John Kynge, brewer, to cate fleshe in the tyme of Lente, by reason of her sicknesse, wch lycence beareth date the xxixth day of Ffebruary; and further, that she the sayde Clemence doth as yet contynue sicke, and hath not recovered her health: Knowe ye therfor, that the sayd lycence continueth still in force, and for the more efficacie therof, ys here registred according to the statute in the psence of Thomas Mosar, Churchwarden of the said parishe of Croydon, the vijth day of Marche, in the xxxviij yeare of the Queene's ma^{ts} moste gratious raigne, And for the registringe therof ther is paid unto the curate ivd."

—"John Whitgifte, Archbushop of Canterburie, deceassed at Lambith on Wednesday at viiij of the clocke in the eveninge, beinge the laste day of February. And was brought the day followinge in the eveninge to Croydon. And was buried the morninge followinge by two of the clocke in the chappell where his pore people doe usuallie sitte.* His ffunerall was kepte at Croydon the xxvijth day of Marche followinge. Anno dni. 1604. Anno regni dni nri Regis Jacobi Secundo." †

1607. April.—"Rycharde Esteinge, a young man, beinge killed suddenlye wth a stroke of thunder & lightninge on the [neck] & under the right eare: but nothinge but blacknesse scene, & the . . . . . . of . . . . . swealed, was buried the xixth day: and smelt of Brimstone exceedingle."

December, 1607.—"The greatest ffrost began ye ixth day of this month. Ended on Candlemas-eve."

1609.—"Ffranncis Tyrrell, cytezin & marchante of London, was buried the first day of September, and his ffunerall was kept at London the xiijth day of the same month. He gave two hundred poundes to the parishioners of Croydon, to builde them a newe market-house, and ffortie pounds to repaire our churche, and ffortie shillings a yeare to our pore of Croydon for xviij years, wyth

---

* From the wording, "in the chappell where his pore people doe usuallie sitte," it has been by some supposed that Archbishop Whitgift was not buried in Croydon Church, but in the chapel of the Hospital which he founded. However, any doubt that may have once existed on the subject is now set at rest, since the coffin of the Archbishop was seen under his monument in St. Nicholas's chancel or chapel, during the rebuilding of Croydon Church.

† "The custom of celebrating the funerals of eminent persons some time after their interment in the church of the parish where they had a residence, which continued many years after the Reformation, accounts for the above entry in the registry."—*Gough's Sepulchral Monuments in Great Britain.*

manie other good and greate legacyes to the citie of London."

1614-5, Feb. 12.—"This was the day of the terrible snowe, and the Sonday followinge a greater."

1633, Jan. 30.—Sepult. "Ralph Smith, yeoman of the guard."

—"George Abbot, Lord Archbishop of Cant., deceased at Croydon upon the 4th day of August, 1633. His funerall was with great solemnity kept in the church here, upon the third day of Septemb. following: and the next day his corps was convaide to Guilford, and there buryed according to his will."

1636, Sep. 9.—Bap. "Thomas Harvy, the sonne of Mr. Eliab Harvy." This Thomas Harvy was nephew to Dr. William Harvey, the celebrated discoverer of the circulation of the blood. It is supposed that several of the family are buried at Croydon.

1643, May 12.—"Sir Hugh Wirrall, Knight, was buried."

1649, March 29.—"My Lady Scudamore buried." Lady Scudamore was aunt not only to the patriot Hampden, but also to Edmund Waller, the poet.

1675, Ap. 11.—"Mr. Wm. Crow, Schoolmaster, was buried." He was a Chaplain of Whitgift's Hospital, and was author of a Catalogue of English Writers on the Old and New Testaments, 1659, which has been frequently printed. Melancholy to relate, this gentleman committed suicide.

1677, November 16.—"Gelbert Sheldon, laite Archbishop of Canterbury, buryed."

Under date March 31, 1722, the Croydon Register contains an entry to the effect, that 6 men were executed at Thornton Heath on that day: another entry, dated April, 1723, reports the execution of 4 other criminals, also at Thornton Heath. From such dreadful notes as these it may be inferred that, formerly, highway robbery was a crime of no unfrequent occurrence upon the London road.

—"Dr. William Wake, Archbishop of Canterbury, died at his palace at Lambeth, January 24, 1736, and was brought to Croydon and buried Feby 9, and his lady, which was buried at Lambeth the April, 1731, was taken up and brought to Croydon the next day, and put in the vault with him."

1743, October.—"George Brigstock was killed at Chelsham with a fall from his horse & buried y^o 27."

1745, August.—"Richard Cooper, son of Thomas, was drownded in a hog-tub & buried ye 8."

—December.—"Dame Lady Jane Cox now Collier wife of ye Rev. M^r. Nathaniel Collier (was buried) y^o 29th."

1746, January.—"James Fiz-Partrick a soulder was shott to death for desertion and buried on Bansteed Downs y^o 27."

—"Dr. John Potter, Archbishop of Canterbury, was buried October 27th, 1747."

1748.—"Hugh Benbridge, killed by a soldier the 22 of February, and buried y^o 29."

1749.—"Robert Saxby, servant to John How, Esq., of the parish of Oxteed, in Surrey, was robed and murdred at the end of Breach Lane, on Saterday, y^o 17th of March, and buried y^o 21."

1749, August 30.—"James Cooper, a highwayman, was executed on a gibet in Smithden Bottom, and there hanged in chains, for murdering and robing of Robert Saxby, groom to John How, Esq., of Barrowgreen, in the Parish of Oxteed in Surry, on the 17th of March, 1749, near Crome Hurste."

—"Dr. Thomas Herring, Archbishop of Canterbury, died at his palace at Croydon, and was buried Mar. 24th, 1757.

1760, September.—"John Dowsett was killed by a fall in repearing the roof of the Church, ye 5."

CHAPTER VII.

DOMESDAY BOOK.

From Domesday Book, that coeval monument of the Conquest of England by the Normans, we extract the entry relating to this Parish: the subjoined is a phototype facsimile:—

Of the above the following is the Latin extension:—

"Terra Archiepiscopi Cantvariensis. *In Waletone Hvndredo.* ij. Archiepiscopus Lanfrancus tenet in dominio Croindene. Tempore Regis Edwardi se defendebat pro quater viginti hidis et modo pro xvi hidis et una virgata. Terra est viginti carucarum. In dominio sunt iiii. carucæ et xlviii. uillani et xxv. bordarii cum xxxiiii. carucis. Ibi æcclesia et unus molinus de V. solidis et viii. acræ prati. Silua de cc. porcis.

De terra hujus Manerii tenet Restoldus vii. hidas de archiepiscopo.

Radulfus i hidam; et inde habent vii. libras et viii. solidos de gablo.

Totum tempore Regis Edwardi et post ualuit xii. libras. Modo xxvii libras archiepiscopo.

Hominibus ejus x. libras et x. solidos."

Rendered into English this signifies:—

"II.—THE LAND OF THE ARCHBISHOP OF CANTERBURY. *IN WALE-TONE (WALLINGTON) HUNDRED.**

"Archbishop Lanfranc holds in demesne Croindene (Croydon). In the time of King Edward (the Confessor) it was assessed for eighty hides,† and now for sixteen hides and one virgate.‡ The land is for (or sufficient to employ) twenty ploughs (ox teams). In demesne there are four ploughs, and forty-eight villans§ and twenty-five bordars‖ with thirty-four ploughs. Here a church; and one mill of (or yielding an annual rental of) five shillings, and eight acres¶ of meadow. Wood for two hundred swine.

"Of the land of this manor Restold holds seven hides of the Archbishop. Ralph (holds) one hide; and from thence they have

---

* Wallington is now a hamlet in the parish of Beddington.

† Mr. Kemble, in his learned work on "The Saxons in England," vol. i., pp. 88-121, defines the Hid or Hide of land as the estate of one household, the amount of land sufficient for the support of one family." " It must be borne in mind," he continues, " that the Hide comprised only arable land; the meadow and pasture was in the common lands and forests, and was attached to the Hide as of common right." The extent of the Hide (he argues) would necessarily vary according to the qualities of the soil, etc., but that ordinarily from thirty to thirty-three acres appear to have constituted the amount of the Hide among the Anglo-Saxons. Learned men differ in their explanations of the term " Hida."

‡ The *Virgata* of Domesday signifies the fourth part of the Hide.

§ *Villans*—holders of land by a mixed tenure, not clearly defined. They were burdened with stated services due from themselves and their land.

‖ The *Bordarii* are supposed to have been cottagers (from the Saxon "bord," a cottage) who held small portions of land upon condition of performing certain services to the lord.

¶ The Anglo-Saxon acre does not appear to have differed materially from the statute acre of our day. It seems to have been a fixed and not a variable quantity; apparently, however, there was a small as well as large acre—*Kemble.*

seven pounds and eight shillings for gable.* In the time of King Edward, and afterwards, the whole was worth twelve pounds. Now twenty-seven pounds to the Archbishop: and to his men (homagers) ten pounds and ten shillings."

---

* *Gable* or *Gavel*, a customary rent in money or kind, and sometimes a service performed to the King or any other lord.

CHAPTER VIII.

SITE OF CROYDON CHURCH AND PALACE.

THE accompanying map of the site of Croydon Palace and Church has been prepared in order to show how these were formerly surrounded by water.* The dotted lines indicate the roads in the vicinity as they coursed in the year 1800; doubtless some of these are very ancient paths.

(*a.*) The Church.
(*b.*) Ancient Quadrangular Court of Archiepiscopal Palace.
(*c.*) Old Vicarage.
(*d.*) Scarbrook Pond. ⎫ These were full of springs
(*e.*) " My Lord's Pond." ⎭ and abounded in trout.
(*f.*) Fish-ponds, formerly in the gardens of the Palace. Some of these, perhaps, were originally natural ponds; they were fed by streams issuing from Scarbrook and " My Lord's Pond."
(*g.*) Natural stream, formerly on the north side of Croydon Palace and Church. This stream issued from

---

* *Authorities consulted*—Ducarel's Map, of the year 1783; Map attached to the Award of the Commissioners appointed to Enclose the Common and Waste Lands at Croydon, dated in the year 1800; Plan attached to Auctioneer's Particulars of Palace Estate, dated January 14, 1829; Plan of the Estate opposite the Church, bought by Mr. Harris; Mr. Cox's Plan of the Town of Croydon, which accompanied " Report of Croydon Local Board of Health," dated November 27, 1849; and various living men who remember having seen the ponds, streams, and mills referred to, and who showed the writer arches and other remaining indications of the water-courses delineated.

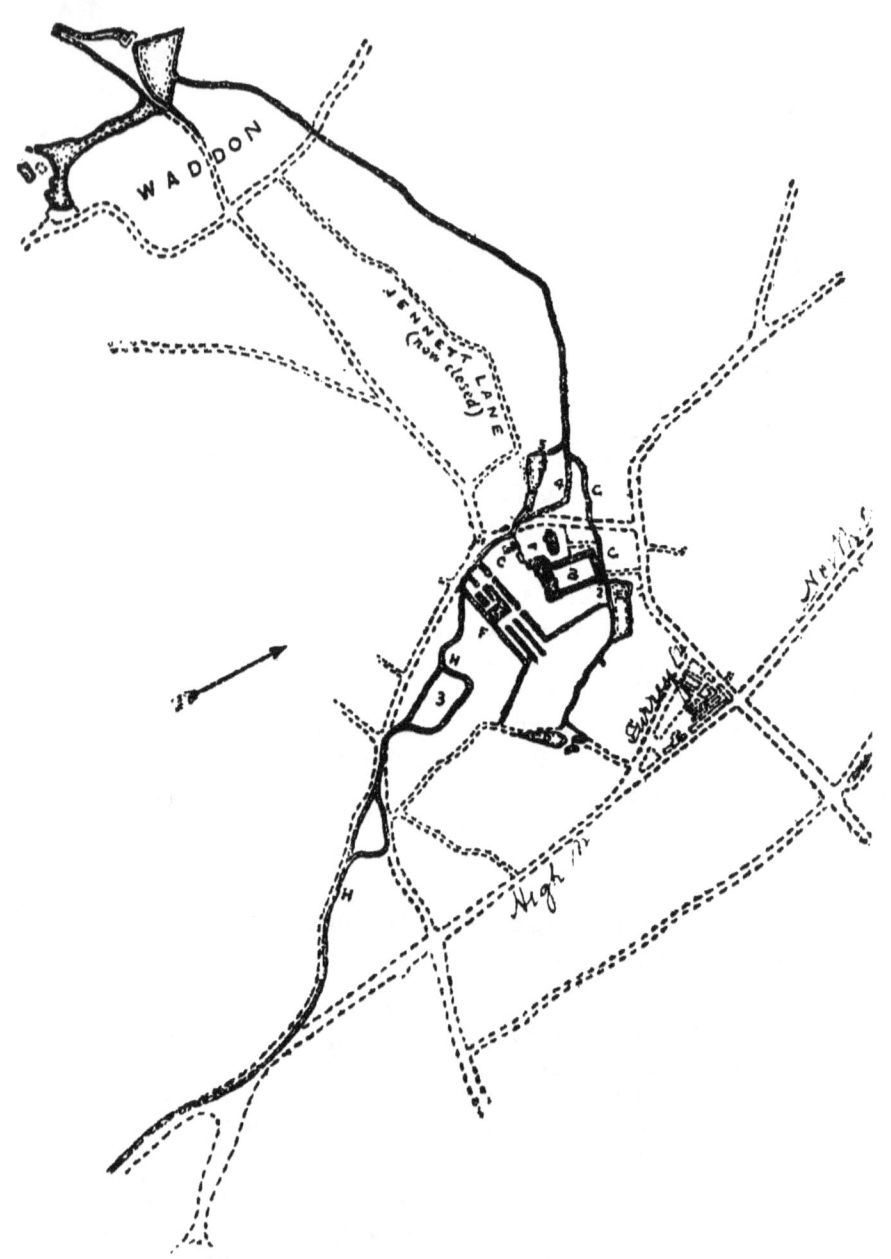

SITE OF CROYDON CHURCH AND PALACE.

"My Lord's Pond;" after coursing along the south side of Church Road (which road, however, is of recent origin) it crossed Church Street in a diagonal line due west, when, passing by the side of the north wall of Elys Davy's almshouse, it ultimately joined the main stream. Not many years since, the extensive machinery of a large calico-printing factory that stood at the spot indicated by the figure 2, was turned by water-power from an artificial branch of this stream. Mr. Edwards tells me he has often caught trout in the stream. The brick-arched watercourse, through which it ran past the north wall of Elys Davy's almshouse, remains to this day.

(*h.*) Natural stream upon the south side of palace and church; at such periods as the overflow of the bourn, this was traceable a distance of five or six miles, as far as Marden Park, on the Godstone Road. The spot shown by the figure 3, where Union Street now stands, is popularly known as "Bog Island:" a nomenclature sufficiently indicative of the original condition of the soil. The course of the stream round a large portion of Bog Island can easily be traced by an existing row of willow trees, and a succession of more objectionable landmarks. Arrived at the corner of the churchyard, this tributary head of the Wandle appears to have crossed the road, when, after coursing a short distance northwards, in front of, and within a few feet of, the tower of Croydon Church, it turned rather abruptly towards the west. The late Mr. Harris informed me he could distinctly remember, sixty years ago, catching trout in this stream opposite our old church. The width and depth of the stream varied according to the season; at the corner of the churchyard where the stream crossed the road, it was ordinarily from ten to twelve feet wide, and from nine to eighteen inches deep; where figure 4 is placed the depth was greater, namely, from ten inches to two feet. In order to obtain more water-power, the late Mr. Starey's father enlarged, or formed, the lake represented west of the church; and figure 5 indicates where a water-mill stood so recently as the year 1849. After Mr. Starey's time, the dimensions of this milldam were curtailed to the size and shape indicated by the dotted line, when a bath-house was erected where the black spot is placed; the site is now occupied by a dwelling-house called Bath Cottage.

In Domesday Book, in the entry relating to Croydon, it says, "here is a church *and a mill.*" Since, however, not one of the ponds or streams described now have any existence, without some reliable chart of the positions these formerly occupied to guide his judgment, fifty years hence a local historian might assign to the mill referred to in Domesday a site more remote from the church than perhaps he would have done had he been conversant with the topography of our parish prior to the date when it was handed over to the care of the Local Board of Health. For, doubtless, to the enlightened labours of the gentlemen composing this board, it is mainly owing that a district, recently traversed by dangerous fever-emitting open sewers, has been transformed into a healthy locality. During the process, however, the surface springs and once pure waters and purling brooks that surrounded Croydon Palace and Church have disappeared; no longer can it be said they stand upon an island.

CHAPTER IX.

THE ARCHIEPISCOPAL PALACE AT CROYDON.

THE capital residence of the Archbishops of Canterbury was anciently the Palace situated near their Cathedral at Canterbury, and given by King Ethelbert, after his conversion to Christianity, to Augustine and his successors for ever. But, besides this palace, the Archbishops had many other castles, seats, and manors where they from time to time resided, as their inclination for retirement or pleasure directed them. Of this number was the manor of Croydon, a place which for many ages has belonged to the See of Canterbury.

Although a considerable portion of the buildings still exist, Croydon Palace, unfortunately, is too much altered and mutilated to tell its history otherwise than in an imperfect manner. Upon the spot now occupied by its remains may once have stood the residence of an Anglo-Saxon chief, the thegn, perhaps, who founded the adjoining church. Yet, whether a dwelling-house stood here in Anglo-Saxon times or otherwise, Domesday Book informs us that, when William the Conqueror's commissioners visited these parts, they found Archbishop Lanfranc in possession of the Manor of Croydon. As a rule, Domesday states in regard to places it describes to whom they belonged in King Edward the Confessor's time; in respect, however, to Croydon, the Norman scribe is silent as to who had been its Saxon owner. Yet, to whomsoever it appertained in Anglo-Saxon times, certain it is that, ere the Surrey Domesday was compiled, Croydon had passed to an Italian ecclesiastic who held the same of the

Norman Duke; for the great battle of Hastings had been fought and won, and William, having slain Harold, was now wearing the English crown.

Appertaining to the Norman manor, in all likelihood, was the capital messuage or mansion of the *scigneur*, or lord of the fee, from whose usual abiding therein indeed, the word manor, *manoir*, is derived; so that this, being essentially connected therewith, probably was coeval with the manor itself, and, consequently, in existence between A.D. 1066 and A.D. 1087, within which years Croydon was presented by the Conqueror to Lanfranc.

Archbishop LANFRANC (A.D. 1070–89) then having received from King William a certain quantity of land here, to be parcelled out amongst inferior tenants holding under the Archbishop, of necessity would require a place in which to assemble those tenants at stated times to pay the rents, and perform such service as by their tenure were due. "I shall, therefore, not scruple," writes the learned antiquary, Edward Rowe Mores, "to set down Archbishop Lanfranc as the first founder of the Palace of Croydon."* Of Lanfranc's presumed building at Croydon not a trace is now visible.

That a house existed here in 1273 appears by a mandate of

Archbishop KILWARDBY (A.D. 1273–78), dated from Croydon on the 4th of September of that year. It shows that this primate once lived at Croydon; and his dwelling here may be received as evidence that this house was then fit for the reception of so great a prelate.

The Archiepiscopal Registers preserved at Lambeth commence only with Archbishop PECKHAM (A.D. 1279–92), who resided much at Croydon. During Peckham's tenure of office occurs the earliest mention of a chapel in this

---

* Quoted in "Some Account of the Palace of Croydon," etc., published by Dr. Ducarel in the twelfth number of the "Bibliotheca Topographica Britannica."

manor of Croydon ; in the record of an ordination holden therein in the year 1283.

Archbishop WINCHELSEY succeeded (A.D. 1294–1313). With the latter part of his pontificate, or, perhaps, with the age of his successor,

Archbishop REYNOLDS (A.D. 1313–27), who also occasionally lived here, coincide certain reparations made at Croydon, the particulars of which are mentioned in the ministers' accounts of the year. The roll is imperfect, and the date wanting, but Richard de Fairford was then bailiff, and Thomas de Bunchesham reeve of Croydon. In that year the kitchen and salsary were repaired, the wardrobe boarded, the bakehouse and stable, together with the sheepcotes and stalls for oxen, weather-boarded, and put into repair. The buildings were then all of timber, no other workmen but carpenters being employed about them. In the same roll is another charge on account of the kitchen-garden and the vineyard.

During the short period of two years (A.D. 1366–68), in which Archbishop LANGHAM enjoyed the See, he was once at Croydon.

Archbishop WHITTLESEY (A.D. 1368–74) appears to have resided here, and to have celebrated three ordinations in the chapel of his manor of Croydon in the year 1371.

Archbishop SUDBURY (A.D. 1375–81) was here four times only ; but his successor,

Archbishop COURTENAY (A.D. 1381–96) came here soon after his election, and received his pall, with great solemnity, in the great hall of Croydon Palace, on May 4, 1382. This prelate spent part of every year of his pontificate at Croydon. It appears that the mansion house of Croydon had, by this time, increased both in its buildings and its conveniences; for, whereas, hitherto the Archbishops had no more than one chamber whither they could retire, namely, their bed-chamber, so that acts are frequently said to be performed *juxta lectum domini* and *ad pedes lecti*, mention is now made of a more honourable apartment called the chief or principal chamber.* Courtenay built a chapel in his manor of Croydon, underneath the privy chamber, near the garden, wherein a special ordination was held on the 28th of May, 1390. This seems to have been a small chapel intended for private use, and after its erection the previously mentioned old chapel appears, by way of distinction, to be called "the chapel of the manor of Croydon, *capella manerii de Croydon.*" In Archbishop Courtenay's time a new granary was erected here, with a chamber over it, and also a wall contiguous thereto, built towards the churchyard. This brings us to the time of

Archbishop ARUNDEL (A.D. 1397–1414). To his pontificate is ascribed the *computus*, or roll of Adam Bochers, reeve of Croydon from Michaelmas, 1399, to Michaelmas, 1400. In the roll referred to, Bochers, by his attorney, John Pieres, accounts for a sum of money expended in building a new stable and chambers at Croydon, of which the particulars are accurately enumerated. This stable is afterwards described as the *new stable*, and the *great stable*, to distinguish it from the *old* stable. Between the two stables there was a wall of lath and plaster, defended at the top with ridge tiles (the ordinary method of constructing walls before the use of bricks was generally introduced); and another wall of the same material connected the great stable with an apartment called the privy chamber: both of these were built in this year. The same roll informs us of another building, which also was then reared from its foundation. This is called the hall, and described as being situate opposite the cellar towards the *herbarium*. The repairs of this year were re-hanging the great gate of the manor, and the racks in the old stable; a reparation of the chamber over the granary; a new door to the cellar, and a new door-case of Caen stone: out of doors, the inclosure about the pond of my lord's

* Reg. Courtenay, fol. 9 a.

garden, and the enclosure of the garden itself were amended; and a new hedge was made from my lord's park to a spot between the corner of the kitchen and the pond.

Soon after these alterations, Archbishop Arundel ordained an oratory within his manor of Croydon, from whence it has been surmised that the chapel belonging to this manor was now either rebuilt or repaired. The arms of this prelate appearing on two corbels in the guard-chamber, also tends towards the supposition that this was erected by him.

Archbishop CHICHELEY, who filled the See of Canterbury from A.D. 1414 to 1443, resided much at Croydon. In his register he appointed Adam Pykman and Richard Pykman *custodes capitalis mansi manerii de Croydon* for life. This act is dated from Lambeth, July 7, 1441. After the decease of Chicheley,

Archbishop STAFFORD (A.D. 1443–52) made Croydon one of his principal residences. The arms of this prelate are more than once repeated in the hall, which seems to indicate that he repaired and beautified it, if it was not entirely rebuilt by him. And if evidence were elsewhere wanting to prove that Archbishop Stafford resided at Croydon, it is found in a carpenter's bill for making my lord's new bed at the manor-house of Croydon. Most of the acts of his successor,

Archbishop KEMP (A.D. 1452–54), are dated from Lambeth and Croydon. We come now to

Archbishop BOUCHIER, who held the See thirty-three years, from A.D. 1454 to 1486. Croydon was one of the chief places of his residence. Early in the pontificate of Bouchier, this manor house and the out-houses belonging to it were new tiled. Among other particulars recorded as having been made at Croydon by the same Archbishop in 1475, mention is made of "work done this year over the altar in the chapel, for placing the jewels upon." The earliest mention of a dove-house at this place is also met with in the accounts of the same year. In 1485, John

Lyttell, then keeper of the manor of Croydon, accounted for lx. s. iii. d. laid out in repairs there done.

Archbishop MORTON (A.D. 1486–1500), who was also a Cardinal, occasionally resided at Croydon.

Archbishop WARHAM (A.D. 1503–32), although he lived chiefly at Lambeth and Knole, yet sometimes dwelt at Canterbury, Charing, and Croydon.

Archbishop CRANMER'S (A.D. 1533–56) arms, formerly emblazoned on the south-east window of the guard-chamber, appear to indicate that he repaired this house. It was at Croydon Palace that the learned and excellent John Fryth, who afterwards suffered martyrdom at Smithfield, on July 4, 1533, appeared before Archbishop Cranmer, Dr. Heath, and others appointed by the King for that purpose, to answer for his opinions concerning Transubstantiation, etc. On the night of his arrival at Croydon, poor Fryth was "well entertained in the porter's lodge."

Cardinal POLE'S (A.D. 1556–58) principal residence was at Lambeth and Westminster, but one act of his is dated at Croydon.

Archbishop PARKER (A.D. 1559–75) often resided at Croydon Palace. In 1567 Queen Elizabeth appears to have visited the prelate at Croydon, where, on the 30th of April, she held a Council. On Wednesday, July 14, 1573, the great Queen came here from her palace at Greenwich, and with all her attendants stayed at Croydon Palace for seven days. It would seem also from the following paper, containing the arrangements for the reception of the Queen's retinue, that Her Majesty was so well pleased with her entertainment that she intended to, if Her Majesty did not actually, re-visit Croydon in the following year:—

"Lodgins at Croyden, the Busshope of Canterburye's house, bestowed as followeth, the 19th of Maye, 1574:—

"The Lord Chamberlayne [*] his old lodginge.

---

[*] Thomas Radclyffe, Earl of Sussex.

The L Tresurer* wher he was
The La Marques† at y⁰ nether end of the great chamber
The La of Warwick wher she was
The Erle of Lecester‡ wher he was
The Lord Admyrall§ at y⁰ nether end of y⁰ great chamber
The La Howard wher she was
The Lo of Honsdane wher he was
Mr Secretarye Walsingham wher Mr Smyth‖ was
The La Stafforde wher she was
Mr Henedge¶ wher he was
Mrs Drewreye wher y⁰ La Sydney was
Ladis and gentylwomen of y⁰ Privye Chamber ther olde
Mrs Abbington her olde, and one other small rome added for y⁰ table
The maydes of honnor wher they wer
Sir George Howard wher he was
The Capten of y⁰ gard** wher my L of Oxford was
The gromes of y⁰ Privye Chamber ther olde
The esquyeres for the bodye ther olde
The gentylmen husshers ther olde
The phesycyas ij chambers
The Quen's robes wher they were
The grome porter wher he was
The clark of the Kytchen wher he was
The wardrobe of bedes.

For the Quen's wayghters, I cannot as yet fynde anye convenyent romes to place them in, but I will doo the best y^t I can to place them elsewher, but yf y^t please you S^r y^t I doo remove them. The gromes of the Privye Chamber nor Mr Drewrye have no other waye to ther chambers but to pas thorowe that waye agayne that my Lady of Oxford should come. I cannot then tell wher to place Mr Hatton; and for my La Carewe here is no place with a chymeney for her, but that she must ley abrode by Mrs Aparry and the rest of y⁰ Pryvy Chambers. For Mrs Shelton here is no romes with chymeneys; I shall staye one chamber without

---

* William Cecil, Lord Burleigh.
† Elizabeth Paulet, Marchioness of Winchester.
‡ Robert Dudley.
§ Edward Fynes, Earl of Lincoln.
‖ Afterwards Sir Thomas, and Secretary of State.
¶ Afterwards Sir Thomas, Vice-Chamberlain.
** Christopher Hatton, Esq., afterwards Sir Christopher.

for her. Here is as mutche as I have any wayes able to doo in this house From Croyden this present Wensday mornyinge, your Honnors alwayes most bowden

S. BOWYER."

The arms of Archbishop Parker were formerly emblazoned on the bow window of the guard chamber of Croydon Palace.*

Archbishop GRINDAL (A.D. 1575–6–1583), when urged to resign the archbishopric, petitioned that he might retain this residence and the adjoining meadow called "Stubbs," Croydon Park, and eighteen acres of meadow at Norbury. "Croydon house," he said, "was no wholesome house, and that, both his predecessor and he found by experience; notwithstanding, because of the nearness to London, whither he must often repair, or send to have some help of physic, he knew no house so convenient for him, or that might better be spared of his successor for the short time of his life." † Archbishop Grindal died here on July 6, 1583.

Archbishop WHITGIFT (A.D. 1583–1603–4) resided much at Croydon, and this mansion is first called *Palatium* in his Register, on the 9th of July, 1599, in the act of the dedication of the chapel of his Hospital of the Holy Trinity. Sir George Paul, in his life of Whitgift, observes, "The Archbishop had ever a great affection to lie at his mansion house at Croydon, for the sweetness of the place, especially in summer time, whereby also he might sometimes retire himself from the multiplicity of business, and suitors in the vacation; yet after he had builded his hospital and his school, he was farther in love with the place than before."

Archbishop ABBOT (A.D. 1611–33) also resided much at this palace. According to the Harleian MSS.‡ "The Archbish. of Canterbury (Abbot) had a house by Croydon, pleasantly sited, but that it was too much woodbound, so

---

* Ducarel. † Strype's "Life of Grindal, p. 284.
‡ No 6395, p. 90.

he cutt downe all upon the front to the highway. Not long after, the L. Chancellor Bacon riding by that way, asked his man whose faire house that was; he told him my L. of Canterburie's. It is not possible, sayes he, for his building is inviron'd with wodde. 'Tis true S`r`, sayes he, it was so, but he has lately cut most of it downe. By my troth (answered Bacon), he has done very judiciously, for before methoughts it was a very obscure and darke place, but no whe has expounded and cleared it wonderfully well." Archbishop Abbot died at Croydon Palace on the 5th of August, 1633. He was succeeded by

Archbishop LAUD (A.D. 1633–44), whose arms were formerly in the north window of the guard chamber, and are still to be seen in the chapel. At the trial of this prelate, Browne, his joiner, being examined at the Lord's Bar against his will, confessed upon his oath, that in the chapel at Croydon there was an old broken crucifix in the window, which he, by the Archbishop's direction, caused to be repaired and made complete; which picture was there remaining very lately; for which work Master Prynn found the glazier's bill, discharged by the Archbishop himself, among others of his papers. Laud put up an organ in the chapel, as appears by his will, a copy of which is preserved in the Manuscript Library at Lambeth.

"In the times of anarchy and confusion," says the learned Ducarel, "which ensued after the death of Archbishop Laud, this palace, with the estate about it, was wrested from the ee of Canterbury, and offered to sales a particular survey for that purpose (wherein the material; of this house, which was to be taken down and sold, were valued at £1,200) being made the 17th of March, 1646, to which time the palace, and everything that belonged to it, had been leased by the then ruling powers to the Earl of Nottingham; after which the possession of it fell to Sir William Brereton, Colonel-General for the Cheshire Forces, who turned the chapel into a kitchen, which, I suppose, continued in that condition till the Restoration, in 1660, when

"Archbishop JUXON (A.D. 1660–63) repaired and fitted it up in a handsome decent manner, as appears by his arms in several parts of it, and in the north window of the guard chamber."

Archbishop SHELDON (A.D. 1663–77) in the latter part of his life retired here, and died in this palace on November 9, 1677. His arms were emblazoned in the north window of the old guard chamber.

Archbishop TENISON'S (A.D. 1694–1715) regard for Croydon was manifested by his founding a charity school in this town; it is uncertain, however, whether or not he resided here.

Archbishop WAKE (A.D. 1716–37) resided several summers at Croydon Palace. It was Wake who rebuilt the long gallery.

Archbishop POTTER (A.D. 1737–47) seldom resided here, although he was buried in the neighbouring church.

Archbishop HERRING (A.D. 1747–57) thoroughly repaired and furnished this palace, and much improved the gardens. In a letter from this prelate to Dr. Ducarel, dated Croydon House, 1752, the Archbishop writes:—"I love this old house, and am very desirous of amusing myself with the history of its buildings, for the house is not one, but most certainly an aggregate of buildings of different tastes and ages." In Archbishop Herring's time the ancient alms, commonly called the Dole, used to be regularly distributed at the gate of Croydon Palace. Archbishop Herring died here on March 13, 1757.

Archbishop HUTTON (A.D. 1757–58) resided at Croydon in the summer of 1757. As Archbishops Secker and Cornwallis, Hutton's immediate successors, did not make Croydon their place of residence, this palace became greatly dilapidated, and, in 1780, an Act of Parliament was obtained by which the palace and appurtenances were vested in four trustees—namely, the Lord Chancellor, the Lord Chief Justice of the King's Bench, and the Bishops of London and Winchester, who, by virtue of such power, sold by auction, October 10, 1780, to Abraham Pitches, Esq., of Streatham (afterwards Sir Abraham)—" The freehold and absolute inheritance in fee simple of the said capital messuage or mansion house, with its rights, members, and appurtenances, and also all houses, out-houses, edifices, buildings, gardens, orchards, tenements, hereditaments, and appurtenances, to the said capital messuage or hereditaments belonging, and their and every of their appurtenances; and also two closes of land, containing by estimation about six acres, contiguous to or near the said capital messuage, with their appurtenances; and also the water conduit or conduits, situate in a mead, called Parson's mead, in Croydon, with the aqueducts and the leaden pipe or pipes leading therefrom to a cistern in the said palace" —for 2,520*l.*

It was not long ere a change took place, in regard to this ancient residence of the Primates of all England: a comparison of the buildings represented on the old, with the present, ground plan of the palace will show the extent of the work of destruction. For some years past the chapel has been, and still is, used as a Girls' School of Industry; and various apartments of the Old Palace, at present, are occupied residentially. But the great hall, and a considerable portion of the remaining buildings, with the gardens, are appropriated to the purpose of washing and bleaching linen. Such has been the fate of Croydon Palace, formerly the seat of learning, and the splendid residence for many centuries of the Archbishops of Canterbury.

Previous to its partial demolition Croydon Palace consisted of one large square court or quadrangle; containing a chapel, a hall, a buttery and kitchen, with other necessary apartments, and a long gallery. The east and west sides of the great court are said to have presented very early examples of buildings built entirely with bricks,* but these have long since disappeared; nor has it fared otherwise

---

* According to Leland, the walls of Kingston-upon-Hull, were made *al of brike* in the time of Richard II. (1377-99).

with the range of buildings that constituted the north side of the great court, including the housekeeper's house and the porter's lodge, which have all vanished likewise, excepting a mouldering stone arch of the inner gate.

Of the surviving portions of Croydon Palace, the great hall is of stone. At the north-east corner stands the porch, that once formed the principal entrance to the mansion. This porch is considered to be older than the hall itself; its outer archway forms a richly moulded pointed entrance; the stone roof is groined. The length of the hall is about fifty-six feet, and its width thirty-eight feet. Its roof, of oak, is a fine example of open timber Perpendicular work; the principals rest on a series of stone corbels, on which are represented angels bearing shields of arms. The windows that light the apartment were probably once filled in with richly stained glass. Originally the hearth was in the centre of the hall, and here they used to pile the blazing logs, until a ruddy glow was diffused into the remotest corner of this large chamber, while the smoke of the fire, curling upwards, escaped through a turret or louvre in mid-roof. No trace now remains of that dais, or raised platform, at the upper end of the hall, where the lord of the mansion and his guests were wont to sit, in days when the proudest noble deemed it no dishonour to eat his meals in the common hall, along with the humblest of his servants; nor is there a vestige left of the orielle, or long passage, formerly at the west end of this apartment. The music gallery was situated at the lower or east end of the hall, and was supported by a screen. Behind this screen were three arched doorways, one leading to the ancient buttery, or place for giving out the beer and other drinks; the second to the kitchen, where the great feasts used to be cooked, and the third to the pantry, whence were distributed the bread and provisions, excepting the meat. The latter offices, which connected the hall with the servants' apartments on the eastern side of the great court, were taken down in 1810. The whole of the east end of the hall fell on the 8th of June, 1830.

Affixed to the upper end of the chamber is the following remarkable coat of arms, supported by two angels—viz., *azure*, a cross fleury, *or*, between five martlets of the second, for Edward the Confessor; impaling quarterly, 1 and 4, *azure*, three fleur-de-lis, *or*, for France; 2 and 3, *gules*, three lions passant guardant, *or*, for England. Under these arms is another angel holding a scroll, which bore* the following now illegible inscription:

Dne salbum fac regem.

" The covered crown," says Steinman, " surmounting the shield, being first used by Henry VI., and his arms on the Charter of foundation of Eton College having the same supporters, this coat has naturally been assigned to that king."

The arms of Archbishop Stafford—*or*, in a border engrailed, *sable*, a chevron, *gules*, charged with a mitre, of the first—formerly occupied a conspicuous position at the east end of the hall, and from this circumstance, joined to the fact that the same arms appear elsewhere in the chamber, it has been inferred that this hall was either entirely renovated or rebuilt by Archbishop Stafford, in place of an older, and it may have been a smaller apartment. On the north-east corbel also were once emblazoned—*or*, a chevron, *gules*—the arms of Humphrey, Earl of Stafford, created Duke of Buckingham in 1444, to whom the Archbishop was related; and opposite, formerly, were the arms of the See of Bath and Wells, of which diocese Stafford was bishop ere he was promoted to the Primacy.

On the second corbel at the east end of the north side of the hall is an unknown coat of arms: quarterly, 1 and 4, *gules*, a chief, *or*; 2 and 3, chequy *or* and *azure*, a chief of the second, over all a bend sinister, *or*. The third, on the same side, contains the armorial bearings of Henry, Earl of Stafford: quarterly, 1, the arms of France and England impaled, in a border, *argent*; 2 and 3, *azure*, on a bend

---

* Steinman, " Hist. of Croydon," p. 106.

cotised, *argent*, three mullets, *or*, between six lions rampant, *gules*, for Bohun; 4, *or*, a chevron, *gules*, for Stafford. The shield on the next corbel bears the arms of France and England quarterly, with a label of three points, supposed to be the arms of Richard, Duke of York, the leader of the party of the Red Rose. The last corbel on this side exhibits the arms of the See of Canterbury impaling those of Archbishop Juxon* — namely, *argent*, a cross, *gules*, between four Moors' heads, fullfaced, proper.

Turning now to the south side of the room, on the second corbel, at east end of wall, are the heraldic insignia of the See of Bath and Wells: *azure*, a saltire, quarterly, *or* and *argent*, impaling the arms of Archbishop Stafford. Next are the arms of the See of Canterbury, impaling those of Archbishop Stafford. Affixed to the fourth corbel are the arms of the same See, and these, according to Steinman, formerly impaled those of Archbishop Herring*—viz., *gules*, semée of cross crosslets, *argent*, three herrings, hauriant, of the last. On the south-west corbel is the device of the same See impaling Archbishop Laud's arms: *sable*, on a chevron, *or*, three cross pattées fitchées, *gules*, between three estoiles *,argent*. Some of the above-named escutcheons are nicely cut out, but the colouring has faded.

Glancing at its position on the older map, it will be noticed that the great hall of Croydon Palace, like those at Haddon and Penshurst, once occupied a central site in relation to other portions of the mansion; a position determined by the requirements of mediæval society, when it was the custom for an entire household to meet at meal time in a common hall. Leading off the dais, or upper end of the hall, some four or five centuries ago, used to be the apartments of the lord and his family; whilst access to the servants' rooms was obtained from the opposite or lower end of the hall. Behind the dais, in olden times, generally were two chambers, one over the other; the lower apart-

* Both Archbishops Juxon and Herring repaired and fitted up this Palace.

ment was called the cellar, and the upper one the sollar; it was from the latter that the lord descended with his family into the hall; and into it, or a chamber similarly adjoining the upper end of the hall, at a later and more refined period, the lord's family used to withdraw, when, under the potent influences of the wassail bowl, the noise and roysterous merriment of the retainers became unbearable; hence our word *drawing*-room.

The apartment thus described, for centuries continued to be the great hall, banqueting, and council chamber of the Archbishops of Canterbury; and, in days when the lord of the manor of Croydon combined in his own person the great position of a prince of the Church with that of chancellor or chief political adviser to the monarch, doubtless many a stirring incident has been enacted within its walls. At this ancient threshold envoys and ambassadors have met a fitting reception, and in this hall many an illustrious noble and scholar have been entertained, and even royalty itself feasted. Oft have the majestic beams of this grand old roof been lit up and warmed by the great crackling yule log beneath, and its rafters rung with acclamations of the Archbishop's guests and retainers, as with cup and horn, well filled, they pledged to the health of that primate whose hospitality knew no bounds, saving the limits of those vast resources formerly attached to the see. But times are changed; and, as the escutcheons on these walls have mouldered, so the tapestry, that once hung down them, all tarnished, has faded away; and this hall is now desolate. Alas! the good and great, as well as all the merry mummers, their revels over, have gone to that bourne whence no traveller returns.

The next great room in Croydon Palace to be noticed is the guard chamber. It is built partly of stone and partly of brick; it is situate on the west side of the great hall, and is about fifty feet long by twenty-two feet wide. In former times this also must have been a noble apartment. The massive oak principals of the roof spring from four

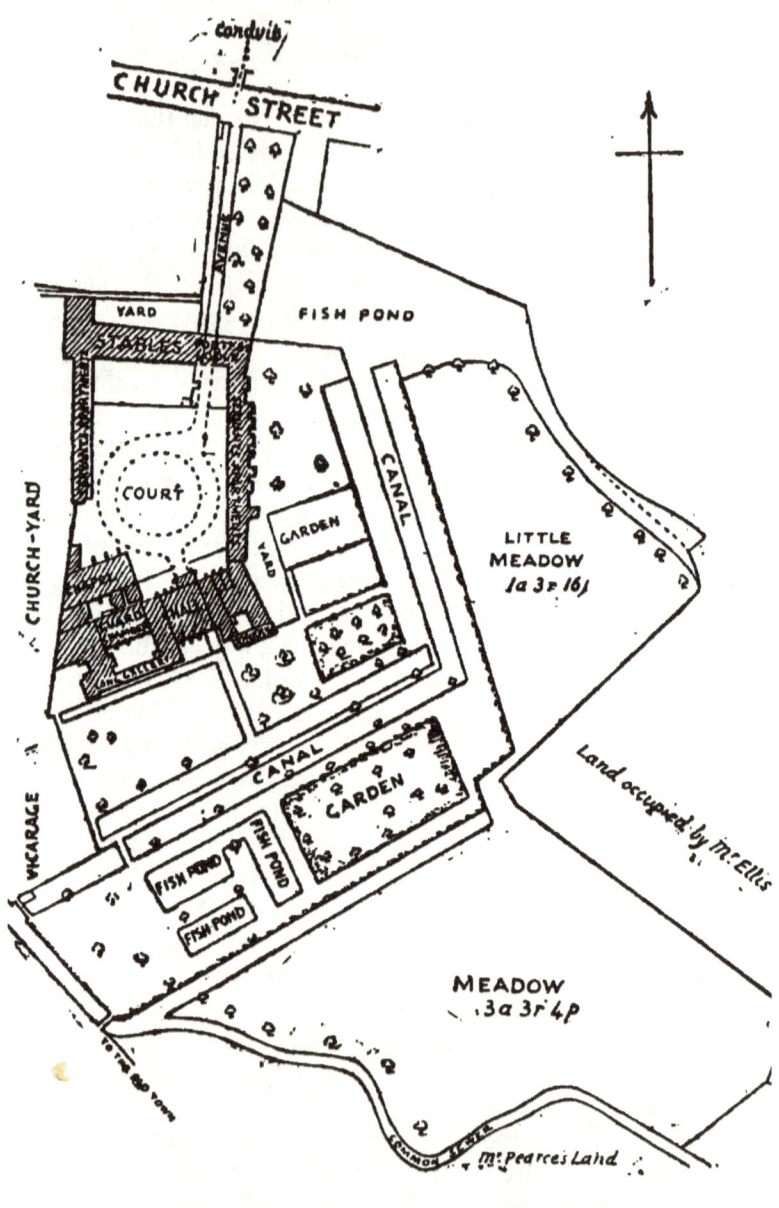

PLAN OF CROYDON PALACE AND GROUNDS IN 1780.

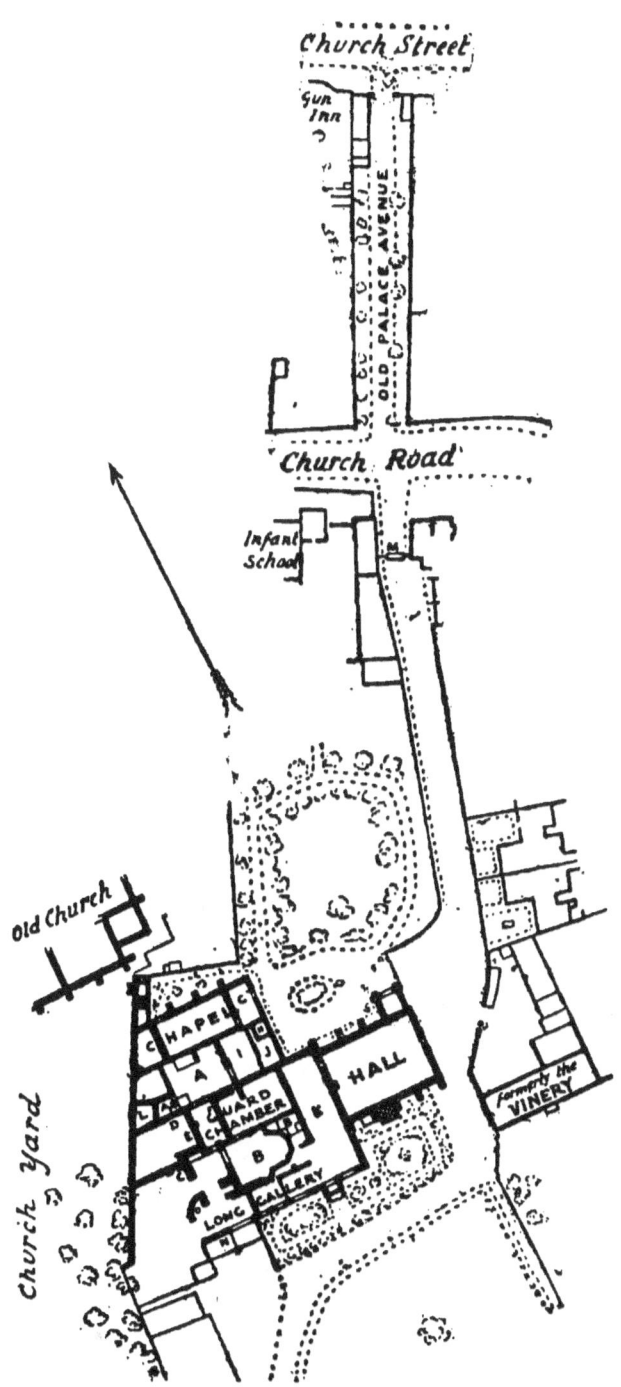

GROUND PLAN OF CROYDON PALACE A.D. 1881.

large stone corbels displaying angels bearing shields, two on either side; and from four smaller corbels, one in each corner of the chamber. These carvings are superior both in design and execution. From the circumstance that the armorial bearings of no other person but those of Archbishop Arundel appear on these corbels, it is concluded that the guard chamber at Croydon Palace owes its construction to this Primate; and he is said to have built it in the place where before stood the principal chamber. The stained glass that formerly adorned the windows of this apartment has now entirely disappeared; and like the great hall, this guard chamber, at present, is so cut up into various compartments, that it is impossible to obtain anything like a just view of its proportions.

The rude *dining-room* which extends from the guard-chamber to the churchyard, as well as the adjoining apartments, are of brick; the ceilings of some of the chambers underneath are of wood, and very low, the windows below stairs small; "And though," adds Ducarel, "they are not of the same make as those of the (now pulled down) east and west sides of the great court, yet I take this building to be near as old, and to have been built some time in the reign of King Henry VI. It hath been so frequently repaired and altered by the several archbishops of this see, that there are at present few or no marks to ascertain the time when it was first erected." Some of the underneath brick and rubble walls in this part of the old mansion are very thick. Where the letter D is placed (see Ground Plan, p. 91) there is an ancient narrow light, and in the same cellar, beneath the dining-room, at the spot indicated by E, is a blocked-up pointed doorway, and there is another pointed archway at F. It is possible that these dimly lighted damp vaults may, at one time, have served as a receptacle for some unfortunate prisoner of State, consigned to the Archbishop's custody; or in the evil times of intolerance they may have been appropriated to be the dungeon of a luckless Gospeller or Lollard: but the secrets of these chambers are like those of the grave.

The *long gallery* forms part of the south front of the palace; it was rebuilt by Archbishop Wake on the site of the ancient one. On the 29th of April, 1587, Sir Christopher Hatton was appointed Lord Chancellor " at Croydon, in the Archbishop of Canterburie's house, where he received the great seale in the gallery there."* A long gallery was considered to be a necessary adjunct to the mansions of England in the olden time; the long gallery at Knole presents a perfect example, but this, at Croydon, is now divided. Structurally speaking, there is a marked difference between the workmanship in the more modern portions of the mansion and that executed during the fourteenth century; for this, of a later period, is mean in conception, and not to be compared with the bold carving and timber work of the earlier time.

The large space indicated by the letter K on the plan is said to have been occupied by the Archiepiscopal Library. AA and BB denote the sites of small open courts.

Formerly there were two, if not three, chapels in this palace, intended for public or private use. The principal chapel, and the chapel of the manor of Croydon, probably were one and the same fabric which stood on the site occupied by the present chapel—namely, north-west of the great hall, and close by the old churchyard. It is approached from churchyard and garden by two small doorways, and a stone staircase at the north-west corner of the chapel. The plan is that of a narrow oblong; the material red brick, with stone casing for doors and windows. There was formerly a small belfry at the west end. Viewed from the adjoining churchyard, the cross-keys and a cross appear wrought with black brick on its western gable. In the south-west corner of the antechapel is a kind of gallery or pulpit of the Renaissance style, overlooking a perforated oak screen, and on it are emblazoned the arms of the Archiepiscopal See impaling those of Archbishop Laud. The Primate's seat, on the

* Stowe's "Annals," p. 742.

right of entrance to choir, has a canopy. On the knobs of the oak benches at the west end of the choir, are carved the arms of Archbishop Laud, impaled successively by those of the Sees of St. David's, Bath and Wells, London and Canterbury; of the deanery of Gloucester; and of St. John's College, Oxford. The east end benches are adorned, on both sides, by the arms of Archbishop Juxon. The interior of the chapel is lit by seven windows, consisting of plain lancet-shaped lights. The roof, of wood, has a depressed slope. The floor underneath the east end bay is raised.

The following Bishops were consecrated in the chapel of Croydon Palace:—

May 6, 1553.—John Harley, D.D., Bishop of Hereford, by Archbishop Cranmer, assisted by Nicholas (Ridley), Bishop of London, and Robert (Aldrich), Bishop of Carlisle.

June 26, 1553.—John Taylor, D.D., Bishop of Lincoln, by the same Archbishop, assisted by Nicholas, Bishop of London, and John (Scory), Bishop of Rochester,

August 2, 1579.—John Woolston, D.D., Bishop of Exeter, by Archbishop Grindal, assitsed by John (Elmer), Bishop of London, and John (Young), Bishop of Rochester.

September 18, 1580.—John Watson, D.D., Bishop of Winchester, and William Overton, D.D., Bishop of Lichfield and Coventry, by the same Archbishop, assisted as before.

September 3, 1581.—John Bullingham, D.D., Bishop of Gloucester by the same Archbishop, assisted as before.

August 24, 1628.—Richard Mountague, D.D., Bishop of Chichester by William (Laud), Bishop of London, Richard (Neile), Bishop of Winton, John (Buckeridge), Bishop of Ely, and Francis (White), Bishop of Carlisle.

September 7, 1628.—Leonard Mawe, D.D., Bishop of Bath and Wells, and Walter Curll, D.D., Bishop of Rochester, by Archbishop Abbot, assisted by Richard (Neile), Bishop of Winton, John, Bishop of Ely, and Francis, Bishop of Carlisle.

October 24, 1630.—William Peirse, D.D., Bishop of Peterborough, by the same Archbishop, assisted by Richard, Bishop of Winton, Theophilus (Field), Bishop of St. Davids, Richard (Corbet), Bishop of Oxford, and John (Bowle), Bishop of Rochester.

The old *greenhouse* or vinery, at the south-east corner of the mansion, is now converted into a dwelling. The orchard has been cut down; the canal and all the fish-ponds have disappeared.

Croydon Palace is lowly situate, and, as a reference to the map on page 72 will show, was once surrounded by running streams. The principal approach was through an avenue from Church Street, formerly guarded by iron gates, the red brick and stone capped piers of which, erected by Archbishop Potter, still bear date, 1742.

Surrounded by woods, trout streams, and vineyards, as it used to be in days of yore, Croydon Palace, during a all long succession of summers, afforded to the Primates of England a very pleasant retreat from care and the multiplicity of business.

CHAPTER X.

LORDS OF THE MANOR.

SINCE the Archbishops of Canterbury were lords of the Manor of Croydon, and for many hundreds of years were accustomed occasionally to reside in their mansion-house here, it follows that their lives are inseparably interwoven with the history of this parish. The Primates who are known to have lived at Croydon, form a majority of the men who have occupied the See of Canterbury since the Norman Conquest. Of these, therefore, we have collected together a series of short biographic notices in the following chapter, well knowing how much the ecclesiastical and political importance of its former lords tends to enhance the interest attaching to this their old manor. There is no evidence that any of the Anglo-Saxon prelates ever had a house here; our narrative, therefore, must commence with a brief reference to Archbishop Lanfranc.

LANFRANC was born at Pavia, in Lombardy, about the year A.D. 1005. In early life, he acquired a taste for literary and scientific pursuits. Devoting himself to the study of the law, he obtained celebrity by the eloquence of his pleading.* He migrated into Normandy, and opening a school at Avranches, thither, attracted by his learning and eloquence, a crowd of scholars soon flocked. Acting on the impulse of religious enthusiasm, suddenly Lanfranc threw up his office of Magister, and quitting the world, sought refuge in the secluded monastery of Bec, of which he became prior. By skilful negotiation at Rome,

* "Ordericus Vitalis," Lib. IV., c. vi.

Lanfranc obtained the Pope's sanction to the marriage, which William, Duke of Normandy, had contracted with his cousin Matilda, an union then within the prohibited degrees of consanguinity; and thus acquiring the friendship of William, in 1066, the Duke appointed him Abbot of his newly erected Abbey of St. Stephen's at Caen. Upon the removal of the Anglo-Saxon Stigand, at the earnest solicitation of William, now King of England, Lanfranc accepted the Archbishopric of Canterbury; and, to a considerable extent, the ecclesiastical polity of William the Conqueror was determined by the advice, the influence, and the wisdom of Lanfranc.* He was loyal to the King, whose supremacy he upheld. On the demise of the Conqueror, Lanfranc was one of the chief instruments of assisting Rufus to the crown, to the prejudice of his elder brother Robert Curthose. This prelate died on the 28th of May, 1089, and was buried at Canterbury. "Lanfranc's death," says Palgrave, "was mourned as the heaviest loss which could befall England. Lanfranc had been placed over the British churches, an alien, yet he lived to become the protector of the English people. Strange in blood to the Norman, strange in blood to the Englishman, both now loved him as their kinsman; his station and disposition combined to render him the mediator between the conquerors and the subjugated." It was this person whom, when they were compiling that great national record "Domesday Book," the Norman scribe entered as lord of the manor of Croydon.

During the long interval that elapsed between the decease of Lanfranc, and the accession of Robert Kilwardby, a period of nearly 200 years, it is probable some of the archbishops of Canterbury, who lived during that time, occasionally visited their manor-house at Croydon, but owing to the loss of their registers the fact cannot now be proved.

* Dean Hook.

ROBERT KILWARDBY. Of the birth place and parentage of Robert Kilwardby, nothing is known. As a Dominican he attached himself to the study of theology at Oxford, taught in the schools, and ultimately was elected Provincial of his Order. Devoted to the interests of the See of Rome, this learned friar, in 1273, was advanced to the chair of St. Augustine. Archbishop Kilwardby officiated at the coronation, in August, 1274, of King Edward I. and Eleanor his Queen, then recently returned from the Holyland. In 1273, he obtained a grant of a market to be held every Wednesday at Croydon;* and in 1276 he also obtained for this town a grant of a fair to be held for nine days, beginning on the vigil of St. Botolph the Abbot, that is to say, on the 16th of May.† Kilwardby was a voluminous writer. On being nominated a cardinal by Pope Nicholas III., he resigned his Archbishopric, and went to Rome. He was poisoned, it was suspected, at Viterbo, in 1279.

JOHN DE PECKHAM was born in Sussex about the year 1240, and probably received the rudiments of that learning for which he afterwards became distinguished at the Cluniac Monastery of Lewes. At an early age he went to Oxford, and, in accordance with the fashion of those times, completed his studies at the University of Paris. Returning to Oxford, Peckham became a Minorite, or Franciscan brother, one of that phalanx of learned friars who successfully laboured to make Oxford famous among the schools of Europe. In course of time, Peckham was advanced to be Provincial Minister of the Franciscan Order in England, and removed to London, where he presided over the large establishment of the Grey Friars. He visited Rome, and happening to be there when Kilwardby arrived, the Pope appointed Peckham to the vacant See of Canterbury. "Peckham," writes his biographer, "was not a true-hearted Englishman, and was invariably

* Cart. 5 Ed. I., m. 24. † Cart. 5 Ed. I., m. 24.

engaged in furthering the interests of the Pope, in opposition to those of the King of England and the country." He died in 1292.

ROBERT WINCHELSEY, according to tradition, was born of humble parentage at Winchelsea, in Sussex, towards the middle of the reign of Henry III. At an early age he was admitted into Canterbury School, and proceeded to Paris where he so distinguished himself that he was appointed Rector of the University. On his return to England he entered Merton College, Oxford, and at length became Chancellor of Oxford. On the death of Archbishop Peckham, in accordance with the wish of King Edward I., Robert Winchelsey was unanimously elected by the prior and convent of Canterbury to fill the vacant See. He received his pall at Rome from the Pope, and, having travelled homewards to England, the enthronement of the new Primate was solemnly celebrated in Canterbury Cathedral on the 2nd of October, 1294. It was a splendid spectacle, the King, attended by his great earls and barons, being present. Profuse in hospitality, this prelate exercised an almost boundless charity towards the poor. Like various of his predecessors, however, Winchelsey was thoroughly un-English. His was a divided allegiance, and he preferred the Pope of Rome to the King of England. He died at Otford in 1313.

WALTER REYNOLDS, who afterwards became Primate of all England, was the son of a baker, and was born at Windsor. Engaging, with distinction, as a lawyer in the King's Courts, he was selected by Edward I. to be tutor to the young Prince, his son; and to the differences that sprang up between the monarch and his foolish son may be imputed the circumstance that Reynolds obtained no further appointment from Edward I. No sooner, however, had Edward II. arrived at the crown than a shower of preferments descended on this favourite. He became Treasurer, Bishop of Worcester, Chancellor, and early in 1314 Archbishop of Canterbury. But during that year the English suffered a disastrous defeat at Bannockburn, and Reynolds resigned the Great Seal. It was a season of much misery and confusion.

In 1314 Archbishop Reynolds obtained a grant of a market to be held at Croydon on Thursday, and a fair to be held here on the vigil and morrow of St. Matthew's Day.*

In mediating between the imbecile King and his barons, the Archbishop appears to have acted with discretion; until perplexed, he espoused the side of Queen Isabella, and acquiesced in that revolution which deposed Edward. Archbishop Reynolds even officiated at the coronation of the young King Edward III., during the life-time of his father. He died at Mortlake in 1327, and, like his predecessors, was buried at Canterbury.

SIMON MEPEHAM, 1328–1333. There is no certain evidence that either this or any of the three succeeding prelates ever resided at Croydon.

JOHN STRATFORD, 1333–1348. Archbishop Stratford in 1343 obtained a grant for a market to be held at Croydon on Saturday, and a fair on the Feast of St. John the Baptist.†

THOMAS BRADWARDINE, 1349.

SIMON ISLIP, 1349–1366. Archbishop Islip, on the 18th of February, 1352, granted to Robert Farnham and William Chober, for the term of their natural lives, a

* Cart. 8 Ed. II., m. 15.   † Riley, p. 586.

messuage and nine acres of land in Croydon, which had escheated to him upon the death of John Latyn, Silvestria his wife, and their son William, to whom a similar grant of the premises had formerly been made by Archbishop Stratford.* And on the 22nd of February, 1362, the same prelate granted to Thomas de Kendale a messuage and nine acres of land, with their appurtenances, in Croydon, which escheated to him on the demise of the before-named John Latyn, Silvestria his wife, and William their son, for a hundred years, at an annual rental of ten shillings.†

SIMON LANGHAM. Of his early life nothing is known. That he was possessed of a great fortune is, however, evident, from the immense sums of money he expended on the building of St. Peter's, Westminster, of which monastery he became first a monk, and afterwards successively prior and abbot. Becoming Treasurer of England, in 1362 he was consecrated Bishop of Ely; and in the following year he became Lord High Chancellor. During Langham's tenure of office, his royal master having received information that the Pope, on the ground that King John had done homage to him for England and Ireland, intended to proceed against the King of England, in order to recover service and tribute, Edward III. prayed the prelates and great men assembled in the Parliament of 1366 to give him their counsel and advice. The decision of the prelates, dukes, earls, and barons was:—"That neither King John nor any other king had any power to place himself, his realm, or his people under such thraldom without their assent and accord." And this having been laid before the House of Commons, was affirmed with a patriotic unanimity. Just at this juncture, John Wiclif, the Reformer, appeared, and he became one

---

* "Reg." Islip, fol. 44a.   † "Cart. Miscell.," vol. x., No. 20.

of the King's chaplains during the Chancellorship of Langham.

In 1366, Simon Langham was translated to the See of Canterbury, but soon after, on the Pope's advancing him to be a cardinal, the King, considering that Langham had ceased to be archbishop, seized the temporalities of the See. Cardinal Langham died at Avignon in 1376.

WILLIAM WHITTLESEY was nephew to Archbishop Islip, and received his education at Cambridge, where he became 'Custos," or Master of Peterhouse. He devoted himself to the study of canon law, and, accordingly, became a student also in the Papal Courts at Avignon. Having returned to England, Whittlesey was appointed Judge of the Court of Arches, Rector of Croydon, and Archdeacon of Huntingdon. In 1361 his uncle gave him the Bishopric of Rochester; in 1364 he was translated to Worcester. Whittlesey is said to have been a man of commanding presence, eloquent, and discreet. In 1368 he became Archbishop of Canterbury; but soon after his elevation he became a confirmed invalid, and for two, out of the six years of his primacy, was confined to his house. He died on the 6th of June, 1374.

SIMON SUDBURY acquired his surname from the place of his nativity, Sudbury in Suffolk. He did not study long at the English universities, for his parents, intending him to be a canon lawyer, sent him to France and Italy. At length Simon's legal attainments attracted the notice of Innocent VI., who became his patron. Sudbury early attached himself to the party of John of Gaunt, Duke of Lancaster, at whose court he met Geoffrey Chaucer, " The morning star of English poetry," and John Wiclif, " The Gospel Doctor." In 1360 Simon became Chancellor of Salisbury; and on the 20th of March, 1362, he was consecrated Bishop of London at St. Paul's Cathedral—

the illustrious founder of New College, Oxford, William of Wykeham, Bishop of Winchester, officiating on the occasion. On the 6th of April, 1376, Sudbury was enthroned at Canterbury, Primate of all England.

At the solemn coronation of Richard II., then only in his twelfth year, Archbishop Sudbury acted a principal part. On the 4th of July, 1379, he received the Great Seal. But educated and long resident in France this created a prejudice against him, added to which, in 1380, as Chancellor, Sudbury presided over the Parliament that decreed the oppressive poll-tax. The country rose in rebellion. After pillaging the Archiepiscopal Palace at Canterbury, the rioters, with Wat Tyler at their head, marched towards London, and having entered it, they surrounded the Tower, to which the King, accompanied by his Chancellor and other great officers of State, had removed for security. On the morning of the 14th of June, 1381, the mob burst into the chapel, when, pinioning the arms of the unfortunate Archbishop, with savage exultation they dragged him to execution upon Tower Hill. Sudbury met his fate like a Christian hero. The insurgents then placed the Prelate's head upon a long pole, and stuck it up on London Bridge, where it remained for nearly a week, until Walworth, the Lord Mayor, substituted for it the head of Wat the Tiler. Such was the tragical end of Simon, lord of the manor of Croydon. It was Archbishop Sudbury who commenced the rebuilding of the glorious nave of Canterbury Cathedral.

WILLIAM COURTENAY was the fourth son of Hugh Courtenay, Earl of Devon, and Margaret, daughter of Humphrey de Bohun, Earl of Hereford: his mother was a grand-daughter of King Edward I. Born at Exeter about the year 1342, on leaving his ancestral home he went to Oxford, where he graduated in law. In 1369 Courtenay became Bishop of Hereford, he was translated to the See of London in 1375. In the early portion of his career Courtenay resisted Romish aggression, but now he showed his subserviency to the Pope by citing Wiclif to appear before him in St. Paul's Cathedral, to answer for his opinions; and attended by John of Gaunt, Duke of Lancaster, and Lord Percy, Earl Marshal of England, the Reformer obeyed the summons. Many angry words, however, passed between the Bishop and the Earl at the meeting, which causing the assembly to grow tumultuous, the court broke up without doing anything.* Upon the murder of the unfortunate Sudbury, the popular Bishop of London was chosen to succeed him as Archbishop of Canterbury. Soon after receiving the royal assent to his election Courtenay accepted the Great Seal, and, as Chancellor, opened the Parliament which met on November 4, 1381. He officiated likewise at the marriage of King Richard II. to Anne of Bohemia, and shortly afterwards the young Queen was anointed and crowned by him in Westminster Abbey.

Archbishop Courtenay received his pall with great ceremony, at his manor of Croydon, from the hands of the Bishop of London on the 4th of May, 1382.

Reference has been made to the changes that took place at the manor-house at Croydon during the life-time of this prelate; and to Archbishop Courtenay has been assigned the credit of commencing that alteration in the architectural character of the old Parish Church of Croydon which resulted in its becoming what is technically known as a Perpendicular structure. He died in 1396.

THOMAS ARUNDEL was third son of the illustrious Fitz-Alan, Lord of Arundel Castle, who commanded the second division of the English army at Cressy; and Eleanor, daughter of Henry Plantagenet, Earl of Lancaster. He was born about the year 1352, and studied at Oxford.

* Lewis's "Life of Wicliffe," p. 53. London, 1720.

Lords of the Manor. 105

At the early age of twenty-one this scion of a great house was made Archdeacon of Taunton; when twenty-two he became Bishop of Ely. During the life-time of Edward III. the Bishop did not busy himself much in public affairs, yet after the accession of Richard II. his name frequently occurs in the Rolls of Parliament, and he became one of the leaders of the Duke of Gloucester's party. On the resignation of Michael de la Pole, the Great Seal was entrusted to Thomas Arundel. In 1388 Arundel was translated to the See of York; it was the year in which the battle of Otterburn was fought between the English and the Scots. In 1396 he was translated from York to Canterbury, the crozier being presented to him in Westminster Abbey by the Prior of Christ Church, Canterbury, in the presence of Richard II., and an august assemblage of nobles.

Civil war breaking out between Gloucester's party and the King, Richard II. arrested and put to death the Earl of Arundel, brother of the Archbishop, and banished the latter. Arundel retired to Florence, there to watch the progress of events. At length the news reached him that his kinsman, Henry Bolingbroke, Duke of Hereford, son of John of Gaunt, and the most popular man in England, had also fallen a victim to the capricious despotism of Richard II. The exiles took counsel together, when having concerted their plan, in company with Bolingbroke, and attended by a mere handful of knights with a small body of archers, at the risk of his life the Archbishop landed at Ravenspur, in Yorkshire, where, raising the standard of revolt, at length that revolution was accomplished which terminated in the solemn deposition of King Richard II., and the placing, by the hand of Archbishop Arundel, of the crown of England upon the head of Henry IV., on October 13, 1399.

Faithful to Henry IV., Arundel accepted the office of Lord High Chancellor in 1407, and again in 1412.

On the 30th of November, 1412, James I. of Scotland,

signed at Croydon a deed of general confirmation to Sir William Douglas, of Drumlanrig, which runs as follows :—

Jamis, throu the grace of God Kynge of Scottis, Till all that this lettre heris or seis sendis gretynge. Wit ze that we have grauntit, and be this presentis lettres grauntis a speciall confirmatin in the maiste forme till oure traiste and wele belofit cosyng Sir William of Douglas of Drumlanrig of all the landis that he is possessit and chartrit of within the Kyngdome of Scotlande, that is for to say, the landis of Drumlanrig, of Hawyke, and of Selkirke; the whilkis chartris and possessiouns be this lettre we conferme, and wil for the mare sekernes this oure confimatioune be formabilli efter the fourme of oure Chaunsellure, and the tenor of his chartris, selit with our grete sele in tyme to come. In witnes of the whilkis this presentis lettres we wrate with our propre hande under the signet usit in selyng of our lettres as now at Croidoune, the last daie of November, the zer of our Lorde 1^{mo}cccc°xij°.*

The unfortunate prince who granted the above, having in the eleventh year of his age been captured on his voyage to France, was detained a prisoner in England fourteen years. When he signed this document the King was about eighteen years old, and evidently at Croydon Palace, in the custody of Archbishop Arundel. Distinguished by mental gifts, highly cultivated by the best teachers that England could produce, eventually James the First of Scotland was murdered at Perth, in 1437.

Archbishop Arundel cruelly persecuted the Lollards; he even went so far as to request of the Pope that the body of Wiclif might be exhumed, and buried in a dunghill; but, for the present, the infamous proposal was deferred. Arundel was also a consenting party to the passing of the Statute, *De Hæretico comburendo*, under which execrable act he adjudged to the flames John Badby, of Evesham, Sir John Oldcastle (Lord Cobham), and many other believers in Christ. This prelate died in 1414, and was interred in the Cathedral at Canterbury, towards the rebuilding of the nave of which he also had munificently contributed.

* This grant is preserved in facsimile in Anderson's " Diplomatum et Numismatum Scotiæ Thesaurus."

HENRY CHICHELEY was originally a shepherd boy of Higham Ferrers, and rose to become Metropolitan of England through the advantage of an education extended to him by William of Wykeham. About 1362-63 has been assigned as the date of his birth, and the year 1373 for his admission to Winchester School; in due course he proceeded to New College, Oxford, where he became a Fellow, and took his degrees. Chicheley studied law; yet, depending on the Church for support, he was ordained. In 1402 the Pope retained him as his lawyer. It was usual in those days for prelates to be politicians; and, accordingly, Chicheley was employed on various embassies and affairs of State by Henry IV. In 1408 he became Bishop of St. David's; and was one of the delegates chosen to represent the Church of England at the Œcumenical Synod of Pisa, wherein the two rival reigning Popes were deposed and solemnly excommunicated, and the Papacy being then declared vacant, a new Pope was elected by the Cardinals, who henceforth occupied the chair of St. Peter under the title of Alexander V.

Chicheley became the friend and adviser of King Henry V., upon whose recommendation he was unanimously elected by the Chapter of Canterbury to the Metropolitan See in A.D. 1414. At an early hour on Tuesday, the 29th of October, 1415, the news reached Chicheley, at Lambeth, that the battle of Agincourt had been fought and won. The Primate met the victorious King at Canterbury, and afterwards at London, where, amid indescribable enthusiasm, a solemn Te Deum was sung. In the truce made with France, Chicheley acted as one of the commissioners; and, on the renewal of the war, he was present with Henry V. when he made his public entry into the city of Rouen. He remained with the army while the English King rapidly extended his conquests over Normandy and Brittany. Peace being signed in 1420, Henry married the princess Katherine, and at her coronation Chicheley officiated. He baptized the infant-heir to the English crown in 1421;

and when, not long after, to the grief of the nation, Henry died in France, Chicheley consigned the body of the hero King to its grave in Westminster Abbey.

Chicheley was munificent; his great work was the foundation of the College of All Souls, Oxford. Among other objects, he gave liberally towards the building of Croydon Church:—"Henry Chicheley, Archbishop of Canterburie, was the new builder or especial repairer of Croydon Church, as appeareth by his arms graven on the walls, steeple, and porch."* "*Ecclesiæ Croydonensi ædificandæ . . . . . multum impendit.*"† In other words, Chicheley completed that work, commenced by Archbishop Courtenay, of transforming the old Church at Croydon into a Perpendicular fabric.

Worn out by infirmities, this worthy old lord of the manor expired on the 12th of April, 1443, and was interred at Canterbury, where there is a monument to his memory.

JOHN STAFFORD was second son of Sir Humphrey Stafford, surnamed "Of the silver hand." After taking his degree at Oxford he practised as an advocate in the ecclesiastical courts. In 1421 he was Keeper of the Privy Seal; in 1422 he became Treasurer of England. On May 27, 1425, Stafford was consecrated Bishop of Bath and Wells, and appointed one of the Lords of the Council, during the minority of King Henry VI. In 1432 he obtained the Great Seal, and "He remained," says Foss, " in this high office uninterruptedly for eighteen years, wanting thirty-two days. He is the first possessor of the office who is known to have been called ' Lord Chancellor'." On May 13, 1443, he was appointed to the See of Canterbury, and about the same time the Pope selected him to be his legate in England. During the long period throughout which he held the Great Seal, it was the misfortune of this

* Stowe's "Annals," p. 107.
† Duck's "Vita Henrici Chichile," &c., 1617.

Archbishop to witness the gradual loss of all those continental territories, the conquest of which had made Henry V. so popular. When the insurrection led by Jack Cade alarmed the kingdom, Archbishop Stafford, at the risk of his life, entered into a parley with the insurgents, and afterwards, by his prompt and bold action, rendered a great service to the country.

The memory of this prelate is inseparably associated with Croydon Palace, the great hall of which he is supposed to have rebuilt. He died at Maidstone on the 25th of May, 1452.

JOHN KEMP was born at Wye, in Kent, in 1380, and received his education at Merton College, Oxford, of which he became a Fellow. He also studied law, and, practising in the ecclesiastical courts, assisted in the proceedings against Sir John Oldcastle for heresy, in 1413. In 1415 he was appointed Dean of the Arches and Vicar-General of Archbishop Chicheley, and in that year also he was employed by Henry V. to negotiate a peace with the King of Arragon, and treat for a marriage with his daughter. His clerical preferments were numerous: successively Bishop of Rochester, Chichester, and London; he succeeded Cardinal Beaufort as Chancellor, in 1426; and in the same year became Archbishop of York. During the six years in which he held the Great Seal, Kemp was one of those peers who signed the answers to the King's uncle Humfrey, Duke of Gloucester, resisting his claim to govern as he liked, and defining the limits of the Duke's authority as Protector: in short, Kemp was the mainstay of the Lancastrians. He was selected to represent the Church and realm of England at the Council of Basle. Raised to the Primacy on July 21, 1452, Kemp continued to discharge the labours of the united offices of Prime Minister and Archbishop of Canterbury, until his decease on March 24, 1453-54.

THOMAS BOUCHIER was great grandson of Sir Robert Bouchier, who, joining the King's army with a very large array, distinguished himself at the battle of Cressy. His father, William, was created by Henry V. Earl of Ewe, in Normandy; and marrying Anne, daughter of Thomas of Woodstock, Duke of Gloucester, sixth son of Edward III. and widow of Edmund, Earl of Stafford, by her had issue, Henry, created Earl of Essex in 1461, and this Thomas, born about the year 1405, who became lord of the manor of Croydon. Entering as a student Nevil's Inn, Oxford, Thomas Bouchier held the office of Chancellor in that university, and becoming Bishop of Worcester, was translated thence to the See of Ely. On the demise of Archbishop Kemp, the council, at the request of the Commons, "For his grete merits, virtues, and grete blood he comes of," joined in recommending Bouchier to the Pope as successor to the Primacy, and, accordingly, he was elected Archbishop of Canterbury on April 22, 1454. A partizan of the Duke of York, at that time protector and defender of the realm, on March 7, 1455, Bouchier was entrusted with the Great Seal, and retained it not quite eighteen months. Gloomy, indeed, were the prospects of the country—defeat abroad, insurrection at home—whilst the functions of government were complicated by the illness of the King. The Archbishop did his utmost to effect a reconciliation between the contending parties, but in vain. Within three months after Bouchier became Chancellor, the first great battle of St. Albans was fought, and it was followed at brief intervals by fierce engagements at Northampton, Wakefield, and Mortimer's Cross. Archbishop Bouchier crowned Edward IV. on June 29, 1461. In 1472 the Pope invested this Archbishop with the red hat. Upon the death of Edward IV., Richard, Duke of Gloucester, "Crookback Richard," as he is styled, induced the Archbishop to urge the queen-mother to give up her younger son into his, the Protector's, care—the elder (namely, Edward V.), being already lodged in the

Tower. But when he pledged his word for the safety of the little Duke of York, and used all his influence to remove him from his mother in the Sanctuary at Westminster, to join his brother in the Tower, the Archbishop does not appear to have had a suspicion of the horrible fate to which the unhappy Princes were doomed. Archbishop Bouchier placed the crown on the head of the usurper, Richard III.; he likewise officiated at the coronation of his successful rival, Henry Tudor, Earl of Richmond, who having won the fight on Bosworth Field, now ascended the throne as Henry VII.; and he united in marriage Henry VII. and Elizabeth, the representatives of the White Rose and the Red.

Cardinal Bouchier died at Knole, on April 6, 1486, and was also entombed in Canterbury Cathedral.

JOHN MORTON was born about the year 1420. Receiving his early education at Cerne Abbey, from thence he went to Balliol College, Oxford, where he took the degree of Doctor, in both laws; and eventually became Chancellor of the University. As an advocate in the Court of Arches, he attracted the notice of Archbishop Bouchier, and in 1456, while that prelate still held the Great Seal, Morton was appointed Chancellor to Edward, Prince of Wales, son of Henry VI., and was also made clerk or master in Chancery. His ecclesiastical preferments were numerous. Staunch to the dethroned Henry VI., Morton was in the bitter field of Towton, on Palm Sunday, 1461, when 40,000 Englishmen lost their lives, fighting one against the other under opposite banners of the White and Red Rose. Escaping from the battle, he accompanied Queen Margaret to Flanders. After the desperate encounters at Barnet and Tewkesbury, and when no immediate representative of the House of Lancaster survived the dreadful revolutions in 1471, Morton sued for, and obtained, his pardon from Edward IV., with reversal of his attainder. In 1472 he was appointed Master of the Rolls, and the Great Seal was several times deposited with him as keeper in 1473. In 1478, Morton was elected Bishop of Ely.

Bishop Morton is said to have been one of the executors of King Edward IV., and this may account for his arrest by Richard, Duke of Gloucester, the Protector. It was on the 13th of June, 1483, that the Protector, apparently in excellent spirits, attended a council in the Tower, to deliberate concerning the coronation of young Edward V. Praising the strawberries which grew in the Bishop of Ely's garden on Holborn Hill, Richard asked the prelate to have some gathered, that he might eat them at dinner, and he then retired. He returned, however, soon after, with eyebrows knit, and biting his lip as if in a passion, when, laying bare his left arm, the Duke declared its withered state was caused by the sorcery of the Queen and Jane Shore, who compassed his destruction by witchcraft. Lord Hastings observed that if they had done this, they deserved to be punished. "What," rejoined the Protector, "thou servest me with *ifs* and with *ands!* I tell thee they have done so, and that I will make good on thy body, traitor!" Whereupon, giving the table a blow with his fist, the chamber was immediately filled with armed men. "I arrest thee, traitor," cried Gloucester to Hastings, "and by St. Paul I swear, that dine I will not, until thy head be brought to me." Lord Hastings was hurried to the green by the Tower chapel, and beheaded on a log of wood that chanced to be lying there. At the same time, Bishop Morton and the Archbishop of York were arrested and confined in separate cells. A petition from the University of Oxford, however, procured Morton's release from that fortress, and he was sent to Brecknock in custody of the Duke of Buckingham. Morton, who was a delightful companion, soon became intimate with his keeper; and when the Duke, on whom the Usurper had lavished both honours and estates, turned

Lords of the Manor. 113

against Richard III., Bishop Morton and Buckingham together planned the sagacious design of raising Henry Tudor, Earl of Richmond, to the throne, and of uniting the rival factions of York and Lancaster by the marriage of the Earl with Elizabeth, eldest daughter of the late King Edward. The prelate contrived to join the Earl of Richmond in Flanders, but his ducal confederate falling into Richard's hands, his head was struck off. Eventually the crown of England was torn from the Usurper at Bosworth, in Leicestershire, and placed on the brow of Henry VII. who soon summoned to his council Bishop Morton. His attainder reversed, on March 6, 1486, Morton was made Lord Chancellor, and a few months after, Archbishop of Canterbury; and thus, placed in the two highest offices in Church and State, this lord of the manor of Croydon retained them both until his death, on September 13, 1500.

Archbishop Morton was a Cardinal, the Pope having conferred on him that title in 1493.

HENRY DEAN, 1501–3. There is no record of this Archbishop of Canterbury having resided at Croydon Palace.

WILLIAM WARHAM. This accomplished prelate was born at Walsanger about the year 1450, and was educated a Wykehamist at Winchester, and at New College, of which he became a Fellow in 1475. It was the era of the discovery of the art of printing; a taste for classical literature was reviving; scholasticism had done its work, and fresh sources of information were opening to the European intellect, through the circulation of Greek literature. As a lawyer and statesman, Warham served King Henry VII. In 1501 he was elected to the See of London; he was appointed Lord Keeper in the year following; then Lord Chancellor; and finally, in 1503.

he was translated to the See of Canterbury. In accordance with the ancient laws of the realm and the canons of the Church of England, Warham received from the king the office of Primate of All England: the King issued his *congé d'elire*, the Chapter at Canterbury and the Pope obeyed, and the usual bull was issued. Even in that age of festivals and ceremonial pomp, the banquet that followed the enthronization of Warham, according to the chroniclers, in splendour was never surpassed. Under ordinary circumstances, Warham was frugal; like his wise but penurious royal master, however, on great occasions he could be munificent, since an archbishop's income then was very large.

Warham officiated at the marriage and subsequent coronation of King Henry VIII. and Queen Katharine, the coronation service of England being the same then as it was in Anglo-Saxon times, and as it still remains.

Archbishop Warham gave the manor of Haling, at Croydon, to Henry VIII., in exchange for other lands.* To the influence of Warham, some of the most distinguished scholars of the day—Linacre, Grocyn, Lilly—were indebted for their introduction, not only to the schools and universities of Italy, but also to the courts of the Medicean and other Italian princes; where, making themselves masters of the "new learning," they returned to diffuse it through the schools of England, and thus raised the intellectual character of this country. Erasmus was especially indebted to Warham. This great prelate died at St. Stephen's, near Canterbury, in 1532.

THOMAS CRANMER was born at Aslacton, Nottinghamshire, in 1484. At the age of fourteen he went to Cambridge, where he resided five and twenty years; and during this time he became a fellow of Jesus College. It would seem that originally Cranmer designed to

* Grants and Exchanges of Lands, Aug. Office.

practise as a lawyer, but altering his intention, he was ordained in 1523, and becoming a professor of theology, or D.D., he lectured on the Holy Scriptures. The subject of the King's divorce being at that time the topic of general conversation, Cranmer argued before the universities of Oxford and Cambridge that the marriage of Henry VIII. with his deceased brother's wife was not merely voidable, but from the beginning void. As advocate for the King, Cranmer also went on an embassy to Rome. In return for such zeal on behalf of his royal patron, Henry VIII. nominated Dr. Cranmer to the See of Canterbury; and his consecration took place on the 30th of March, 1533. On the 23rd of May following, Cranmer pronounced sentence of divorce between King Henry VIII. and the Lady Katherine; two days after, Henry married Ann Boleyn, and Cranmer set the crown upon the head of Ann at her coronation.

The question of the royal supremacy had once more been raised in connection with the King's divorce. It is an historical error to represent England as differing with the Pope for the first time in the reign of Henry VIII., since the anti-papal character of the statute law of England is proved by various Acts of Parliament long ere a Tudor ascended the throne. By a statute of Henry III., the Pope's canon law had no place in England, excepting so far as the King and Parliament permitted.* In the Parliament holden at Carlisle in the year 1306, being the 35th of Edward I., it was enacted that from thenceforth the usurpations of the Bishop of Rome in respect to English benefices should not be suffered.† By the Statute of Provisors, passed in 1350, it was decreed that the Bishop of Rome should not be permitted to dispose of the livings of the Church of England:‡ the Statute of Præmunire, passed in 1353, enacted that no one hence-

---

* 20 Henry III., c. 9.   † Coke's "Reports," i. 14.

‡ Statute of Provision of Benefices, 25 Edw. III., 6, and Statute of Provisors, 38 Edw. III.

forth should draw any plea out of the realm, the cognizance of which appertained to the King's Court, on pain of forfeiture of goods and chattels to the Crown.* The Statute of Præmunire, passed in the reign of Richard II., asserted that "The Crown of England hath been so free at all times, that it hath been in no earthly subjection, but immediately subjected to God in all things touching its regality, and no other, and ought not to be submitted to the Pope." Henry VIII., therefore, claimed no powers beyond those which belonged to his ancestors, although in various instances they had failed to exercise them. The breach between England and Rome widened; and under Henry and Cranmer's direction, legislation in ecclesiastical affairs proceeded gradually further. At length, an Act of Parliament conceded to the King the title of Supreme Head of the Church, together with power to correct grievances and call defaulters to account.

The monasteries had been the nurseries of much that was great and good, but they outlived their usefulness, and in the time of Henry VIII. had ceased to meet the requirements of the age. In the work of the Dissolution of the Monasteries, however, Cranmer took no active part; that iniquitous proceeding was accomplished by the King's Vicegerent, Thomas Cromwell.

Wiclif's noble labours to furnish the people of this country with a manuscript translation of the Holy Scriptures in their own tongue, coupled with the circulation of the first *printed* Bibles in English by Tyndal and Coverdale, had aroused a spirit of inquiry regarding the Word of God, and the corruptions of the Church, to satisfy which Archbishop Cranmer obtained the royal assent for an authorized English Version. Accordingly, in 1537, a folio edition of the Bible appeared under the assumed name of Matthews; it was a revision of Tyndal and Coverdale's translation; and a copy of this book was

* Præmunire for Suing in a Foreign Realm, 27 Edw. III., c. i.

ordered to be set up in some convenient place in every church. In 1540 appeared that further revision known as "Cranmer's Great Bible."

The King's assumption of infallibility failing to satisfy a large portion of the nation, a serious insurrection ensued, and multitudes were hanged or burned in consequence. To this dreadful severity, and likewise to all the domestic changes in the chequered life of that fickle tyrant, Henry VIII., the Archbishop was a witness. Cranmer became godfather of Edward VI. He married, and soon afterwards divorced, Henry and Ann of Cleves. The Archbishop laboured, but in vain, to save the unhappy Katherine Howard from the block. He interceded for the Lady Mary, when the King, her father, threatened to send her to the Tower, for refusing to relinquish the title of princess, or renounce the supremacy of the Bishop of Rome.

Cranmer was pursuing his studies at his manor of Croydon, when, on the 28th of January 1546-7, he received a summons to attend immediately upon the King at Westminster; but before he could arrive Henry was speechless. When Henry VIII. was interred at Windsor, Cranmer sang Mass; he also officiated at the coronation of Edward VI. Soon after the accession of the youthful monarch, Cranmer renounced the dogma of transubstantiation. The Archbishop now directed his attention to that revision of the ancient devotional offices of the Church, which finally resulted in our Book of Common Prayer. In order to enforce a uniformity of teaching in matters of faith, forty-two articles, afterwards reduced to thirty-nine, were also prepared by Cranmer. The primate was engaged on his great work of the revision of the old canon law, when he was called to the chamber of the dying Edward VI., to append his name to a document, the purport of which was no less than to divert the succession to the Crown in favour of Lady Jane Grey. At the earnest request of his dying godson, Cranmer at last signed the fatal document,

After the death of the young King, Queen Mary and her Government carried on their bloody work against heretics with a barbarous severity. Cranmer was odious to Mary, not only as the author of her mother's divorce, but as the Pope's enemy, and for conspiring to place the crown of England upon the head of Lady Jane. Accordingly, he was arraigned, condemned, and sentenced to death. From the Tower he was removed, in company with Ridley (alas! not as they had formerly met in the Chapel of the old Palace, at Croydon), and Latimer, under a strong guard, to Oxford, where, on the 21st of March, 1556, he was chained to the stake, and consumed amid faggots. The last words of this venerable martyr were, "Lord Jesus, receive my spirit."

REGINALD POLE. It appears that during Pole's brief occupancy of the See of Canterbury he was here, since one, at least, of his acts, was dated from Croydon.

On the father's side, Reginald Pole claimed to be related to Henry VII.; his mother was niece of Edward IV. He studied, first at Oxford, and afterwards at Padua, where, through the liberality of Henry VIII., he was enabled to maintain a princely establishment. The refined profligacy of the Court of Leo X. had caused a reaction among the more serious members of the Roman Church, and the company with whom Pole associated were favourably disposed to a reformation. Pole and the Italian reformers accepted the grand doctrine of justification by faith; yet, although doctrinally agreeing with the German reformers, unlike Luther and Cranmer, Pole determined to uphold the Pope's supremacy and the sacerdotal system. In 1536, Pole was created a cardinal. From the Simancas Papers we glean that, at the very time Pole was so much indebted to Henry VIII., he was conspiring to dethrone his benefactor and restore the papal power in England. The treasonable correspondence of Pole sent his brother, his kinsman, and his noble mother to the scaffold, and Reginald's own attainder followed soon after. As one of the papal legates, Cardinal Pole presided at the Council of Trent.

On the death of Henry VIII. Protestantism triumphed in England in the person of his youthful successor, but the early demise of Edward VI. revived Pole's long cherished expectations of reintroducing the Papacy into England. Anxious to see this country purged of schism, as Legate of Pope Julius III., Pole set out on a mission to his cousin Mary, who received him with reverence. The statutes against the Pope's supremacy were now repealed, and those hideous laws for the repression of heresy, passed in the reigns of Richard II. and Henry IV. and V., were re-enacted. Lambeth Palace, splendidly furnished at Queen Mary's expense, became the residence of Pole. His election to the See of Canterbury took place even while Cranmer was alive; the consecration of Pole, however, did not occur till the 22nd of March, 1556, the day following that on which poor Cranmer suffered. It was during Pole's ascendency in the Councils of Queen Mary that the great majority of "Gospellers," as they were nicknamed—a frightful list—were sent to the stake. Cardinal Pole breathed his last on Nov. 18, 1558, just two-and-twenty hours after the decease of Queen Mary.

MATTHEW PARKER was the son of a substantial tradesman of Norwich, at which city he received the rudiments of his education. From thence he went to Cambridge, where he became a Fellow of Corpus Christi College. His zeal, eloquence and learning, recommending him to Ann Boleyn, he became Chaplain to the Queen, and afterwards to Henry VIII. Master of Corpus Christi; soon after receiving this honour he became Vice Chancellor; and to Parker's judicious management it was mainly owing that the estates belonging to the University and Colleges of

Cambridge were not swallowed up by the hungry courtiers of Henry VIII., in the same way as these had devoured the possessions of the religious houses throughout the kingdom. As Dean of Lincoln, he acquiesced in all the reforms that took place in the reign of Edward VI.; yet such was his attachment to Cambridge that, rather than leave Benét College, he refused a bishopric; having married, however, on the accession of Queen Mary he was deprived of all his preferments. During the reign of Mary, Parker lived in retirement. Soon after the accession of Elizabeth, Matthew Parker, D.D., was consecrated Archbishop of Canterbury, on the 17th of December, 1559. Although not a man of brilliant talents, Archbishop Parker possessed a sound judgment, and could distinguish between things essential and non-essential. He was in favour of the Reformation in the Church, for, having studied the early Fathers, and being well versed in all that related to the first four general Councils, he knew the deviations of the Church of Rome from primitive truth; Parker had likewise studied the writings of Luther, Zwinglius and Calvin, and could espy their faults as well as their merits; accordingly, he wished to avoid extremes. For the revision of the Book of Common Prayer his antiquarian researches eminently qualified him. Archbishop Parker was also mainly instrumental in procuring the publication of the "Bishop's Bible," as it was called, which was carried on under his direction. Parker was not only a translator, but he was an original author; he was, moreover, an indefatigable collector of ancient manuscripts. Respecting that most valuable bequest of manuscripts made by Archbishop Parker to the library of Corpus Christi College, Cambridge, Masters has observed that "it contained more materials relating to the history of this kingdom, both civil and ecclesiastical, than could before have been met with anywhere else." A prince of the Church, Archbishop Parker at all times maintained a great, yet decorous and orderly establishment; and the public entertainments given by the Archbishop were usually on a scale of great splendour. We have already adverted to his hospitable reception of Queen Elizabeth in the grand old hall of Croydon Palace.

Having presided over the Church of England during a stormy period of her history, Archbishop Parker died on the 17th of May, 1575.

EDMUND GRINDAL. Of the family and early history of this next Lord of the Manor of Croydon little is known. Edmund Grindal was born in the parish of St. Bees, in Cumberland, A.D. 1519. After passing through the Grammar School, he was sent to Magdalen College, Cambridge; from thence he removed to Christ's College, and afterwards to Pembroke Hall, where he was chosen Fellow in 1538, and of which eventually he became President. "Before he came to be taken notice of in the Church," observes Strype, "he made a figure in the University as one of the ripest wits and learnedest men in Cambridge." In 1549, when the Commissioners of Edward VI. held a Royal Visitation of Cambridge, Grindal, still a young man, was one of the four selected out of the ablest scholars in the University to debate the questions:—" Whether transubstantiation could be proved by plain and manifest words of Scripture?" and "whether it might be collected and confirmed by the consent of Fathers for a thousand years after Christ?" Grindal so ably maintained the negative, that Ridley, Bishop of Rochester, one of the Visitors on this occasion, on his translation to the See of London soon after, made choice of him for his chaplain. In 1551, Grindal became chaplain to the King, and in the following year he obtained a stall in Westminster Abbey. On the death of King Edward, in 1553, foreseeing the storm gathering over the Reformed Church, in company with many others of piety and learning, Grindal fled to the Continent. He made Strasburg his sanctuary, and while in Germany applied diligently to the study of its language, in order that he might be qualified to preach in the churches of that country. One of his chief employments also, during his exile, was to collect "the writings and stories of the learned and pious sufferers in England, and to publish them; for which purpose he had a great correspondence here." The results of these inquiries were incorporated by John Foxe into his "Acts and Monuments." Mr. Grindal was also concerned about the controversies that were springing up at Frankfort, in the year 1554, about a new model and form of worship, varying from King Edward's second book. Queen Mary dying in 1558, Grindal returned to England, and was soon called upon to take a part in the settlement of important ecclesiastical affairs. He was one of the Commissioners charged with the revision of the Book of Common Prayer, which in its amended form was to be presented to Queen Elizabeth's first Parliament.* In the summer of 1559, he was also employed as a Royal Commissioner in the North, to require the oath of supremacy, and to inspect the cathedrals and manners of the clergy.

The cruel Bonner, being deposed from the Bishopric of London, Grindal, B.D., was consecrated to the vacant see, December 21, 1559, being at the time forty years of age. On Wednesday, the 4th of June, 1561, the Bishop's Cathedral of St. Paul's was struck with lightning and burnt. The Queen, deeply affected with this misfortune to the chief church in her metropolis of England, gave

* The original papers, containing suggestions in Grindal's handwriting, are preserved among the Petyt MSS. in the Library of the Inner Temple. The Liturgy of 5 and 6 Edward VI. was reestablished, with some few alterations and additions, by 1 Eliz. cap. 2. The Book of Common Prayer, thus enacted to be used throughout the Churches of England, was used for the first time on Sunday, May 12, 1559, in the Queen's Chapel. On the following Wednesday it began to be read at St. Paul's, upon which occasion Mr. Grindal preached before an august assembly of the Court, the Lord Mayor, Aldermen, &c.

orders for its immediate repair, and Grindal expedited the work. Our Bishop was much engaged in the famous Convocation of the year 1562 : by it the forty-two articles of religion, framed under King Edward, were reduced to their present number—namely, thirty-nine. In the year 1563, that awful scourge, the plague, again broke out violently in London, carrying off 17,404, out of the 20,372 people who died in that year within the city. A red cross was fixed on the door of every house where the plague was, with a writing underneath to signify that the infection was there, and to avoid it. At this juncture, Bishop Grindal urged the duty of repentance, prayer and fasting ; nor did he neglect the suffering poor, but advised that of the provisions saved by this fasting, a good portion should be weekly bestowed in the back lanes and alleys of London, among the poor strangers who were sorest visited.

About this time, the bishop was much concerned in endeavouring to allay and repress the differences which had sprung up among the clergy of his important diocese. During the past fiery trials, a mutual sympathy had bound together the suffering reformers, and together they had drunk deeply of the cup of persecution ; but now, when the fierce and bloody struggle with the Papists had somewhat subsided, although there still continued to be an agreement among the reformers in England in matters of doctrine, yet there arose a controversy about what should be the discipline of the newly-reformed Church—a controversy which, unhappily, quickly led to the destruction of the visible unity of the reformed Church of England. Croydon old Church must for ever be interesting to the antiquary and historian, Churchman and Dissenter, since within its hallowed walls lies the dust of Grindal, Bishop of London when the High Commission Court suspended thirty of the London ministers, and put some of them under arrest, for refusing to wear the ecclesiastical dress, and to comply with the ceremonies enjoined by Queen Elizabeth. "After prayer," says Neal, "and a serious debate about the lawfulness and necessity of separating from the Established Church," the deprived ministers resolved on quitting it; and laying aside the English Liturgy, they began to celebrate public worship after the Genevan model. From that day dates English Protestant Nonconformity.

Grindal had the honour of assisting in the work of translating the Holy Scriptures into our language, for in the year 1568, the first edition of the "Great Bible," commonly called the "Bishop's Bible," was published, of which work he executed a portion.*

In 1570, Grindal was translated to the Archbishopric of York, and on the demise of Parker he became Archbishop of Canterbury. Yet scarcely a year elapsed ere this prelate had the misfortune to fall under the displeasure of Queen Elizabeth, an occurrence which was the source of much trouble and sorrow to him. In his zeal to advance religion, Grindal, on first coming to the See of Canterbury, earnestly set himself to encourage and regulate the exercises called "prophesyings," which had been used before, but with some abuses in most dioceses, and had the countenance of the respective bishops. In this, however, he was angrily checked by the Queen, she supposing the heads of most of those who resorted to these exercises would be filled with notions that might render them at length turbulent in the State. In June, 1577, the Archbishop was, by order of the lords of the Star Chamber, confined to his house, and sequestered for six months. In the year 1579, either his confinement was taken off, or he had leave to retire for health to his manor-house at Croydon, as in that year he consecrated

---

* Grindal appears to have executed the minor prophets, that portion of the work bearing his initials, "E. L." "The tenth (allotment) contained Hosea, Joel, Amos to Malachi inclusive, and had the letters "E. L.," for "Edmundus London."—STRYPE's *Parker*, vol. ii. p. 222.

the Bishop of Exeter here; and in the year following, the Bishops of Winchester and of Lichfield and Coventry. We find the Archbishop also consecrating the Bishop of Gloucester, in the Chapel of Croydon Palace, in 1581. He still exercised this part of his ecclesiastical functions by commission from the Queen, but the other affairs of his See, during his sequestration, were managed by two civilians appointed for that purpose. In 1582, the Archbishop was to a certain extent restored to his ecclesiastical jurisdiction, but the aged primate did not long enjoy it, as, in addition to his other complicated bodily disorders, he now had the affliction to become totally blind; and all hope of recovering his sight having vanished, he tendered his resignation to the Queen. He hoped, however, that he might be permitted to retain the Archbishopric until the following Michaelmas, when the audit of the See was kept for the whole year; he also asked to be allowed to retain the manor-house at Croydon for his residence, with a few acres of land attached. Queen Elizabeth was pleased to accept Archbishop Grindal's resignation, and assigned him a pension; but it is not certain that the business of his resignation and pension were completed before his death. Fuller quaintly observes:—" Being really blind, more with grief than age, he was willing to put off his clothes before he went to bed, and in his lifetime to resign his place to Dr. Whitgift, who refused such acceptance thereof; and the Queen, commiserating his condition, was graciously pleased to say, that as she had made him, so he should die, an Archbishop; as he did, July 6, 1583."

The poet Spenser frequently quoted Grindal's sayings as current at the time, and alluded to his troubles in passages which shew the high estimation in which Grindal was held by his contemporaries.* He was the author of a dialogue between Custom and Verity, published in Foxe's "Acts and Monuments."

* He is the "Algrind" of Spenser, which is the anagram of his name.

It has been already mentioned that this excellent man, the bosom friend of Ridley and Myles Coverdale, drew his last breath at Croydon Palace. He was buried in the adjoining church, where a characteristic and splendid monument was reared over his grave; but this, as we have related, unfortunately perished in the flames that consumed the old church of St. John the Baptist, at Croydon.

JOHN WHITGIFT, whose name, on account of his munificence to this parish, is immortalized at Croydon, was descended from an ancient and wealthy Yorkshire family. His father, Henry Whitgift, had settled as a merchant at Great Grimsby, in Lincolnshire, and there the subject of this notice, being the eldest of six sons, was born, about the year 1530. His childhood was spent under the care of his uncle, the Abbot of Welhove; but about the second year of King Edward VI., 1548, Whitgift entered at Queen's College, Cambridge, from whence he removed to Pembroke Hall, of which college the famous Ridley was then master, and Grindal and Bradford (afterwards martyred), fellows, the latter becoming his tutor. Throughout the dangerous reign of Queen Mary, the subject of our notice kept himself reserved, plying his studies, and by narrowly examining the controversies between the Romanists and the Reformed, he became confirmed in the truth. In 1560, on the accession of Queen Elizabeth, Whitgift entered into Holy Orders, and soon after preached his first sermon at St. Mary's, before the University, from these words of the Apostle Paul: "I am not ashamed of the Gospel of Christ," &c. (Rom. i. 16). Shortly after, he obtained preferment from Dr. Coxe, Bishop of Ely, who made him his chaplain, and conferred on him a prebend in that church, having previously given him the rectory of Teversham, in Cambridgeshire. In 1563, he commenced B.D., and in that year also was appointed Margaret Professor of Divinity. In 1565, he was sworn chaplain to the Queen, who having heard him preach, and taking a liking to him, punned upon his name, declaring that he had a *white gift* indeed. Maintaining the character of a good preacher and vigorous disciplinarian, his salary as professor was augmented, and a licence from the University was granted him to preach in any part of the realm. According to the University register, Whitgift commenced D.D., 1567, and on his appointment to keep the Act, he chose for his thesis, *Papa est ille Antichristus,* "the Pope is the Antichrist." Being President of Peter-house, in 1567, he was made Master of Pembroke Hall, but about three months afterwards — namely, on July 4, Whitgift succeeded to the Mastership of Trinity College. Here he assiduously attended to the duties of his station, watching over the students of his house, attending their public disputations; generally dining and supping with them in the College Hall, and being present at prayers. In 1570, Whitgift was made Vice-Chancellor of the University: about this time he carried on a hot controversy with the learned Thomas Cartwright, and the Puritans in general. As a reward for his pains in vindication of the Church of England, in its doctrines, worship, and government, in 1573 Queen Elizabeth conferred upon Whitgift the Deanery of Lincoln, and highly valuing his abilities in learning and government, she further promoted him, in 1576, to the See of Worcester. Shortly after he was made Vice-President of the Marches of Wales.

Grindal's remissness in executing the laws against the non-conforming clergy displeasing the Queen, she suspended him from his functions, and confined him to his house. Upon Grindal's disgrace, Whitgift was chosen Archbishop of Canterbury, and the Queen desired her pleasure should be communicated to him; but, in her presence, he besought permission to decline the appointment during the lifetime of his friend. "Yet," as Fuller says, "what he would not *snatch* soon after fell into his hands." It was upon the 23rd of September, 1583, that he was confirmed Archbishop of Canterbury. The Queen charged Archbishop Whitgift " to restore the discipline of the Church, and the uniformity established by law, which (said her Majesty), through the connivance of some prelates, the obstinacy of the Puritans, and the power of some noblemen, is run out of square."

In judging of Whitgift's measures to accomplish the end which Queen Elizabeth had in view in appointing him to the highest office, under her, in the Church of England, much doubtless should be allowed for the times and circumstances under which he acted. Intolerance was the order of the day then, irrespective of party; each party, when it could grasp the power into its own hands, was but too eager to assert the necessity of a uniformity of public worship; nor scrupled at using the sword of the magistrate to prevent that liberty of conscience and freedom of religious profession which is every man's right, so far as is consistent with the peace of the civil government he lives under. Those were times, too, of dark plots and conspiracies. In the days of the Tudors, moreover, the notion was generally entertained that the royal prerogative was unlimited; as yet, the great body of the people were unprepared for those advanced principles of civil and religious liberty which now, happily for us, generally prevail; these were then practically unknown, and almost as uncared for. Our Archbishop's zeal and laborious pains for the establishment of the Church of England brought down upon him, even in his own day, no small amount of animosity and abuse; nor is it to be wondered at that the judgments of succeeding historians have greatly varied respecting his conduct. Whitgift's public character is thus briefly but graphically rendered by Strype: " Invincible patience was conspicuous in this . . . . . Archbishop, under those many oppositions, taunts, reproaches, calumnies, clamours, lies, and insufferable abuses, he underwent in Parliaments, in court, in city, in country; and for nothing else but for labouring to preserve and keep the

Church of England as it was legally established in the first reformation of it. All which, notwithstanding, he went on steadily, and with meekness and forbearance persevered in his pious purposes, and succeeded, at length, beyond expectation ; making good his motto, 'That he that beareth patiently, overcomes at last.' "*

" Whitgift," says Fuller, " was a man of a middle stature, black heired, of a grave countenance, and brown complexion ; small timbered, but quick, and of indifferent good strengths, and well shaped to the proportion of his bulk : of a milde and moderate disposition, of a free minde, and a bountifull hand towards his household servants, his poore neighbours, but especially towards schollers and strangers ; many whereof resorting hither out of *France* and *Germany* (among whom that famous man *Drusius*, *Renicherus*, and others) he most courteously entertained, and very liberally relieved : a diligent preacher, as well after his preferments as before, seldome failing any Lord's Day, while he was Bishop of *Worcester*, notwithstanding his important and incessant emploiments otherwise, but that he preached in some of the parish churches there abouts, and no lesse frequently when he was Archbishop, visiting the church and pulpit at Croydon, during the time of his residence there in the vacations from attendance at Court."† Occasionally, this prelate maintained an unusual degree of State, and required to be attended with bended knee. At Christmas he kept open house. Every third year he went into Kent, when he was usually followed by his retinue, amounting to two hundred persons; and in addition to these, he was honourably escorted by the gentry of the county, so that he sometimes entered the city of Canterbury with a procession of eight hundred or a thousand horse. For the purpose of encouraging military discipline, the Archbishop had a good armoury and a competent number of horses ; so that he was able, from

* " Life of Whitgift," Ded. Epis. vol. i.
† " Life of Whitgift :" Fuller's " Abel Redivivus," Lond., 1651.

amongst his own servants, to equip, at all points, a regularly trained little force of one hundred foot and fifty horse. At the momentous period when the *Invincible* Spanish Armada, as it was vainly called, was almost upon the shores of Britain, this little force, with Whitgift at its head, was ready to take its share in defence of the sovereign and country; but happily the dreaded invasion was frustrated; the event, as is well known, being, that under the providence of the Almighty, the leviathan Armada was ignominiously vanquished and miserably scattered. Upon the revolt of the Earl of Essex, Whitgift's armed force was the first to enter the gates of Essex House, and to secure the premises. The Archbishop's military preparations were somewhat carped at by his enemies.

Archbishop Whitgift delighted to reside in his mansion-house at Croydon. He was a great benefactor to this town. He founded the Hospital of the Holy Trinity here. It was finished on the 29th of September, 1599, and endowed with lands for the maintenance of a warden, schoolmaster, and twenty-eight poor brethren and sisters, or a greater number, not to exceed forty, if the revenues should admit of it. The building of this hospital cost him above £2,700. "This memorable and charitable structure of brick and stone," says Strype, " one of the most notable monuments founded in these times for a harbour and subsistence for the poor, together with a fair school-house for the increase of literature, and a large dwelling for the schoolmaster, the Archbishop had the happiness, through God's favourable assistance, to build and perfect in his own lifetime. And the reason why he chose to do it himself, while he was alive, was, as Mr. Stow, the historian, had heard from his own mouth, '*because he would not be to his executors a cause of their damnation;*' remembering the good advice that an ancient father (St. Gregory) had left written to all posterity, '*Tutior est via, ut bonum quod quisquis post mortem sperat agi per alios, agat dum vivat ipse, per se'*—*i.e.,* The good that any one hopeth will be done by others, after he is dead, that he do it himself while he is alive is much the safer way." Of the condescension of this prelate to the inmates of this hospital, we are told by Izaak Walton, in his "Life of Hooker," that he visited them so often, "that he knew their names and dispositions, and was so truly humble, that he called them brothers and sisters; and whenever the Queen descended to that lowliness to dine with him at his palace at Lambeth, which was very often, he would usually the next day shew the like lowliness to his poor brothers and sisters at Croydon, and dine with them at his hospital, at which time you may believe there was joy at the table."

On the 14th of August, 1600, Queen Elizabeth again visited Croydon Palace, to enjoy the hospitality of this, her favourite, prelate. The Archbishop was much with Queen Elizabeth during her last hours, performing the offices of religion. Whitgift likewise set the crown upon the heads of King James and Queen Anne, his royal consort, at Westminster, on St. James's Day, July 25, 1603, with all the pomp accompanying that solemnity.

The closing years of Whitgift's life were somewhat oppressed with fears respecting the safety of that Church, the establishment of which had been the great object of his life; indeed, to his concern for it may be attributed that paralytic stroke which hastened him to his end. In answer to King James, who visited him on his deathbed, at Lambeth, Whitgift's last words were, "*Pro Ecclesia Dei, Pro Ecclesia Dei;*" "for the Church of God, for the Church of God." Archbishop Whitgift was honourably interred in the parish church of Croydon, on March 27, 1604, his banners being carried by two noblemen who had formerly been his pupils—namely, the Earl of Worcester and Lord Zouche.

RICHARD BANCROFT, 1604–10, cannot be reckoned among the archbishops resident at Croydon, since none of his Acts are dated from here.

GEORGE ABBOT, the son of a clothworker, was born at Guildford, in Surrey, on the 29th of October, 1562. He received the rudiments of education at the Grammar School of his native town, whence he removed to Balliol College, Oxford, of which, in time, he was chosen Fellow. In 1585, Abbot became M.A.; he took his degree of D.D. in 1597, and in the same year was elected Master of University College. In 1599 he was installed Dean of Winchester, and Vice-Chancellor of Oxford in the year 1603, and again in 1605. A popular preacher, soon after he was ordained, Abbot became chaplain to Thomas, Lord Buckhurst, upon whose decease, in 1608, he was appointed chaplain to George Home, Earl of Dunbar, and Treasurer of Scotland. By the prudence of his suggestions, Dr. Abbot rendered important service to this royal favourite in the endeavour to establish Episcopacy in Scotland, thus paving the way for his own rapid preferment.

In 1604, the translation of the Bible now in use was ordered by King James, and fifty four divines were selected by the King for the work, of whom Dr. Abbot was appointed one. In December, 1609, Abbot was consecrated Bishop of Coventry and Lichfield; yet, holding this bishopric for one month only, in 1610 he was translated to the See of London; and soon after—namely, in March, 1611, King James nominated him to the Primacy of All England.

Archbishop Abbot's theology was of the Calvinistic stamp, and throughout life he continued a staunch advocate of the principles of the Puritan party. Being at Croydon when King James's proclamation for permitting sports and pastimes upon the Lord's Day was ordered to be read in the churches, Archbishop Abbot peremptorily forbad its being read there. His Grace, who used to go into Hampshire in the summer for the sake of recreation, was invited by Lord Zouche to hunt in his park at Bramshill, when he accidentally shot one of that nobleman's gamekeepers with an arrow from a cross-bow, which he discharged at a buck : and the keeper bled to death in an hour. This sad accident threw our Archbishop into a state of deep melancholy, and ever afterwards he kept a weekly fast on Tuesday, the day on which the fatal mischance occurred; he also settled a handsome annuity upon the widow. Archbishop Abbot founded a noble hospital at Guildford. In King James's last illness he was sent for, and attended with great constancy till His Majesty expired, on the 27th of March, 1625. He performed the ceremony of the coronation of King Charles I., although at the time very infirm, and much troubled with the gout. The Primate departed this life at Croydon Palace, A.D. 1633.

WILLIAM LAUD. Amid jarring testimonies of prejudice and passion, the facts concerning this unhappy prelate must be sought.

William Laud, the son of a substantial clothier, was born at Reading, in 1573. He received the rudiments of his education at the Free School of his native town, and was sent from there to the University of Oxford. His first preferment was the vicarage of Stamford, which he received in 1607. After exchanging various livings, and having proceeded D.D., he obtained a Prebendal Stall in Westminster, and was elected President of St. John's College, Oxford. He became also one of the royal chaplains, Prebendary of Bugden, Lincoln, and Archdeacon of Huntingdon. At length, Dean of Gloucester, in 1616, . Laud accompanied King James I. on a visit to Scotland, whom he pressed to bring the Scottish Church to a nearer conformity with that of England. He was nominated to the Bishopric of St. David's, but owing to the circumstance of Archbishop Abbot having accidentally killed one of Lord Zouche's gamekeepers, Laud scrupled to receive consecration at the hands of the primate, until the latter had been cleared of irregularity. On his elevation to the Episcopate, Laud resigned the Presidentship of St. John's, and many of the minor benefices he possessed.

By appointment of King James, a conference took place between Fisher, the famous Jesuit, and Laud, concerning the errors of the Church of Rome. An account of this celebrated controversy was published in 1624, and a justification of it by Laud himself, in 1639. The ingenuity and learning that Laud displayed at this conference acquired for him the friendship of the Duke of Buckingham, who made him his chaplain; yet, notwithstanding this connection, he had the courage to oppose the Duke in his design to appropriate the funds of the Charter House for the maintenance of the King's army.

Charles I. having ascended the throne, Bishop Laud became his principal adviser in affairs of the Church; but the general history of this momentous period was agitated with a spirit of religious and political fermentation. On the 16th of August, 1626, this prelate was translated to the See of Bath and Wells; in 1629, he became Bishop of London. Laud was at Croydon, assisting at the consecration of Bishop Montague, when he heard of the assassination of his friend the Duke of Buckingham; and the grief he experienced on the occasion is expressed in the prayers he inserted in his manual of private devotions. After the death of the duke, the King entrusted the chief management of English affairs to Bishop Laud. James, Marquis of Hamilton, administered the government of Scotland; the third great personage at the Court of Charles I., to whom was committed the affairs of Ireland, was Wentworth, Earl of Strafford, between whom and Laud an extraordinary friendship existed : it is a remarkable circumstance that these three statesmen were all destined to fall victims to popular fury.

In 1630, Laud was elected Chancellor of the University of Oxford. As Dean of the Chapel Royal, he baptized the infant Prince, afterwards Charles II.; he also baptized James II. In 1633, Laud again attended his Sovereign on a visit to Scotland, when Charles I. was crowned King of Scots, at Holyrood Palace, on the 18th of June. On this visit the English Liturgy was read at Divine Service in the Chapel Royal; it gave much offence to the Scots; and Edinburgh was also erected into an episcopal See, to the still greater exasperation of the Presbyterians. Bishop Laud was formally translated to the See of Canterbury on September 19, 1633. The year 1635 found the Archbishop busy in his design of restoring to its ancient splendour the church at Canterbury, and those other cathedrals which had fallen into decay ; he also repaired the chapel of Croydon Palace, for to this quiet place he used often to retire. On the 29th and 30th of August, 1636, Charles I. and his Queen were entertained at Oxford by the Primate, as Chancellor of the University ; and on this occasion the royal party visited the inner quadrangle of St. John's College, which, then recently finished, remains a monument of the taste and munificence of Laud.

The Archbishop was again concerned in the ecclesiastical affairs of Scotland. In 1635, after a revisal by Laud and Bishops Juxon and Wren, the Book of Canons was finished. Not long after, the Liturgy, also revised by the same prelates, was, by a royal proclamation, commanded to be read in all Scottish churches. This liturgy, however, met with an unfavourable reception, and dangerous tumults arising, led to the introduction of the well-known "Solemn League and Covenant," and a concurrence between the Presbyterians of the North and the leaders of the Puritan party in England: it terminated in the destruction of the Archbishop, and the overthrow of the monarchy.

The House of Commons voted Laud a traitor, and the order for the Primate's committal being carried up to the House of Lords, he was given into the custody of Black Rod. On the 26th of February, 1640–1, the articles of the Archbishop's impeachment—in number, fourteen—were carried up to the Lords, and they were severally read to him at the bar. It was charged to Laud that he had traitorously endeavoured to subvert the fundamental laws and government of the kingdom, and instead thereof to introduce an arbitrary and tyrannical government; and that he had wickedly endeavoured to reconcile the Church of England to that of Rome, &c. In the history of his "Troubles and Trials" the Archbishop has separately answered these articles. Laud was committed to the Tower, where he languished for nearly three years ere his enemies brought him to trial. His trial lasted five months, and in the end he was condemned to suffer death. With undaunted courage and a cheerful countenance, in the presence of a vast mob, Laud mounted the scaffold on Tower Hill, January 10, 1644–5. Having finished his dying address, and prayed, the Archbishop laid his head on the block, and when he had said, "Lord, receive my soul," which was the signal for the executioner, his head was struck off at one blow.

Oxford is much indebted to the munificence of Laud, who presented to that University no fewer than 1,300 MSS. in the Hebrew, Syriac, and other languages; he also founded there an Arabic Lectureship, and annexed a Canonry to the Professorship of Hebrew.

After the impeachment of Laud, a gap of twenty years, from 1640 to 1660, occurred in the Archiepiscopal occupation of Croydon Palace. During the earlier part of the period referred to, this mansion, with the adjoining lands, was leased to Charles, Earl of Nottingham, and afterwards the estate was granted by the Parliamentary Commissioners to Sir William Brereton, Bart., who resided here during the Protectorate.

WILLIAM JUXON was born at Chichester in 1582. He received his education at Merchant Taylors' School, whence he removed to St. John's College, Oxford, of which he became a Fellow, and eventually President: at last, Juxon became Vice-Chancellor of the University. He studied law, and, after holding various church preferments, early in 1633 he became Dean of the Chapel Royal, and was elected Bishop of Hereford; yet, before he was consecrated, the Bishopric of London becoming vacant by the promotion of Laud to the Primacy, Juxon was translated to the latter See. On the recommendation of Archbishop Laud, in 1635, Bishop Juxon was appointed Lord High Treasurer of England: no ecclesiastic had held this office since the days of Henry VII.; yet Juxon filled it with prudence, until the disturbances having commenced, in 1641 he resigned the White Staff. When the question of the Earl of Strafford's attainder was perplexing Charles I., and the Bishop was applied to for advice, unlike other counsellors who pressed the King to comply with the votes of Parliament, and sign the warrant for the execution of that noble, Juxon told his Majesty that " he ought to do nothing with an unsatisfied conscience, upon any consideration in the world."

In 1646, that ordinance was made by which the name, dignity and function of all archbishops and bishops were abolished, and their lands were alienated to be vested in trustees, or to be sold to meet the public expenses. Two years afterwards, Juxon was with the King in the Isle of Wight. On the removal of Charles I. to the metropolis, the Bishop was summoned by the King, upon whom he tenderly waited from the commencement of his trial till the 30th of January, 1649, the day on which Charles was executed in front of Whitehall. On that dreadful morning, Bishop Juxon accompanied his Sovereign on to the scaffold. A dignified calmness characterized the demeanour of the King, who viewed undismayed the apparatus of death, and the countless crowd of spectators that, far as the eye could scan, surged behind the swords of the soldiery. While the King was preparing himself for the block, Bishop Juxon said to him, "There is but one stage more; it is a turbulent and troublesome, but a short one. It will soon carry you a great way. It will carry you from earth to heaven, and there you will find, to your great joy, the prize to which you hasten—a crown of glory." "I go," replied his Majesty, ",from a corruptible to an incorruptible crown." "You exchange," rejoined Juxon, "an earthly for an eternal crown—a good exchange." Charles having taken off his cloak, delivered the insignia of the Garter, usually called the George, to the prelate, pronouncing the word "Remember." Being ready, the King laid his neck on the block, when, stretching out his hand as a signal, the axe descended, and the head rolled from the body. A deep groan bursting from the multitude testified their horror at the sad spectacle. The faithful Bishop, and Mr. Herbert, then took their deceased master's body and head, and after embalming them, placed them in a coffin, and reverently buried them in St. George's Chapel at Windsor.

Another name, besides that of Juxon, is associated with the martyrdom of Charles I., and with the history of our immediate neighbourhood; but to it a sterner interest attaches. Within a few yards of the southern boundary of the parish of Croydon stands Purleybury, the house, it is said, in which once lived Sergeant John Bradshaw,[*] who presided over the so-called High Court of Justice that pronounced Charles Stuart " a tyrant, traitor, murderer,

[*] See Introduction to Horne Tooke's "Diversions of Purley."

and a public and implacable enemy to the Commonwealth of England;" and for his "treason and crimes" condemned the King to death.

During the Commonwealth Juxon retired to his estate in Little Compton, Gloucestershire, where he lived like a country gentleman, excepting that every Sunday, at Chastleton House, in the vicinity, in spite of the penalties attached to an attendance on Divine service according to the rites of the Church of England, the Bishop did not scruple to perform that service. In this retirement he composed his sermon on the death of Charles I. We are informed by Whitelock "that Juxon delighted in hunting, and kept a pack of good hounds, so well ordered and hunted, chiefly of his own skill and direction, that they exceeded all other hounds in England for the pleasure and orderly hunting of them." On the Restoration, in 1660, Juxon was appointed to the primacy; he had become, however, an old man, and laboured under an incurable complaint. He placed the crown upon the head of King Charles II.; it was his last public appearance. Besides other munificent acts, Archbishop Juxon spent a considerable sum in the repair of Croydon Palace. He expired on June 4, 1663, and was buried in the chapel of St. John's College, Oxford.

GILBERT SHELDON, was born at Stanton, in Staffordshire, in 1598. His father, although descended from an ancient family, was but a menial servant of Gilbert, Earl of Shrewsbury: Sheldon took his name from the Earl, who was his godfather. Having laid the foundation of a good education, he was entered of Trinity College, Oxford, in 1613, and taking the usual degrees, was elected Fellow of All Souls' College in 1622. After he had obtained orders he became chaplain to Lord Keeper Coventry, who made use of him on various important occasions. As a reward for these services, he presented him with a prebend of Gloucester, and recommended him to Charles I, as one well versed in political affairs. On the 2nd of May, 1633, His Majesty presented him to the Vicarage of Hackney, in Middlesex: Sheldon was also rector of Ickford, in Buckinghamshire; and Archbishop Laud gave him the rectory of Newington, in Oxfordshire. Proceeding B.D. on Nov. 11, 1628, he took the degree of D.D. June 25, 1634; and in 1635 he was elected Warden of All Souls' College. He was also Chaplain in Ordinary to the King, and Clerk of his Closet, and on the road to further preferment when the Civil Wars broke out, and checked his career. He was a zealous adherent to the royal cause, and was one of the chaplains whom His Majesty sent for to attend his Commissioners at the Treaty of Uxbridge. On account of his loyalty, Sheldon was ejected from his Wardenship, and imprisoned for six months; but, on the Restoration, he received ample rewards for his sufferings, and was promoted to the See of London.

The conference between the Episcopal and Presbyterian Divines, in 1661, was held at the Savoy, of which Sheldon was Master. By the opposite party he is accused of want of fairness on this occasion. To conciliate was not his object, for when it was debated in Council, in August, 1662, whether the Act of Uniformity should be punctually executed that month, or be suspended for a time, Bishop Sheldon pleaded against the suspension, and carried the Council with him. In 1663, Sheldon was translated to the See of Canterbury.

On the removal of Lord Clarendon from the Chancellorship of the University of Oxford, Archbishop Sheldon was elected to succeed him, and he immortalized his name in that university by the erection, at his sole expense, of the celebrated theatre which bears his name. Immediately after the opening of this edifice, the Archbishop resigned his Chancellorship, and retired from public business. During the latter part of his life he chiefly resided at Croydon, where he died, November 9, 1677, in the 80th year of his age.

Sheldon was a generous prelate. During the time of the Great Plague he continued at Lambeth, notwithstanding the danger, and with diffusive charity preserved numbers alive that would otherwise have perished. He rebuilt Lambeth Library. The monument reared over Archbishop Sheldon's grave, in Croydon Old Church, was a fine specimen of carving. Alas! that so great a triumph of the sculptor's art should have been subjected to such a fire.

WILLIAM SANCROFT, 1678–1691.
JOHN TILLOTSON, 1691–1694.
THOMAS TENISON, 1694–1715.

The two first-named prelates do not appear to have lived at Croydon Palace, and of Archbishop Tenison's residence here we can say nothing.

WILLIAM WAKE descended from the same noble families whence sprang the Saxon Hereward, famous for daring patriotic exploits against the Norman oppressor. Hereward, surnamed de Wake, or le Wake, was lord of Brunne (now Bourn, near Croyland Abbey, not far from the marsh-environed Isle of Ely) and of Depyng; the latter estate continued in the family of Wake until the early part of the sixteenth century. William was born in the year 1657, at Blandford, in Dorsetshire. He made rapid progress through all parts of school learning. Taking his degrees at Oxford, and obtaining ordination in 1682, as chaplain, he accompanied Viscount Preston, Envoy Extraordinary from Charles II., to the Court of France. Soon after the commencement of the reign of James II., he was elected preacher to the Honourable Society of Gray's Inn. Wake sided with the Revolution, and after that event became Deputy Clerk of the Closet to King William and Queen Mary. Having been created D.D., and collated to a Canonry in Christ Church, Oxford, and also presented to the rectory of St. James', Westminster, in 1701, Wake was installed Dean of Exeter. Upon the 21st of October, 1705, he was consecrated Bishop of Lincoln, whence, after the accession of George I., and on the demise of Dr. Tenison, he was nominated to the Metropolitan See, and confirmed, January 16th, 1715-16.

Wake was the author of many controversial and theological works. In 1703 appeared his celebrated book entitled "The State of the Church and Clergy of England, in their Councils, Synods, Convocations, Conventions, and other Public Assemblies, historically deduced from the Conversion of the Saxons to the Present Times. With a large Appendix of original Writs and other Instruments." Folio, London. In Mill's "Essay on Generosity," dedicated to Archbishop Wake, it is stated as a fact, that he expended £11,000 on the repairs of the two palaces of Lambeth and Croydon. Worn out by age and infirmities, this prelate died at Lambeth Palace, on the 24th of January, 1736-37. He was interred in a private manner in Croydon Church.

JOHN POTTER, who succeeded the last-named Archbishop as Lord of the Manor of Croydon, was born at Wakefield, in 1674. He early discovered a great aptitude for learning, particularly in the Greek language. At fourteen years of age Potter was sent to Oxford, where, having taken the degree of B.A., in 1694, he was elected Fellow of Lincoln College; and he proceeded M.A., on October 16th of the same year. In 1697 appeared his beautiful edition of Lycophron's "Alexandra," and, in the same year, the first volume of his "Archæologiæ Græcæ;" these productions established his reputation as a scholar. He was ordained priest by Bishop Hough, January 4, 1699. Commencing B.D., July 8, 1704, that same year he was appointed chaplain to Archbishop

Tenison, to reside with whom he then removed to the palace at Lambeth. Upon the 18th of April, 1706, Potter proceeded D.D.; and soon after he became Chaplain in Ordinary to Queen Anne. In 1708, through the influence of the great Duke of Marlborough, he was appointed Regius Professor of Divinity, and Canon of Christ Church, Oxford. It was King George I. who raised Dr. Potter to the See of Oxford, of which he was consecrated Bishop on the 15th of May, 1715.

In the celebrated Bangorian controversy Bishop Potter took an active part. He preached the coronation sermon on the accession of George II., who, upon the death of Dr. Wake, promoted Bishop Potter to the See of Canterbury; he was confirmed February 28th, 1736-37. He died on October 10th, 1747.

THOMAS HERRING, the son of a clergyman, was born in 1693. He received the rudiments of education in the Grammar School, at Wisbeach, and then entered Jesus College, Cambridge. After being successively minister of various parishes, in 1726 he was nominated preacher to the Honourable Society of Lincoln's Inn; and about the same time was appointed Chaplain in Ordinary to the King. In 1737, Dr. Herring was promoted by King George II. to the See of Bangor, whence, in 1743, he was translated to the Archbishopric of York.

It was fortunate for the kingdom that a prelate so noted for his attachment to civil and religious liberty filled the important office of Archbishop of York at the critical moment of the Jacobite Rebellion. Amidst the consternation occasioned by the rout of the Kings' troops under Sir John Cope, at Prestonpans, on the 21st of September, 1745, Archbishop Herring patriotically rallied the nobility, gentry and clergy of the North. In an animated speech, delivered at a great meeting held at York, his Grace called upon all true Britons to rally round their happy constitution, and unite as one man against the Pretender. The vast assemblage warmly entered into the Archbishop's views, and a large sum of money was subscribed on the spot, to raise troops for the defence of the country.

Upon the decease of Archbishop Potter, in 1747, Dr. Herring was elevated to the See of Canterbury. This prelate spent upwards of £6,000 in the reparation and fitting up of Croydon Palace; and here he drew his last breath.

MATTHEW HUTTON was the lineal descendant of Dr. Matthew Hutton, Archbishop of York in the sixteenth century. He studied at St. John's College, Cambridge, and became first, Bishop of Bangor, then Archbishop of York, and lastly Archbishop of Canterbury. He died March 19, 1758; having filled the chair of St. Augustine less than a year.

With the above mere reference we conclude our series of biographic notices of bygone Lords of the Manor of Croydon, since Hutton was the last Archbishop who took up his abode in the old Palace here, ere it fell into decay. Learned prelates, head-shepherds of the flock of Christ, and illustrious statesmen in their day and generation, have been these old Lords of the Manor of Croydon, whose chief glory it is to be associated with their memories.

CHAPTER XI.

MANORIAL.

WE will now attempt to give what may be termed a brief manorial account of the parish of Croydon, and accordingly commence with the

Manor of Croydon.

From time immemorial Croydon was, and continues to be, in the hundred of Wallington.

It has been already mentioned that, when Domesday Book was compiled, the manor of Croydon belonged to the Archbishop of Canterbury; nor does it appear to have been ever separated from the See of Canterbury, except for a few years during the Commonwealth, although, in common with other possessions of the Church of England, the management of this archiepiscopal estate, by legislative enactment, is now lodged in the hands of the Ecclesiastical Commissioners for England and Wales.

The original extent of the estate described in Domesday Book as the manor of Croydon is uncertain. Whether the estate, defined in a lax manner as such by the Norman scribe, was at one time co-extensive with the boundaries of our parish, and comprehended all those lesser manors which we now find separated from it; or whether Haling, Waddon, and some of the smaller estates in this parish may not have enjoyed a still more ancient manorial existence than even the Norman manor itself, are questions which probably will remain for ever undetermined. From the entry in Domesday we glean that, in Saxon times, the manor was worth £12; but that it had increased so much in value as to be worth, when the Commissioners of William the Conqueror surveyed it, £27 to the archbishop; to his men, £10 10s. In 1291, it was taxed at £20; in 1322, at the same; in the time of Archbishop Bouchier it was valued at £55 3s. 11d. per annum; and from a survey of the manor, taken in the year 1646, we learn that the archiepiscopal manor, palace, and lands in Croydon, were then computed to be worth £274 19s. 9½d. per annum, exclusive of the timber. During the interregnum, the ancient residence of the archiepiscopal lords of this manor, with its orchard and vineyard, was, as we have related, leased, first to Charles, Earl of Nottingham, and afterwards, to Sir William Brereton, until the return of Charles II., when the manorial residence, along with the manor itself, was restored to the Archbishops of Canterbury. But in 1780, Croydon Palace, the old home of the lord of the manor was sold, and the mansion and estate of Addington having been purchased with the proceeds, henceforth the archbishops ceased to reside in the manor or parish of Croydon.

Formerly, the archbishop's bailiff had return and execution of the King's writs.

Within the parish and manor of Croydon are seven boroughs—namely, Coombe, Selsdon, Bencham or Whitehorse, Addiscombe, Woodside, Shirley and Croham; and from each of these a constable used to be annually appointed at the court-leet for the manor of Croydon, held in Easter-week; when a head constable, two petty constables, and two head-boroughs were nominated for the last-mentioned of these places.

There are eight beadlewick lands, the owners of which, in their turn, used to serve the office of beadle; they collected the fines and amercements.

There are also eight reeveswick lands—that is, eight estates the owners of which are liable to be chosen to serve the office of reeve. The quit-rents are collected by the reeves anually chosen by the homage jury, at the general court baron; the reeves are generally chosen in rotation. To neither the office of beadle or reeve was or is any emolument attached.

The last time that the customs of the manor of Croydon were presented here was in the year 1793, when they were as follows:—

1. One heriot—being the best beast of every copyholder dying seised of any messuage or tenement, not lying within the four crosses*—shall be paid for every such messuage or tenement; and if he have no quick cattle, then three shillings and sixpence for a dead heriot.

2. On the death of every copyholder for life, three shillings and sixpence for a dead heriot, and no more.

3. If any person to whom a right of copyhold shall descend, shall die before admittance, one quick heriot is due for every messuage or tenement, and no more; and for want of a quick heriot, three shillings and sixpence for a dead heriot. (This is understood to mean for every distinct copyhold.)

4. If a surrender be made to any person being no copyholder before, then he is to fine at the will of the Lord, and to pay three shillings and sixpence for a dead heriot, and no relief.

5. If a surrender be made of a copyhold to any copyholder, there is due to the lord three shillings and sixpence for a dead heriot, and a relief, which is the extent of the rent (*i.e.*, the quit rent) by the year due to the lord, and no more.

6. Copyholds descend to the youngest son; and if

---

* The precise spot at which the four crosses referred to stood cannot now be identified, but the copyhold estates which lie within the square originally formed by these crosses are known; they enjoy exemption from heriots, but were subject to all other services. In 23 Elizabeth the crosses were thus described:—" The 1st is at Burchall's House, in an elm tree; the 2nd is at the pound; the 3rd is at Little Almshouse Corner; and the 4th at Dodd's Corner, in an elm against the Catharine-wheel Corner."

no son, then to the youngest daughter, and so to the youngest in every degree.

7. All copyholders who have any estate of inheritance, may strip and waste, but the tenant for life may do neither.

8. No copyholder may let a lease of his copyhold without licence of the lord, for more than three years, and is to give to the lord, for every year that he is to have licence to let his copyhold, sixpence, and no more.

9. That all copyholders taking any surrender out of court, if there be no condition mentioned to the contrary, shall make due presentment thereof at the next court.

10. No fine is to be paid for any messuage or tenement lying within the four crosses.*

The manors, or reputed manors, of Ham, Palmers or Tylehurst, and Selhurst, are now incorporated with the principal manor of Croydon.

HAM.—This estate, situated on the north-east side of the parish, towards Beckenham, was granted by the Crown in 2 Philip and Mary, to Sir Anthony Browne, Knt., Viscount Montague, by the description of all that demesne and manor called *Estham, alias Escheham, juxta Croydon*, being then part of the Honor of Hampton Court. In 1809, it belonged to Lord Gwydir, who inherited it from his grandfather, Peter Burrell, Esq., of Beckenham. About the year 1835, Lord Gwydir sold Ham Farm to Mr. Morris, who sold it to Lord Overstone, from whom it was purchased by its present proprietor, Lewis Loyd, Esq. J.P.

PALMERS, or TYLEHURST, sometimes described as a manor, yet in reality only a farm, comprised about seventy acres, pleasantly situated on the southern skirts of Norwood hills. By an Inquisition in the year 1595, it appears that Richard Forth, LL.D., died seised of this estate. It was afterwards the property of the Newlands, the coheiresses of which family sold it to Mr. Bulkley, in 1769,

---

* Some of the above customs are now almost obsolete, whilst others have been modified so as to conform to modern convenience.

who disposed of it to Mr. Samuel Cotes. At the time of the inclosure, Mrs. Cotes claimed and had an allotment for the estate, as a farm.

SELHURST, was granted by King Henry VIII. to Archbishop Cranmer, in 1541, and the estate continues to be attached to the See of Canterbury. Several acres of wood still remain at Selhurst.

Besides these three, there was another manor within the manor of Croydon—namely, that of " Croydon otherwise Bermondsey in Croydon." It extended from Broad Green, opposite the "Half Moon," down the western side of the main road to " Crown " Corner, then down Crown Hill into Church Street, when turning to the right past the "Derby Arms," it reached back again to the "Half Moon." The common belonging to this manor formed the triangle of Broad Green with Mr. Chatfield's premises, and all the space of ground from Mr. Chatfield's southern fence to the Manor House, North End (lately occupied by Mr. Till). This common was inclosed by a separate Act of Parliament subsequent to the great Croydon Enclosure Act, and on that occasion the turnpike road, from near the West Croydon Station up to Mr. Chatfield's, was widened to its present width, and allotments were made to the parties entitled to common rights over this common, and whose estates were within the manor above described; the allotments being situate between the Manor House and West Croydon railway bridge, which accounts for the minute division of property there.

CROYDON PARK, represented in part by Park Hill—a large portion of which has been leased out and is built over—has from time immemorial belonged to the Manor and See of Canterbury, excepting for two brief intervals, one during the reign of Henry VIII., when Archbishop Cranmer exchanged it with that monarch for other lands; but it reverted to the Archbishop by another grant in the reign of Edward VI.; and the other in the time of the Commonwealth. The office of keeper of Croydon Park was granted for life, or terms of years, to various individuals, at different periods. Thus, in 1326, Archbishop Reynolds conferred the keepership of this park for life on — le Barber. Sir William Walworth, the renowned Lord Mayor of London, who struck down Wat the Tiler for insulting King Richard II., was appointed keeper of this park by Archbishop Courtenay, in 1382, and here he probably resided. In the reign of Edward IV., John Lyttyll was keeper of Croydon Park, and so forth. When Croydon Palace was sold, it was at first proposed to erect the new archiepiscopal residence at Park Hill. Eventually, however, Addington was preferred, and an Act of Parliament having been obtained in 1807 for purchasing the mansion and estate of Alderman Tricothick, on that site arose the present archiepiscopal seat.

On the enclosure of the common and waste lands of Croydon, in 1797, claims were made and allowed for the following manors:—

1. Croydon, by the Archbishop of Canterbury.
2. The Rectory, by Robert Harris, Esq.
3. Waddon, by the Archbishop of Canterbury.
4. Whitehorse, by John Cator, Esq.
5. Norbury, by Richard Carew, Esq.
6. Haling, by William Parker Hammond, Esq.
7. Croham, by the warden and poor of Whitgift's Hospital.

Concerning the manor of Croydon we have just treated. An account of the Rectory, and further particulars relating to the Manor of the Rectory of Croydon, will be found under their proper heading of Advowson.*

Waddon.

This manor, anciently styled Woddens, is of considerable extent; it lies on the west side of our parish, towards Beddington. King Henry I. gave Waddon to the monks of Bermondsey, in 1127. In 1390, the convent gave the

* See page 35 and following.

manor to Archbishop Courtenay, in exchange for the appropriation of the church of Croydon, and with the See of Canterbury it has ever since remained, except for a short time during the interregnum.

The stream of the Wandle, pent up here into a lake, propels the machinery of a large mill standing on the far shore: it is supposed to occupy the site of that mill mentioned in Domesday Book in connection with the manor of Croydon.

In the time of Archbishop Bouchier, the manor of Waddon was valued at £8 12s., and in that of Archbishop Parker, at £22 6s. 8d.

A court baron used to be annually held here in Easter week.

Norbury.

The manor of Norbury, or Northborough, was situated on the north-west side of this parish; it extended over both sides of London Road, and part of Thornton Heath, and there were several detached houses and lands in and near Croydon which paid quit-rents to it. In the 48th year of the reign of King Edward III., Nicholas Carew, of Beddington, Keeper of the Privy Seal, obtained a grant of free-warren on all his lands in Croydon; and died, August 17, 1391, seised, *inter alia*, of the manor of Norbury. It remained in the possession of the Carews until the attainder of Sir Nicholas Carew, K.G., in 1539; for in the bailiff's account of "the estates of Sir Nicholas Carew, attainted of treason, from Michaelmas 31 to Michaelmas 32, Henry VIII," amongst others is the manor of *Norburye*, in Croydon.

Sir Nicholas, at one time the boon companion of Henry VIII., and a partaker with him in all the tournaments and other diversions of that age, was related to Ann Boleyn; so the king promoted him to be master of his horse. At length, however, with the Marquis of

Exeter and others, Sir Nicholas was charged with conspiring to set Cardinal Pole on the throne; and after a summary trial, he was beheaded on Tower Hill, March 3, 1539. Henry VIII. then annexed Norbury to his newly created Honor of Hampton Court; and Edward VI., in the first year of his reign, granted it, with the meadow called Pyrle-Mead, in Croydon, to the Archbishop of Canterbury, in performance of an agreement of his late father. In the same year, Francis Carew obtained a reversal of his father's attainder, and either the grant just mentioned did not take effect, or the manor was resumed into the king's hand, for in 6 Edward VI. we find Norbury held by Thomas, Lord Darcy, of Chiche, who married a sister of Francis Carew. But Queen Mary, in the second year of her reign, having previously obtained a re-conveyance from Lord Darcy, re-granted to Sir Francis Carew his father's forfeited estates. It was this lord of Norbury who magnificently rebuilt the mansion-house at Beddington, and took so much delight in its gardens. He first planted orange-trees in England, raising them from seeds imported by his niece's husband, Sir Walter Raleigh. Planted in the open, in winter, these orange-trees were preserved by a movable shed; and thus they flourished for about a hundred and fifty years, until the hard frost of the years 1739–40 cut them off. Queen Elizabeth paid a visit of three days' duration to Sir Francis, in August, 1599, and again in the same month of the following year. On one of these occasions he showed the Queen a cherry-tree, with its fruit ripe a month after the usual time. Sir Francis had contrived this botanical curiosity by straining a wet canvas over his tree, by which means both the growth and colour of its fruit were checked, until, assured of the Queen's coming, he removed the canvas, when a few sunny days matured the fruit. The favourite walk of Queen Elizabeth is still pointed out at Beddington.

Sir Francis Carew died on the 16th of May, 1611, and

a splendid monument on the south side of his chapel, in Beddington Church, denotes the place of sepulture of this old lord of Norbury. Along with Beddington, Norbury descended to Captain Charles H. H. Carew, R.N., in whose time the patrimony of this branch of the great house of Carew was broken up, and, pursuant to a decree of the Court of Chancery, the manor of Norbury, with all the family possessions at Beddington, was sold under the hammer, to defray debts contracted by gambling.

When Norbury was sold, the mansion, built by the late Mr. Coles, and above eighty acres of the adjoining land, including the lake, were purchased by William Goldsmith, Esq., who resides in the house. Opposite the front entrance grow some fine cedars of Lebanon, and a magnificent specimen of a Scotch fir.

Whitehorse.

The manor of Benchesham, Bunchesham, or Whitehorse, lies northward of our town, towards Norwood. It appears from a chartulary of Rochester, printed in the "Textus Roffensis," that, soon after the Conquest, the tithes of this manor were given to that monastery by Godfrey de Straenbrook; and this grant was confirmed by successive archbishops, the estate being within their diocese. In 1287, Jeffry de Haspale held the manor in fee, to be inherited by William and Philip de Padyndenne; and the latter held it on his decease, in 1309. Yet Peter Chaceport had a grant of free warren here in the reign of Henry III., and in 1299, Richard Gravesend, Bishop of London, had a similar grant. In 1338, on the death of Stephen de Gravesend, who was also Bishop of London, it was found that he died seised of the manor of Benchesham, in Surrey, held of the Archbishop of Canterbury, as of his manor of Croydon, by the service of 21s. a year, and suit of court to the archbishop at Croydon, from three weeks to three weeks; that there was a capital messuage of no value beyond reprises; 200 acres of arable land, worth 58s. 4d. a year, of which 100 was valued at 4d., and the other at 3d. an acre; the pasture, of 8 acres of wood, worth 12d.; the pannage when it happens *communibus annis*, 18d.; the underwood, 4s.; 8 acres of meadow, 8s.; 20 acres of pasture, at 2d. an acre, 3s. 4d.; rents of assize, as well from free tenants as from natives, 70s.; and at Christmas, 24 hens and 1 cock, worth 2s., at 1d. each; six ploughshares at the same time, 4s.; pleas and perquisites of Courts, 3s. 4d. It was also found that the reversion belonged to Hugh de Nevill, by fine levied in the King's Court, and that he was then 30 years of age.

In 29 Edward III., Chirbury was owner of the manor. In 1368—that is, in the 41st year of King Edward III.'s reign, Chiriton alienated it to Walter Whitehorse, the King's shield-bearer; and from him the manor is said to have acquired its name of Whitehorse. Two years after, Walter obtained a charter of free warren here. He appears to have sold to Arnold Holker, who had a confirmation in fee of free warren herein from Henry IV. In the reign of Henry VI. Edmund Brudenell had a further confirmation of this free warren. But in the sixth year of the reign of Henry VIII., Sir Robert Morton, Knt., nephew of Cardinal Morton, Archbishop of Canterbury, died seised of this manor; and it was held by his relative, William Morton, in 1566, whose grandson Thomas, dying in 1678, left five daughters, among whom the estate was divided. Four of the shares were purchased by John Barret, Esq., in 1712; and his grandson, to whom the property descended, having bought the fifth share, in 1787, eventually sold the whole to John Cator, Esq., of Beckenham. Dying in 1806, he left the estate to his nephew, John Cator Esq., who sold it to John Davidson Smith, Esq., since whose time Whitehorse

Manor has been cut up and sold, not to one, but probably five hundred different owners.

Bencham Manor House, as it used to be called, stood just a little off the road, on the south, where Whitehorse Lane joins Whitehorse Road. The date, 1604, was wrought in brick-work on the south gable, but the old house has been pulled down.

Haling.

We have already dilated upon the peculiar significance of this name.* The manor of Haling is situated on the S.W. side of this parish, and comprises a mansion and park. The fine plantations here form the subject of a poetical "Epistle from a Grove in Derbyshire to a Grove in Surrey," with the "Answer," by William Whitehead, formerly poet laureate. In the latter part of the fifteenth century this manor appears to have been in the possesion of Thomas Warham, one of the twelve principal inhabitants of Croydon, found presenting to the Chauntry of St. Mary, in our old church, in 1458, and again in 1476. Citizen and carpenter of London, it would seem from an imperfect Roll of the year 1456 (34 Hen. VI.), that this Thomas Warham was professionally employed on the archiepiscopal residence. He is presumed to have been uncle to William Warham, afterwards Archbishop of Canterbury. The ancient tomb, still remaining on the south wall of Croydon Church, is supposed to have been erected in memory of this old lord of Haling.

"Amongst some papers at the Chapter House at Westminster," observes Mr. Bray, "is a copy of the will of Thomas Warham, of Croydon, dated 3 Sept. 1478, and particulars of his estate there. By his will he directs that his body should be buried in the parish church of St. John the Baptist of Croydon, in the Chapel of St. Nicholas, before the image of Our Lady of Pite. He

* See page 11.

gives legacies for masses, &c., with a distribution of torches used at his month's mind, amongst different churches, one of which is Tanrigge. He gives in lead for covering the north aile of the Church of Croydon, 4 marcs. By the papers we find that he held the Manor of Haling of the Archbishop by the rent of 21s. 0½d.; that the free-rents and quit-rents paid to the said manor amounted to 12s. 8d.; that the clear yearly value amounted to £35 16s. 10½d., the house not accounted; and that he had woods then worth, and which within ten years would be worth, 400 marcs per annum. It is likely that he was father of William Warham, of whose lands of the manors of Halyng and Selerste, and of his lands in the towns of Croydon, Whaddon and Mycham, there is an account amongst the above papers, in which it is stated that the manor place of Halyng, with two orchards, two gardens, a culver-house with the bank of conies, were let to Sir Nicholas Carew, Knt., at 40s. a year; the land of the said manor and game of conies, at £12 (Little Dubbers Hill is mentioned amongst the land), and the farm of Selherste, £12".

The William Warham referred to here was either that archdeacon of Canterbury who died in 1557, or his cousin, Sir William Warham, of Malsanger, in the parish of Oakley, Southampton, whose father, Hugh Warham, one of the brothers of Archbishop Warham, was certainly a possessor of Haling, as his pedigree is to be found in one of the early Visitations of the county. This William Warham, styling himself of Malsanger, sold the Manor, with other lands in Wodden and Mitcham, by deed bearing date the 1st of March, 1536, to Henry VIII., for the sum of £710. In 1554, Queen Mary granted to Sir John Gage, K.G., the manor of Haling, valued with its appurtenances in all issues beyond reprises, at £15 per annum, to be held by the said Sir John and his heirs, by the tenure of knight's service *in capite*—viz., for the fortieth part of a knight's fee. Of this lord of the manor, his son, Robert Gage, Esq., of Haling, has left the following MS. account :—

"*Sir John Gage, of Furle, his Preferment at Court.*

"Sir John Gage, Knight, my good father, whose soul God pardon, was, after my grandfather's death, warde to the Duke of Buckingham; who, after my father was married to my mother, daughter to Sir Richard Guilfourd, Knight, was preferred by him to King Henry the Eighth his service; and after, he being at the wininge of Turwin and Turrein, was first made captain of the Castle of Callis; after he was made deputy of the Castle of Owns under my lorde Vawse. Shortly after he was sent for home, and presently made Knight, of the privy counsell, vize chambelaine, and captain of the guard; within few yeares after, for service he did in the borders of Scotland, at his returne home was made controwler and chancellour of the Dowchye in one day; within few dayes after he was made counstable of the Tower of London; and the next St. George's feast after, Knight of the most noble order of the garter. On goinge to wininge of Bullen (Boulogne) he was joyned in the commission with Charles duke of Suffolke, lord leauetenant of the King's majesty's campe, for sundry services there; with Sir Anthony Browne, Knight, master of the horse and generall captayne of the bands of horsemen. After the death of our Sovereign lord King Edward the Sixth, at the cominge in of queen Mary, he was made her lord chamberlaine. Thus haveing served in all these roomes and offices truely and paynefully from the first yeare of the reign of our sovereigne lord King Henry the Eighth of famous memory, unto the fifth yeare of the reign of our sovereign lady queen Mary (1558) untouched with any reproch or unfaithfull service in this time, being 77 yeares old, he ended his life, in favour of his prince, in his owne house at Furle in Sussex, committing his soul there to God's mercifull tuition."*

* *Vide* Collins's "Peerage."

This Sir John Gage, in 22 Henry VIII., whilst Vice-Chamberlain, was one of the knights deputed by Parliament who, with the two archbishops and the principal nobility and clergy, signed that memorable letter to the Pope, desiring him to comply with the King's divorce, threatening him, if he refused, that they should consider themselves as committed to their own hands, and should seek their remedy elsewhere. He was one of those warriors and favourites of royalty whose portraits Henry VIII. commissioned Holbein to paint. He left issue four sons and four daughters, of whom Robert, his third son, succeeded him at Haling. He represented Lewes in Parliament in 1533, and died seised of this manor, in 1587. He also had four sons and a daughter—namely, John, Robert, Edward, William, and Mary Gage, all of whom were probably born at Haling; but almost certainly the last named three, to judge from the accompanying extracts from our parish register :—

"Mary Gage was chrystened the iijrd day of October, 1563."

"Edward Gage the son of M^r. Robert Gage was christened the xxvi. day of Augt 1567."

"Wyllm. Gage, the son of Robert Gage, Esq., was christened the third of October, 1568."

John, the eldest son, succeeded his father at Haling, for his brother Robert, having connived at Babington's conspiracy to assassinate Queen Elizabeth, and liberate Mary Queen of Scotland from her confinement, had been executed at St. Giles's-in-the-Fields, on the 21st of Sept. 1586. "It does not appear, however," remarks Steinman, "that he actually entered into the conspiracy, but rather that he suffered as an accessory after the fact, in concealing the conspirators when their treasonable design had been discovered. In a MS. account of their several trials and confessions, we read " that when all the matter was discovered, he lent Savage (who suffered for the same cause) a horse to flye to Croiden, and directed him to one off Savage's father's men, who should help him away." Among the charges urged against him at the trial, was that he attended Ballard, as his man, when he went into the North to provoke the people to rebellion. He was discovered hid in a barn, in Cannock's apparel, having lent his own to Babington. When asked on his trial wherefore he fled into the woods, he stoutly and fiercely answered: 'For company.'"

John Gage, of Haling, was committed to the Tower, by warrant dated the 10th of January, 1590, for harbouring G. Beesley, a missionary priest. "He suffered," writes his descendant, "great hardships for the Catholic faith, and was long in confinement."* From the memoir of his son, it appears that John Gage remained in durance upwards of thirty years, outliving the "remainder of his subsistence" and the several annuities "his noble allies and kindred had bestowed upon him." He occupied apparently the "Broad-Arrow Tower," on the left-hand side of which room is still extant a defaced inscription, subscribed "January 1591, I. Gage." This unfortunate lord of the manor of Haling left issue by his two wives (Margaret, daughter of Sir Thomas Copley, Knt., of Gatton, Surrey, and a lady of the name of Barnes) six sons, the eldest of whom lived abroad for several years, in the Court of the Archduke and Duchess Albert and Isabella, at Brussels. Returning to England, Sir John Gage entered the service of King Charles I., and became a colonel in the Royalist army. He was Governor of Oxford, twice relieved Basing House, and ultimately lost his life in a skirmish at Culham Bridge, near Abingdon, on January 7, 1644. He was interred at Christ Church, Oxford, where the inscription on his tomb designates him :—"*Filius ac Hæres Johannis Gage de Haling, in Agro Suriensi, Armigeri.*"

By the attainder of John Gage, Esq., the manor of Haling became forfeit to the Crown.

* Gage's "Hist. and Antiq. of Hengrave," 1822, p. 231.

Under letters patent of the 34th of Elizabeth (1592), and again of the 9th of King James I. (1612), Haling, with all the lands and tenements attached, was let on lease by the Crown to Charles, Lord Howard of Effingham (afterwards Earl of Nottingham), Lord High Admiral of England, at a rent of £15 per annum. About four years before he came to reside at Haling, this celebrated admiral had put to sea against the huge Spanish Armada. Whilst the "Invincible Armada," as it was vainly called, moved proudly up Channel, in form of a crescent, the horns of which were seven miles asunder, the superior seamanship of the brave English admiral, seconded as it was by those distinguished naval officers, Drake, Hawkins and Frobisher, who held commands under Lord Howard, gave the English fleet a considerable advantage over the unwieldy galleons of Spain, and several of them were captured or disabled. On the night of the 29th of July, 1588, the English sent eight fire-ships into the Armada, as it lay at anchor near Calais; the Spaniards, in terror, cut their cables, and dispersing, on the following morning two more galleons fell into the hands of the English. On the 31st a storm came on that necessitated the return to Spain of the shattered navy of Philip, the English pursuing it in its inglorious flight as far as Flamborough Head, when want of ammunition compelled them to give over the chase. Not long after the memorable event, Queen Elizabeth raised her admiral to the dignity of Earl of Nottingham. This famous Lord High Admiral of England drew his last breath in our parish, at the mansion of Haling, on the 14th of December, 1624. Sir William Howard, his brother, also died here, on September 1, 1600; and his second son, Charles, afterwards third Earl of Nottingham, was born at Haling in 1610.

Notwithstanding the forfeiture of Haling by John Gage, the manor appears to have been ultimately restored to his family, and with the generous consent of his eldest son, he alienated by indenture dated the 12th of July, 1626, the fee simple of the estate to Christopher Gardiner, Esq., of Dorking, Surrey, in consideration of the sum of £2,350, Soon after, taking leave of this troubled life, John Gage, Esq., died at Croydon on the 6th of Dec. 1626. The manor of Haling remained in the family of Gardiner till 1707, when it was conveyed to Edward Stringer, Esq., who, dying without issue, left it to his widow; and she marrying — Parker, Esq., her grandson William Parker Hamond, Esq., inherited it. He was succeeded by his son of the same name, born November 24, 1793; upon whose decease on the 24th of April, 1873, his son, also named William Parker Hamond, became the present proprietor.

No courts are held for the Manor of Haling.

But great changes have taken place within the last forty years in respect to Haling, and the Lord of the Manor is gradually alienating this estate. The mansion, and about seventy acres of the adjoining land, including the grove with its rookery, have been purchased by James Watney, Esq., father of the present member of parliament for East Surrey, and he resides here. The house which was small has been much enlarged, roads also have been cut through various portions of the old manor, and numerous freehold plots have been alienated to others.

Croham.

The manor of Croham, Cronham or Cranham lies south-east of Croydon. It consists of a messuage and farm comprising the wood known as Croham-hurst and the valley known as Croham Deane, in all about 400 acres, which extend into the adjoining parish of Sanderstead. Quit rents are payable to it from several houses and lands in the town of Croydon. On an extent made in the year 1287, it was found that Jeffry de Haspale held certain lands for life, to be inherited by William and Philip de Padyndenne; and of those held in fee was the manor of

Croweham. In 1368, a person named Chiriton alienated the manor to Walter Whithors, the King's shield-bearer; it appears however to have reverted to the family of Chiriton. But in the first year of the reign of Henry IV., being then in possession of the Crown, the King granted the custody of it to William Oliver. From the Court Rolls of the Manor, it appears that in the reign of Henry VII. Croham belonged to Dame Anne Peche. In the reign of Henry VIII. the manor was held by Sir John Danet in right of his wife, daughter and heir of Thomas Elynbrigge. Afterwards, Croham belonged to Sir Oliph Leigh of Addington, by whom it was sold to Archbishop Whitgift, who gave it to his Hospital of the Holy Trinity, as part of its endowments, attached to which it still remains. Courts are sometimes held for this manor.

ADDISCOMBE.

No better proof could be adduced of the change which has taken place in regard to this parish, than the contrast between Addiscombe of to-day, and the same district as it appeared thirty years ago, when its noble mansion stood amidst a well-timbered domain, where now little else is visible but bricks and mortar.

Addiscombe is situated from a mile, to a mile and a half north-east of the Town Hall of Croydon, on the roads to Shirley and Beckenham. In the reign of Henry VIII., this estate belonged to Thomas Heron, son of an opulent citizen of London, and he may have erected that older mansion of Adgcomb, the foundation walls and other relics of which were discovered during the course of some recent building operations. Dying here in September, 1518, he appears to have been succeeded by another Thomas Heron, Esq., who died on October 2, 1544. This Thomas left issue by his wife Elizabeth, daughter and co-heir of William Bond, Esq., clerk of the Green Cloth, two sons, namely, William, justice of the peace for Surrey, who died without issue, in 1562; and Nicholas, afterwards knighted, and who dying here, was buried in Croydon Old Church, on September 1, 1568. Sir Nicholas was probably succeeded by his eldest son, Capt. Poynings Heron, who had a daughter baptized at Croydon in 1579. Addiscombe afterwards became the residence of Sir John Tunstall, who must have resided here after 1619, as on the 13th of September in that year, he subscribed his name to Alleyne's Quadripartite deed of Dulwich College, being then of Carshalton. Of a Durham family, Sir John was gentleman usher and esquire to Queen Anne, consort of James I. His eldest son Henry, then residing at Croydon, in 1647 was appointed one of the Committee for inquiring into the conduct of the clergy of Surrey. Sir John Tunstall, Knt., died in February, 1650, and his son in August following, leaving John his son and heir. But in 1662, Addiscombe belonged to Sir Purbeck Temple, Knt., a member of the Privy Council of Charles II., who dying without issue, in August, 1695, the estate came into the possession of his widow, who, on her decease in February, 1700, left it to her nephew, William Draper, Esq., who married Susanna, daughter of the celebrated John Evelyn.

"19 July, 1695.—I dined," writes Evelyn, in his Memoirs, "at Sir Purbeck Temple's, neare Croydon; his lady is aunt to my son-in-law, Draper; the house is exactly furnished."

Again Evelyn remarks:—

"29 August, 1695.—Very cold weather. Sir Purbeck Temple, uncle to my son Draper, died suddenly. A greate funeral at Adscombe. His lady being owne aunt to my son Draper, he hopes for a good fortune, there being no heir."

And again:—

"13 February, 1700.—I was at the funerall of my Lady Temple, who was buried at Islington, brought from Adscomb, neare Croydon: she left my son-in-law Draper (her nephew), the mansion-house of Adscomb very nobly and completely furnish'd, with the estate about it, with plate and jewels to the value in all of about £20,000; she was a very prudent lady, gave many greate legacies, with £500 to the poore of Islington, where her husband Sir Purbeck Temple was buried, both dying without issue."

Mr. Draper rebuilt Addiscombe House. Sir John Vanbrugh is said to have been architect of the new mansion, the building of which was commenced in June, 1702, and finished in the latter half of the following year, as we learn from these additional extracts from Evelyn's diary :—

"27 June, 1702.—I went to Wotton with my family, for the rest of the summer, and my son-in-law Draper, with his family, came to stay with us, his house at Adscomb being new building."

"11 July, 1703.—I went to Adscomb, 16 miles from Wotton, to see my son-in-law's new house, the outside to the covering being such excellent brick-work, cased with Portland stone, with the pilasters, windows, and within, that I pronounc'd it in all points of good and solid architecture, to be one of the very best gentlemen's houses in Surrey, when finished. I returned to Wotton tho' weary."

On the east front of Addiscombe House was carved the following inscription in Roman capitals :—

NON FACIAM VITIO CULPAVE MINOREM.

The walls and ceilings of the grand staircase, and saloon of the mansion, are said to have been painted by Sir James Thornhill.

By marriage with an heiress of Draper, this estate afterwards went to Charles Clarke, Esq., of Ockley, Surrey, whose only son Charles died in the lifetime of his father, leaving an infant son named Charles John, who, in right of his mother, became heir of the Farnaby family, of Sevenoaks, and of the Radcliffe's, of Hitchin. He went to Paris on the Peace of Amiens, and there lost his life, through the falling of a scaffold at some public show. He left no child, and his only sister and heir, Anne Millicent Clarke, marrying Emilius Henry Delmè, Esq., who afterwards took the name of Radcliffe, Addiscombe became the property of this gentleman. He was Master of the Stud to King George IV., and his successor William IV.

During the course of the 18th century Addiscombe House became alternately the residence of Charles, Lord Talbot, Lord High Chancellor, who died here in 1737; Lord Grantham, who died in 1786; and Charles Jenkinson, first Earl of Liverpool, who had a lease of it for life, and died in 1808. Wraxall relates how the redoubted William Pitt, Lord Chancellor Thurlow, and Mr. Dundas, the Treasurer of the Navy, returning after dinner from Addiscombe, found a turnpike open, and galloped through it without paying the toll. The turnpike-man fancying they were highwaymen, fired a blunderbuss after them, but missed them; whereupon the poet sang:—

> "How, as Pitt wandered darkling o'er the plain,
> His reason drown'd in Jenkinson's champagne,
> A rustic's hand, but righteous fate withstood,
> Had shed a Premier's for a robber's blood."

In 1809, Mr. Radcliffe sold Addiscombe to the Honourable East India Company, who founded here a military seminary for the education of the Company's cadets. Various unconnected additions were now made to the premises, in order to adapt them for the purposes of a military college. The establishment of the seminary consisted of a Public Examiner, an Oriental Examiner, a Lieutenant-Governor, Staff-Captain, two orderly officers, a broad-sword master, fifteen professors and masters (one of whom, being in orders, officiated as chaplain), six non-commissioned officers, a bugler, and a proportionate number of servants. The course of studies consisted of mathematics, fortification, military drawing, military surveying, Hindustani, civil and lithographic drawing, French and Latin; and lectures on experimental philosophy, chemistry and geology were delivered at stated periods. An occasional detachment of sappers and miners used to be employed in throwing up field and other works, which, in their general progress, offered valuable instruction to the cadets. The total annual expense of the seminary was about £20,000, of which, the proportion allowed by the Company was between £11,000 and £12,000. Two public examinations were held during the year at Addiscombe, in the presence of the members of the Court of Directors. Captain George Thompson, who stormed Ghuzni, Lieutenant Eldred Pottinger, the defender of Herat, and a long list of distinguished Anglo-Indians received their education at Addiscombe. It used to be one of the sights of Croydon to see the Addiscombe cadets march, with band playing, to the old parish church on a Sunday morning.

On the dissolution of the powerful East India Company, after the Mutiny, the estate of Addiscombe College was sold in upwards of two hundred lots, during the years 1862–63; various newly made roads having been previously cut through it. No bidder, however, was found willing to offer the reserved price fixed for the purchase of the mansion, which soon after was levelled to the ground; and thus Croydon was deprived of a structure that, for more than a century and a half, had been one of its stateliest ornaments.

COMBE, delightfully situate on the skirts of Addington Hills, lies in a south-eastern direction from the Town Hall of Croydon. The estate comprises between 200 and 300 acres of land, well studded with trees of large growth, beeches, limes, elms, and oaks. Combe House, a capital mansion, is now in the occupation of Baron Heath; the whole estate belongs to Mrs. Sutherland, who resides at Combe Lodge; Combe Farm is the only other dwelling on the estate. Opposite the entrance to

Combe House grows a magnificent Portugal laurel. Originally one root, from this parent stem branches have shot out in all directions, which, overhanging the ground, in numerous instances, have taken root again, yards even from the original stem; and these fresh roots, shooting upwards and developing their branches, the whole together form one grand shrub, the circumference of which is about sixty yards. In front of the mansion are three cedars of Lebanon; of these, the centre one is the finest in the parish. Not far off, on the south-east side of the house, is an ancient well, and by it are the remains of three old elm trees. This well in former times was nearer to the road, the track of which has been shifted farther off the mansion. It is said that the pilgrims on their journey to the shrine of Thomas à Becket, at Canterbury, used to drink of this way-side well. The pilgrims' way can still be traced in the neighbourhood of War-Coppice, Caterham, and at Titsey; to join which route, pilgrims from places nearer Croydon than the "Tabard" at Southwark, could not do better than go *via* the old Palace of the Archbishop, and thence by Combe Lane, partaking, as they passed this retired spot, of the pure refreshment such a well might yield them.

SELSDON. In treating of the soil of this parish and its ownership, we must not overlook Selsdon. This considerable estate occupies the detached portion of the parish, about three miles southward of Croydon Town Hall. The mansion was built by William Coles, Esq., about the year 1809, who sold Selsdon to George Smith, Esq., M.P., brother to the late Lord Carington; he added the drawing-room and library. To George Smith, Esq., who died on the 26th of December, 1836, succeeded George Robert Smith, Esq., who also altered and enlarged the mansion. Dying on the 23rd of February, 1869, he was succeeded by his son, Ernald Mosley Smith, Esq., who died on the 8th of December, 1872, when the estate became the property of his brother Walter Caradoc Smith, who died at Paris, on the 13th of March 1876. Selsdon then passed to the present heiress, Mabel, only child of the above-named Ernald, a minor.

The mansion contains a valuable library of works, chiefly relating to India, collected by the late George Smith, Esq., who was a Director of the Honourable East India Company. There is also a curious and nice collection of coins at Selsdon, collected by the late George Robert Smith, Esq. In one respect Selsdon is perhaps unique, there being no place probably, equally near to London, that commands such an extensive view and yet retaining so much of a rural character. During the minority of the present owner, the Bishop of Rochester has a lease of the mansion, and resides here.

SHIRLEY HOUSE is situated on the skirts of the Heath. Built by John Claxton, Esq., in 1720, this mansion was sold by his grandson of the same name to John Maberly, Esq., from whom it descended to his son Colonel Maberly, who was principal Secretary of the General Post Office. After a long residence here, during which he enlarged and beautified the grounds by diverting the course of the public road further from the mansion, and by enclosing and planting on a great slip of what until then had been merely barren heath, the assigns of Colonel Maberly sold the estate to S. Skinner, Esq., who disposed of it to the late Lord Eldon. This nobleman died here, when his son, the present earl, succeeded to the property. Sir John Anson occupied Shirley House for some years, during the minority of the present noble owner.

Besides the Ecclesiastical Commissioners, the Whitgift Charity, and the previously named proprietors, among other considerable landowners in the parish may be mentioned the names of Lewis Loyd, Esq., J.P., Lady Ashburton, William J. Blake, Esq., the Farley family, the family of Teevan, Mrs. Newman Smith, Mrs. Russell, the Morland family, &c.

CHAPTER XII.

ANCIENT DESCRIPTION AND CHRONOLOGY.

FROM what has been previously advanced, it may reasonably be concluded that a human settlement of some kind has existed at Croydon from a remote period. Passing over some pre-historic relics, if the discovery of numerous Roman coins scattered over its area indicates that this neighbourhood was at least known to the Romans, the mention of Elfsies' priest of "Crogdene" in A.D. 962 implies the existence of a church and parishioners, at Croydon, more than nine hundred years ago; whilst the entry in Domesday Book concerning "Croindene" is conclusive as to the population of this manor in the time of William the Conqueror. Camden and, long after him, Gale mentions a tradition that a royal palace formerly stood on the west part of the town, near Haling; in reference however to Camden's observations on the point, "this indeed," says Ducarel, "he quotes as a tradition; and it can be no other, for I believe no historian has ever told us that the Saxon Kings had any palace near this town." At present the more ancient portions of our town appear to cluster in the neighbourhood of Middle Row, or to lie in the direction of the old church, southward of which is the ancient thoroughfare known as Old Town; and at the South End of High Street. But there is a tradition that, at one time, our old town extended westward a great way towards Beddington, and the ruins of this bygone extension were described by Ducarel as standing in 1783. It is said also that the present High Street was originally merely a bridle-way running through fields; leading over higher ground, however, and in a more direct course than the crooked roadway through the old town, by usage, this became the principal route, and at length was built along.

That, in former times, the Archiepiscopal Palace and undrained old town of Croydon were damp and unwholesome may be surmised from the answer which Henry VIII. somewhat sharply addressed to Cranmer. "I was by," observed Morice, "when Otford and Knol wer given him. My lord (Cranmer) minded to have retained Knol unto himself, said that it was too small a house for his Majesty. 'Marry,' said the King, 'I had rather have it than this house (meaning Otford) for it standeth on a better soil. This house standeth low and is rheumatick like unto Croydon, where I could never be without sickness.'" A notice of Croydon, written in the reign of Queen Elizabeth, says that—"The streets were deep hollow ways and very dirty, the houses generally with wooden steps into them, and darkened by large trees growing before them—and the inhabitants in general were smiths and colliers." The term *collier*, here used, was synonymous with that of *charcoal-burner*; and, previously to the introduction of mineral coal from Newcastle or elsewhere, there is little doubt that one of the chief occupations of the natives of old Croydon was to convert the wood which grew so plentifully in the neighbouring forest into charcoal, for the purpose of supplying the requirements of the metropolis. In the name "Colliers water," still applied to a place in this parish, we have a memento of the once thriving but now extinct charcoal-burning or colliery trade of the district.

The sooty looks of the colliers or charcoal-burners of Croydon long furnished a topic for merriment to poets and playwrights. Richard Crowley in his satirical epigrams, published about the year 1550 has one on

THE COLLIER OF CROYDON,

which runs as follows:—

> It is said that in Croydon there did sometyme dwell
> A Collyer that did al other Colyers excel,
> For his riches thys collyer might have been a Knight,
> But in the order of Knighthood he had no delight;
> Would God al our Knights did mind coling no more
> Than thys collyer did Knighting, as is sayd before;
> For when none but pore collyers did with coles mell,
> At a reasonable price they did their coles sell;
> But synce our Knight collyers have had the first sale,
> We have pay'd much money, and had few sacks to tale;
> A lode, that late years for a royal was sold,
> Wyl cost now XVI. shillings of sylver or gold.
> God graunt these men grace their polling to refrayne,
> Or else bryng them back to theyr old state agayne;
> And especially the Colliar that at Croydon doth dwell,
> For men think he is cosin to the collyar of hell.

About the same date were published the 'Egloges' of Alexander Barkley, who thus refers in one of these to our town:—

> "And as in Croidon I heard the Collier preache."

It was the era of the Reformation, and, to judge from the foregoing, its influences seem to have stimulated into activity the religious life of one at least of the sooty denizens of old Croydon; the man, indeed, may have been a Bunyan in his way.

Thomas Peend, in his fable of "Hermaphroditus and Salmacis," published in 1565, observes that Vulcan

> A Croydon Sangwine right did seme.

Again, in "Damon and Pythias," a comedy written by Richard Edwards, and first acted in 1566, one of the characters introduced is Grimme the Collier of Croydon. Ulpean Fulwel likewise, in his comedy of "Like wil to like quod thee Devil to the Colier," published in 1568, makes three of his *dramatis personæ*—namely, Tom Collier, Nichol Newfangle, and the Devil—dance together to the tune of "Tom Collier of Croidon hath solde his cole." There is also a play entitled "The Historie of the Collyer," relating to the same worthy, which was acted in 1576—1577 before Queen Elizabeth. Greene, in his "Quip for an Upstart

Courtier" (1592), writes, "Marry, quoth hee that lookt like Lucifer, though I am black, I am not the divell, but indeed a Collyer of Croydon." And in the tragedy of "Locrine," published in 1595, occurs this distich:—

> The Colliers of Croydon,
> The Rustics of Roydon.

No-ways more favourable than the preceding strictures on its grim inhabitants, is the following doleful reference to Croydon and its colliers, culled from a poem written by Patrick Hannay, Gent., and printed in 1662:—

> In midst of these stands Croydon cloath'd in black,
>   In a low bottome sinke of all these hills ;
> And is receipt of all the durtie wracke,
>   Which from their tops still in abundance trils ;
> The vnpau'd lanes with muddie mire it fills,
>   If one shower fall, or if that blessing stay,
> You may well smell, but neuer see your way.

The satirist has one more hit at the dusky imps of this valley in the comedy of "Grim, the Collier of Croydon, or the Devil and his Dame, with the Devil and St. Dunstan, by J. T.," dated 1662.

The woods about Croydon formerly were of vast extent, and long it was ere the charcoal-burning trade decayed. Writing so late as in the year 1783, Ducarel noted that "the town is surrounded with hills well covered with wood, whereof great store of charcoal is made." The once famous staple of this neighbourhood, however, even then must have been nearly extinguished, since in a description of Croydon given in the second edition of the "Ambulator," 1782, it is said "the adjacent hills being covered with wood, great quantities of charcoal are made and sent to that city," namely London ; but in subsequent editions this passage is omitted.

Very different to the ill-drained, smoky and dirty village alluded to in the previous quotations, is its successor, the well-drained and paved, lighted and healthy large modern town of Croydon. Formerly the town, in respect to shape, used not inaptly to be compared to a triangle, of which, the two streets meeting opposite the "Swan and Sugar Loaf," at the South End, formed the sides, and Church Street the base; but owing to an amazing recent extension in all directions of the habitable area of Croydon, such a simile can no longer be applied.

Turning from the dismal retrospect of old Croydon presented to us by the pens of bygone satirists, let us now review, in chronological succession, some of the more prominent events of its past history. In the year 1185 the town was amerced one mark for a default:—"*Croinden Archiepiscopi Cantuariensis, r. c. de j marca pro defalta: In th. b. et quieta est.*"* The following entry evidently refers to the same fine:—" 31. H. 2 *Crouinedna Archipi. Cantuar. deb.* 1. *m. per def.*"†

In A.D. 1200, two women who had stolen some clothes in *Croindone*, having been pursued by the men of this place to Southfleet, were there seized, imprisoned, and afterwards tried by the Lord Henry de Cobham, and many other discreet men of the county, who adjudged them to undergo the ordeal of fire—namely, to carry hot iron *ad portandum calidum ferrum*. By this superstitious, foolish, and cruel test of innocence, one of the women was acquitted, but the other, being condemned, was afterwards drowned in a pond.

On the 14th of May, 1264, as the Londoners were flying from the battle of Lewes, where they had sided with the Barons against King Henry III., they were intercepted at Croydon by a body of Royalists from Tonbridge Castle, who routed them again with great slaughter. It is not improbable that the human remains found near Whitgift's Hospital, or those skeletons which were dug up by Mr. Turner in 1814, in his paddock on the south side of George Street, were remains of the unfortunate Londoners who fell in this sanguinary skirmish.

* Madox's "Hist. of the Exchequer," p. 384.
† "Records of Surrey and Sussex," by Le Neve.

In 1270, after the outrage on Alan Lord Zouche, John de Warrenne, Earl of Surrey and Sussex, dated an Instrument from *Creyndone*, stating his intention to stand to the judgment of the Court on pain of excommunication and forfeiture of his estates. The celebrated Earl Warren referred to, married the half-sister of Henry III.; he fought in the first division of the Royalist army at Lewes along with Prince Edward. The quarrel between Earl Warren and Lord Zouche arose concerning some land, and the dispute being carried before the King's Justiciaries at Westminster, the Earl, apprehensive lest a verdict might be given against him, attacked in Court Lord Zouch and his son, both of whom he wounded, the father indeed desperately, and then rushing violently into the King's palace, afterwards fled to his castle at Reigate, whither, however, he was soon pursued and brought to terms by Prince Edward. According to the anonymous continuator of Matthew Paris's Chronicle—" John de Warenne, Earl of Surrey, slew with his own hand in Westminster Hall, Alan de la Zouche, the King's justiciary, in consequence of some words which passed between them." But the lawless incident appears to be more accurately related by the cotemporary continuator of Florence of Worcester's Chronicle, who says that, " Earl Warrenne assaulted the Lord Alan de Zouche in Westminster Hall, on the bench, before the justiciary, on the octave of St. John, and so severely wounded him, that he died on the feast of St. Lawrence (that is about six weeks afterwards). His eldest son Roger had recourse to flight, but narrowly escaped."

Melancholy to relate, the only son of this irate seventh Earl of Warren was killed in a tournament held at Croydon. To the same unknown monk who continued the last named Chronicle we owe the following record of the circumstance:—" The Lord William de Warrenne, son and heir of John de Warrenne, Earl of Surrey, was encountered and cruelly slain, as it is said, by his enemies, in a tournament held at Croydon, in the month of December," A.D. 1286. The sad mischance occurred probably on the elevated plateau of Duppa's Hill, the firm level of which seems well adapted either for a tilt *à l'outrance* or in the gentler mode.

The privilege of holding market and fair at Croydon, obtained in the years 1273, 1276, 1314 and 1343, by the interest successively of Archbishops Kilwardby, Reynolds, and Stratford, from the Kings Edward I., II. and III., no doubt tended to enhance the importance of our town.*

The Master and Brethren of the Hospital of St. Thomas the Martyr, in Southwark, held certain lands and tenements in Croydon, Bedyntone, Bandon and Mycham, which they gave to Gilbert, the third or the Red, Earl of Gloucester and Hereford, and Lord of Bletchyngelegh, in exchange for the advowson of Bletchyngelegh, as appears by a deed of that Earl dated 20 Nov. 7 Edward I., stated by inspeximus in a confirmation granted by Edward II., anno 8°; but this exchange seems to have been afterwards cancelled.

Passing on, we note the circumstance that, on the 20th of March, 1382, Sir William Walworth, the same who, when Lord Mayor of London, had boldly plunged his sword into the throat of Wat the Tiler, and arrested the progress of that revolutionary movement of which Wat was chief, by Archbishop Courtenay was appointed Keeper of Croydon Park. That there were anciently some grammar schools in this town, appears from another entry in Archbishop Courtenay's Register, to the effect that, on the 31st of May, 1393, this Prelate ordained John Makheyt, a deacon at Maidstone, master of the grammar schools of Croydon; yet what became of the school or schools in question nobody can tell.

1414.—" Sir Robert Morton, Knight, servant to King Henry, ob. 1414," and was buried in Croydon old Church.

* See pp. 98 and 100.

In Fuller's "Worthies of England," among the Surrey gentry returned by the Commissioners in the year 1443 (12 Hen. VI.) are mentioned the names of the following gentlemen of Croydon:—

   Roger Elingbrig, Arm.
   Thomas Hering, de Croydon.
   Robert Dogge, de Croydon.
   Jacob Janyn, de Croydon.
   Roger Longland, de Croydon.

1544.—Under this year an entry in Croydon parish register informs us that:—"Thomas Heyrne obiit 2 die Octobris"; it was Thomas Heron, Esq., the rich owner of Adgecome or Addiscombe. 1545: on the 16th of October, a commission of array was issued for raising four hundred able men, when this town was required to furnish four archers and six billmen. "1550, Aug.—Mr. Tonstall buryed the 21." So runs another entry in our parish register; the Mr. Henry Tonstall referred to was eldest son of Sir John, by his wife Penelope, daughter of Sir Walter Leveson, Knt. of Lilleshall, Salop.

In the month of September, 1550, a poulterer of Surrey named Grig, regarded by the ignorant as a prophet able to cure diseases by words and prayers, for which he said he would take no money, was, by commandment of the Earl of Warwick and others of the King's Council, set on a scaffold in the town of Croydon, with paper on breast, whereon was written concerning his deceitful and hypocritical dealings. He was afterwards put in the pillory at Southwark, during the Lady-day fair.

On the 25th of May, 1551, an earthquake was felt at Croydon.

The entry in our parish register relating to the poet Barkley gives 1552 as the date of his interment. Anthony à Wood says he was buried in Croydon Church. Alexander Barkley or Barklay appears to have been by birth a Scot. He studied at Oriel College, Oxford, and was afterwards successively a Benedictine monk at Ely, and a Franciscan at Canterbury. He is best known by his poem called "The Gret Shyppe of Fooles of this Worlde," taken from a work of the same name, written in German by Sebastian Brandt; it is a satire upon the follies of the age. Warton, in his "History of English Poetry," says the stanzas are verbose and prosaic, but that it is a work deserving of attention, as it exhibits, like other satires, a picture of familiar manners and popular customs. Barkley mentions "Croidon" more than once in his Eclogues; we have already quoted from this source. From another line we glean that Barkley resided here in early life :—

"While I in youth in Croidon towne did dwell."

Again this poetaster wrote :—

"He hath no felowe betwene this and Croidon,
Save the proude plowman, Gnatho of Chorlington."

It was in the month of July, 1573, that the great Queen Elizabeth halted for seven days at Croydon Palace. The fact has been noticed that Richard Gornarde or Gurney, as he called himself, was baptized in our old Church, in 1579. According to Lloyd's Memoirs, Sir Richard Gurney, Lord Mayor of London, was born at Croydon on the 17th of April 1577. He was son of Bryan Gornarde, of Croydon, a descendant of the Gurneys of Kendal, Westmoreland. The name Gornarde occurs several times in our Register, from whence also it appears that this Richard had two brothers, John, baptized 9th Dec. 1576, and Robert, baptized 28th May, 1581. Richard was apprenticed to Mr. Coleby, a silk-mercer in Cheapside, who bequeathed to him his shop and effects, estimated to be worth £6,000; and, still increasing in wealth and reputation, he became one of the leading citizens of London, and ultimately head of that Corporation. On Nov. 25th, 1641, being then Lord Mayor, he entertained Charles the First, on his return from Scotland, at a cost of about £4,000, when the King was pleased to confer on him the honour of Knighthood; and on the 14th of the following month the higher distinction of a Baronetage. In that same year Sir Richard Gurney caused the Royal Proclamation against the militia to be publicly read in the City. For this devotion to royalty he was deprived of his mayoralty, rendered incapable of holding any public office in the kingdom, fined £5,000, and ordered to be imprisoned in the Tower during the pleasure of both Houses of Parliament; and there he remained till within a month of his death, a term of seven years. After having, on account of his attachment to the Royal cause, suffered in his estate to the extent of £30,000, Sir Richard died on Oct. 6th, 1647. He was one of the trustees nominated by Henry Smith, Esq., for the management of his large property left to this and other towns in Surrey.

On the 17th of July, 1584, Archbishop Whitgift issued a commission to Samuel Finch, Vicar of Croydon, to claim, receive, and examine, all clerks sued, indicted, or convicted before any justice, or upon any felonies within Croydon; and to require such clerks to be received and admitted to the benefits and privileges of the clergy. The same prelate issued a similar commission to Finch and Hammond on the 20th of June, 1588.

It is affirmed that in the reign of King James I., when public horse-racing was first regularly established, Gateley, in Yorkshire, Theobalds, on Enfield chase, and Croydon, were held in the greatest estimation, as resorts for this pastime.

"1625, July 21.—Richard Vaughan sonne to the Lord Vaughan and Mrs. Bridget Lloyd were marryed." This Richard was only son of John, first Baron Vaughan and Earl of Carberry of the Kingdom of Ireland. Created a Knight of the Bath at the coronation of Charles I., as the Royalist Lieutenant General of Carmarthen, Pembroke, and Cardigan, he became distinguished, and receiving as his reward the title of Baron Vaughan of Emlyn in the County of Carmarthen, after the Restoration he was appointed Lord President of the Principality of Wales.

He married, says Steinman, first, Bridget, daughter and heir of Thomas Lloyde, Esq., of Llanlees, Cardigan, as above; second, Frances, daughter and co-heir of Sir John Altham, Knight of Oxby Hertfordshire; third, Lady Alice Edgerton, daughter of John Earl of Bridgewater, and died in 1687, having issue by his second wife only.

Yet two more entries in our Parish Register connect Croydon with the calamitous vicissitudes of that dreadful civil war in the days of Charles the First. Bap. "1637, May.—Christopher Heydon, the sonne of Sr John Heydon Knt." Sir John Heyden of Barkinstrop, Norfolk, was Lieutenant of the Ordnance to Charles I. "1639, June 18.—Basset Col, gentleman and the Lady Aymie Mordant, Knight and Baronet were maryed." She was mother of Sir Charles Mordaunt, Bart., one of those Cavaliers who paid the penalty of their loyalty by the forfeiture of their estates.

"1645.—On the 15 of April the order undergiven was issued by the Parliament for the withdrawel of a detachment of 200 horse and 100 dragoons, which had till then been quarter'd in this town—there awaiting the concentration of the County forces.*

"Sir,—We have now received some intelligence that the rebells of Kent are in some measure dispersed. And therefore there being no further use of yor Horse and Dragones that we wrot unto you to send towards Croydon, we desire you, they may bee recalled and disposed as you please.

    Signed in the name and by the warrant of the Committee of Both Kingdomes by your very affectionate friends and humble servants,

                      Manchester, Loudoun."†

"Darbie House,
   15 April, 1645.
      Sr Thomas Fairfax."

* *Vide* a Diary, or an Exact Journal, No. 48.
† "MSS., Brit. Mus. Ayscough's Cat." No. 1519, p. 44.

On the 10th of August, 1647, General Fairfax marched from his head-quarters at Croydon to Kingston, where, on the following day he held a Council of War.

Writing of the Black Assizes at Oxford, in 1577, and of the Assizes at Hereford in the reigns of King James and Charles I., Dr. Fuller adds:—"The like chanced some four years since at Croydon, in Surrey, where a great depopulation happened at the assizes of persons of quality; and the two judges, Baron Yates and Baron Rigby, getting their banes there, died a few days after." The exact date at which this fatal catastrophe occurred has not been ascertained, but Ducarel supposes that Yates and Rigby " were some of Oliver's judges."

1670.—On the 1st of June, Nathaniel Hardy, D.D., Dean of Rochester, died in this town. He was present with the Commissioners at Uxbridge; and in 1660, along with others, went to the Hague to invite Charles II. to return, and take possession of the Government. "At length," says Wood, "this active and forward man, who had little or no character among the true loyalists, especially that part of the clergy who had suffered in the times of usurpation, giving way to fate in his house, at Croydon in Surrey, on the 1st day of June 1670 was buried on the 9th day of the same month, in the chancel of St. Martin's Church in the Fields."

On January 27, 1721–2, a child having two heads, four arms, four legs, one body, one navel, and distinction of two male children was born here. 1728.—On the 12th of May a tempest of hail and rain, accompanied with thunder and lightning, swept over Croydon. The storm was so violent that hailstones from eight to ten inches round were struck some inches into the earth; cattle were forced into ditches and drowned; glass was shattered, and otherwise great damage done. In 1744 much destruction was effected by lightning in and near Croydon. Another great thunderstorm broke over Croydon on Sunday afternoon, June 23rd, 1878, when Handcroft Road and other low-lying parts of the town were flooded, as were also the basements of numerous premises situated in all parts of the parish, owing to the incapacity of the drains to carry off the immense volumes of water that suddenly descended. Considerable damage also was caused by lightning; whilst the destruction of glass by hailstones, many of which were three inches in circumference, was immense. The amount of rain measured during the storm by scientific observers was found to be: at Addiscombe, during the two hours that the storm lasted, 1·412 inches; at Park Hill, 1·285 inches; at the Sewage Filter Works, where the downpour seems to have been very heavy, the quantity measured was 2·22 inches.

CHAPTER XIII.

PAST TOPOGRAPHY.

SINCE the introduction of railway communication between the metropolis and Croydon, and the formation of our Board of Health, the changes in respect to this locality have been manifold and great. Who that now visits the neighbourhood of our old Church would dream that the site on which both it and the remains of the Archiepiscopal Palace stand was formerly an island, surrounded by clear running streams, out of which trout were fished; that a big pond once existed by the side of the road called Scarbrook; that adjoining the avenue leading from the old Palace into Church Street was a still larger expanse of water known as "My Lord's pond"; that opposite, and within a few yards of the west door of St. John's Church, a great mill-dam extended; or that a broad natural stream used to course through the Old Town? Nevertheless such were the facts, and, as previously explained, it is entirely owing to a recent superior system of draining the lower parts of this town, that the streams, ponds, and surface waters referred to have disappeared.*

The springs of those tributary heads of the Wandle which arose from under the western side of High Street, and fed the Scarbrook, were powerful. A noted spring of water also formerly gushed up opposite the west end of Sheldon Street, and a reminiscence of it still lingers in the name Pump-pail. Benson Spring likewise was a fine and very clear one: this arose about fifty feet north of

---

* See chart and accompanying explanation, pp. 71–74.

the water-works' engine-house, and the path leading to it from Surrey Street used to be called Spring Walk ; another path that led from Surrey Street to this spring is represented by Sturt's Yard. Benson Spring was never frozen over, not even in the year when the Thames was frozen: it is the source of the present water works.

With respect to that other tributary of the Wandle which flowed from the southern end of the parish, this stream ran along the Brighton Road, between the footpath on the west, and the roadway. Arrived at the "Anchor" it coursed along the passage at the back of that inn, running immediately alongside the wall on the east, yet leaving a space of ground four or five feet wide, in front of the doors of those little ancient tenements which still face the passage. The stream continued its course for a short distance along what is now the path on the west side of Southbridge Lane, when, crossing the road,* and entering the meadow, it separated into two branches, one of which ran through the field, while the other skirted the east side of Southbridge Lane. As it gurgled through the meadow, the bourne appeared a lovely rivulet, about five feet wide, and from one to two feet deep, with a nice gravelly bottom for trout to spawn in; and here, sixty years ago, they used to catch trout a foot long. The eastern fork of the stream flowing round by the line of St. Andrew's Street (which however at that time had no existence) eventually met the western branch of the stream in front of, where now is, the north door of St. Andrew's Church ; and, at this point, a wide plank, with a single hand-rail on a couple of posts, was thrown across the stream, to enable our Croydonians to pass dry-shod in the direction of Combe Lane.

A little further on, just opposite the N.W. angle of St. Andrew's School, the stream was spanned by another bridge, called the " Six Arches Bridge ;" for here, over the

---

* Just by the Nursery Garden. the Merstham tram went across an open arch over the stream, until a child happening to get drowned here, they covered the arch with a grating.

water one had to cross to get to Meadow Stile.* At this point the bourne was some twenty feet in breadth, and the bridge, constructed of brick, about three feet wide, with hand-rails, was placed obliquely to the stream. Doubtless, it is to one or other of these now defunct bridges that we are indebted for a nomenclature still preserved in South-*bridge* Lane, South-*bridge* Place, &c. A third bridge, also regularly built of brick, with a parapet of the same material, communicated between Pump-pail and Duppa's Hill Lane, for it was a main route.

And now the stream ran close under the west wall of the old "Running Horse," one of the windows of which, supported on posts, projected over the minnowy flood; nor could the front entrance of this hostelry be gained, except by a wooden bridge; another tiny bridge led to the skittle-ground. Having parted again, in order to encircle "Bog Island," eventually the combined stream arrived at the old Churchyard, when, deviating towards the west, its waters mingled with those from the Scarbrook and formed the Wandle.

On the rising of the bourne, which, on an average happened every fourth or fifth year, the Old Town used to be inundated, so much so, that the natives had to cross over the flood on planks, to get from the houses on one side of the road to those on the other; and this condition of affairs lasted sometimes five or six weeks. Meanwhile the water on the Brighton Road, in the neighbourhood of Purley Oaks, reached even up to the horses girths. At Pump-pail burial ground, in those palmy sanitary times that preceded extra-mural sepulture, coffins have been seen to float, and actually require to be forced under water while they were shovelling the earth into the grave! Fancy the inhabitants of neighbouring houses or ourselves being compelled to drink water that had been filtered through such a process! Cremation itself would

* Living men can well remember when there was really a stile at the end of the path through the meadow, where it joined High Street.

be preferable. In Boswell Court House, old Kilmister saw a servant at the cellar-door get into a floating tub, and push herself with a stick across to where the barrel stood, in order to draw the beer; "this," said he, "happened when the bourne was up, yet the adjoining roadway was dry." Of the bourne, Camden thus writes: "For the torrent that the vulgar affirm to rise here sometimes, and to presage dearth and pestilence, it seems hardly worth so much as the mentioning, though perhaps it may have something of truth in it." As for dearth it may have been superstitious to connect such a calamity with the periodic inundation of the bourne, yet who, on reading the above, can doubt that ere the huge culvert was constructed which now arrests and carries off its waters along with the sewage of Croydon, in former times, the "Rising of the Bourne," but too surely portended a harvest of sickness and death.

The name Wodden's Marsh, which on some of the older maps is given to a wide district on the west side of our parish, implies, a much less favourable condition of the soil there than is now exhibited. In short, the huge marsh pond by the side of Mitcham Road has disappeared. A sheet of water formerly in the grounds of Addiscombe College has also passed away. The more circular south end of Addiscombe pond was fed by springs and constituted one of the heads of the Ravensbourne, the main stream of which was reached at Catford bridge. The great pond referred to was crossed mid-way by a brick bridge that stood exactly where Lower Addiscombe Road now passes two rows of chestnut trees, still growing by the once hollowed out moat, eastward of the house named "The Chestnuts."

In the immediate neighbourhood of where now stands West Croydon Railway Station, forty-five years since was a large basin of water forming the head of Croydon Canal. It was in the year 1801 that the Act of Parliament for making and maintaining this canal was obtained;

the canal itself was opened in 1809. A fork of that iron tram which then communicated between Croydon and Merstham, following the line of the present Tamworth Road ran up to the said canal basin. This tram was laid down by Messrs. Jolliffe and Banks about the year 1804, and, consequently, it was an early specimen of an iron railroad. It ran originally from Merstham to Wandsworth *via* the course now named Church Road, and afterwards a branch was carried up to the Croydon Canal; the junction of the lines being at the Old Gun Orchard in Pitlake. The trucks were generally drawn by large mules. Nearing the wharf, the trucks used to be hauled by a windlass up a short incline, on to the platform, where their contents of lime, timber, stone or fuller's earth, as the case may have been, were unloaded into barges, that afterwards came back from Deptford laden with coals. Fragments of the bank on which this old Croydon tram ran are still visible on the west side of Brighton Road. The bank or footway running along the right hand side of the railway between St. James' Bridge and Gloucester Road is the old towing path of the Croydon Canal; of the canal itself, vestiges remain to the north of Portland Road, S. Norwood, and at Anerley.

Some of the wells, out of which our forefathers used to draw water, still remain, and from time to time others are discovered. The town pump used to stand at the angle formed by the junction of Market Street and Middle Street. There was also a parish pump at Pump-pail, and another in Handcross Alley. Some of the houses in High Street used to be supplied with water from a pump that stood up the yard of the Old King's Arms: a woman went round to the houses with pails of water.

Various living persons can remember when there was not a single house standing between the recently pulled down Rectory Manor-house, No. 38 on the west side of North End, and the Mansion known as Broad Green House. Broad Green, as its name indicates, sixty years ago was really an unenclosed greensward where boys used to play cricket. Here also, on the first of May, a fair was held. There was a rookery by the Green, and when this was destroyed an effort was made to re-establish it in the park of Brickwood House, but the rooks declined. According to Garrow, in the year 1818, there were about eighty-five houses at Broad Green. The old path is still remaining which led between the London and Mitcham Roads, for there was no Sumner Road then. Sumner Road was so named in honour of Archbishop Sumner, at whose cost the adjoining structure, Christchurch, was erected. Beyond the "Half Moon Inn," forty years ago, were not more than three houses on that side of the road ere you came to the pond at Thornton Heath. One of these old tenements, now pulled down, was called Weller House. In it lived Mr. Weller, the originator, it is said, of the "Gin Palace" system, by which he amassed a fortune which he laid out in fields at Croydon. Old Weller aspired to having a coat of arms painted on his carriage, with a motto in Latin, of which, says popular tradition, the English was: "Gin bought it, who'd have thought it." On Weller's decease his estate was claimed by his medical attendant, by name Wildbore, on the ground that the same had been left to him by will; this led to a lawsuit between the doctor and the relatives; and hence Wildbore's name came to be affixed to this section of our parish.

We read that, in the year 1818, the hamlet of Thornton Heath contained about sixty-eight houses.

In a rate-book, of the years 1756-7, under the heading North-End, Jos. Willoughby, Esq. is rated for Oakfields; the site is now cut up into a variety of roads and known as the Oakfield Estate. On this, the east side of the London Road, thirty-five years since, there were no houses between where Croydon Hospital now stands and Broad Green Place; but some cottages stood at Broad Green, and at the corner of Bensham Lane.

Sixty years ago an open common, covered with furze and gravel pits, stretched away from North End in the direction of Norwood and Selhurst. Upon this common were four windmills. One of them stood on the left hand side of Windmill Road near where it joins St James' Road. The sails of another mill revolved higher up on the left, not far from the junction of Whitehorse and Windmill Roads; Windmill Cottage, Beulah Grove, is the identical mill-house. A third windmill stood on the right-hand side of Gloucester Road, as you came towards Croydon town, not far from the Whitehorse Inn: and the fourth windmill, Noakes', stood also on the right-hand side of Gloucester Road. It was from the windmill first referred to that Windmill Road derived its name; this mill being the only one of the four marked on the Enclosure Map of the year 1800.

Near the locale of the present "Windmill Inn" a small inconvenient tenement may be seen, perched up on a solitary slip of land left by the spade of the gravel digger. It is the old 'Pest House', to which in less enlightened sanitary days they consigned those patients who were suffering from small-pox, and here, huddled together, for want of proper ventilation doubtless a considerable percentage of them died.

Opposite the Mansion known as Dingwalls, fifty years since might be seen arable land ploughed by ox-teams. As for the district known as Bedford Park, not one of the roads on it excepting the Sydenham Road, at the date we speak of, had any existence, but the winding round of this old pathway over the common is clearly indicated on the Enclosure Map. The residence situated on the West side of Sydenham Road North, known as 'Middle Heath Cottage' is appropriately so-named. The names Bedford Park, Tavistock and Woburn Road, &c., have obviously been applied in remembrance of that Russell family whose interests hereabouts were formerly considerable. St. James' Church, the result of one of the earliest ecclesiastical mutations of what until then had been the undivided parish of Croydon, was built on the common in 1827–9. At that date, in the lane leading past it,* now named St. James' Road, there was hardly a tenement on either side from Broad Green Place to what, owing to the name of the family now owning the estate, is called Morland Park; and not a dwelling between Morland's and Woodside Court, except an old farm house still standing near Addiscombe Railway Station, The rows of houses known as Canning, Clyde, Elgin, Havelock, Outram, and Ashburton Roads had no existence prior to the year 1862, when the stately mansion at Addiscombe was pulled down.

The lane or road, called Cherry Orchard, derives its appellation from the circumstance that, in former times, and indeed until the cutting of the railway, an orchard full of cherry-trees extended from where Messrs. Hall's coal-office now stands, to the Upper Addiscombe Road, and thence in the direction of George Street, past where Dingwall Road now runs. When cherries were ripe, a cherry fair used to be celebrated annually on the spot where the lane joins Upper Addiscombe Road. Some fifty years since, there was only one little cabin between Fairfield House (opposite the Literary Institution) and that old house just over the railway bridge; and nothing beyond it excepting a barn and small wooden cottage, till you reached those two ancient residences situated opposite the upper ends of Outram and Ashburton Roads. On the north side of Upper Addiscombe Road stands Ashburton House, so named because here resided the first Lord Ashburton, and adjoining it the farm cottage bearing date, 1676. Between Ashburton House and Addiscombe College there were no houses, nor any between the College and Brickwood House, saving a couple of tenements, and that dwelling adjoining Brickwood, reached by the lane.

---

* Some of the trees that used to grow in the hedge of the old lane alluded to, remain on the north side of St. James' Churchyard.

The reason this estate is called "Brickwood" is because it formerly belonged to a gentleman of that name.

The greater portion of the field on which Croydon Fair used to be held has been hollowed out into a huge gravel pit, for the present appearing an unsightly object in the centre of Croydon. This fair used to commence with a goodly display of cattle; it lasted three days. Until recently the fair field was a lovely green sward. But, after the suppression of Fairlop and Greenwich Fairs, the fast Londoners used to run down by train, in thousands, to Croydon Fair; and here they carried on such a saturnalia that the respectable inhabitants of the parish rejoiced when this pleasure fair also was done away. An excellent cattle fair, however, still continues annually to take place at Croydon, on October 2nd, the day on which the old fair used to commence.

Formerly a row of lime trees extended from where the residue of them still grows in High Street, opposite the end of West Street, up to Mint Walk. Patches of limes, until very recently, also remained in North End. Poplar Walk derives its name from the row of poplars which formerly grew there.

In reference to the south end of Croydon, fifty years since there was scarcely a house between the "Swan and Sugar-loaf" and Purley.

The avenue to Haling House used to run from Duppa's Hill Lane, through the Waldrons, and that portion of the park now covered by residences on Bramley Hill. Nor were there any buildings on the Waldrons, save the entrance lodge in Duppa's Hill Lane; for, seventy years ago, the Waldrons, as its name imports, was a wild waste, in which gravel was dug, and rabbits ran wild, with plenty of snakes, adders and newts. At that time there was neither roadway nor houses where Duppa's Hill Avenue now is; but Violet Lane was then, and on either side of it grew plenty of broom. When Napoleon contemplated invading Britain, at the beginning of the century, lest the French might succeed in stopping our supplies, among many similar precautionary measures adopted in other parts of the kingdom, that old row of wooden tenements on the east side of Duppa's Hill Terrace was turned into a granary, and so also was Whitgift's School in George Street.

By the way, in Southbridge Lane, opposite Parker Road, stands a brick and flint structure, and over the door a mouldering stone, on which is carved :—

T
W + E
1553

It was the eventful year in which King Edward the Sixth died, and Queen Mary ascended the throne.

From the "Running Horse" Inn up to the Old Union House, now an Infirmary, on both sides were fields fenced in with wooden palings. Fifty-five years since a large tract called "Penfold's Field" extended from Duppa's Hill Lane to Tanfield Lodge. Opposite was Ridley's, which, from Hill Place in the Old Town, with the exception of one tenement, a cowkeeper's just at the bottom of Hill Place, extended one continuous field right round to the Old Union House. From the "Running Horse," in the direction of the Old Church there was not a house till you came to the four little red-brick cottages nearly opposite the "Globe Inn:" between these and the "Running Horse" intervened a bleaching field, and through the midst of it meandered the Wandle. Every house on "Bog Island" has been erected within the memory of living man.

It would appear from the parish rate-book that, in the year 1756, there were about thirty-one tenements in Waddon.

Westward of Pitlake is a district known as Barrack Fields, it derives its name from the Barracks formerly adjoining. A populous neighbourhood now occupies the site of those fields, on which living men can remember horse-races taking place. On the north side of Handcroft Road extended an open meadow, called Parson's Mead, so called because, as we have seen, it formerly belonged to the Manor of the Rectory of Croydon. The meadow stretched from Handcroft Road on one side to the London Road on the other; and from Broad Green House to the Manor House in North End. Fifty years ago it was customary after hay-harvest—viz., on Lammas-day—for those who enjoyed the right, to turn out one or two head of cattle into this meadow. The name Handcroft may be merely a corruption of Hand-Cross. One of the four crosses in the Manor of Croydon was described in the reign of Elizabeth as standing at the Little Almshouse Corner; and adjoining the spot is that ancient passage called Handcross Alley. On the enclosure map of the year 1800 Parson's Mead is delineated as consisting of thirty acres, three roods and twenty-two perches. Not until many years after the above-named date was there a single house upon it, nor was it intersected by any path, excepting that ancient short cut from the Common to the Old Church, part of which still remains at the back of North End. Tamworth Road was cut through Parson's Mead when the tram was laid down. Tamworth and Drayton Roads acquired their names in this way. The late Mr. Walter N. Wright owned some property at the south end of the first-named street, and as his father had known the first Sir Robert Peel, he suggested these names in remembrance of the circumstance, and so named the roads were.

Handcroft Road is doubtless very ancient, and at one time was connected with Bensham Lane, which appears to be a continuation of it. The more ancient route from Croydon to London would seem to have led from our old town past the old church, up Handcroft Road, and Bensham lane, and so across to Streatham, *viâ* that Green lane, one end of which is named Parchmore Road. One of the links of this route appears to be now lost. But that the Green lane referred to is very ancient those aged pollard oaks and huge stems of thorn trees growing on either side bear witness. It seems originally to have been an old trackway through what at one period was the forest or great North wood. The lane winds its devious course generally over the highest ground through which it passes, for the man—and Celt he may have been—who first trod it, found on this elevation the ground harder and firmer than on the lower level upon either side; and, ere the surrounding country was drained, muddy indeed in winter must have been the lower parts of this forest. To reach Croydon by the present route, in very ancient times, at certain seasons of the year, one must have been compelled to ford quite a morass in the low-lying neighbourhood of Streatham Bridge; and this is an argument for the superior antiquity of the higher road. Again, the very winding of the lane suggests how old it is, for its crookedness was, in all probability, occasioned by obstacles in the way of the original tracker; here he may have met a great oak tree and further on a pond, neither of which he could pass except by going round them; and thus, although both pond and oak have disappeared they have left their permanent impress on this way. Man in a savage state is not likely to carry a roadway in a straight line through such obstacles as would naturally exist in a forest like the North-wood: the straightness of the present road between Croydon and Streatham, therefore, is another proof of its more recent formation. Unless indeed this is that old Roman Via, part of which is said to have been visible at Broad Green, towards the close of last century. But Roman roads were not always straight, as witness portions of the Watling Street; nor did our Roman Conquerors disdain occasionally to utilize the old British lines of communication. It is pretty certain that the High Street of Croydon and North End formed at one time merely a bridle-way across the fields. Nor, in estimating the probable antiquity of the way by Handcroft

Road and Bensham Lane, ought the circumstance to be overlooked, that a number of Roman and Saxon coins have been found in various spots not far off this route. A Roman coin is in my own possession which was found in a garden off Handcroft Road. A coin of the Emperor Vespasian, and also one of Domitian, were discovered in the manor of Bensham. A coin of Hadrian was dug up in our cemetery, and one of Ælius Cæsar on the site of the Union House, both of which stand just a little to the east of Bensham Lane: and it was not far off Collier's Water Lane, where it joins Parchmore Road, that a quantity of Anglo-Saxon coins were found. Discoveries such as these seem to bespeak, for the spots on which these coins were picked up, a proximity to some old highway.

Not a vestige remains of "The Vicar's Oak," that remarkable tree which anciently grew at a spot, where, according to old Aubrey, "four parishes (including Croydon) meet in a point." It appears to have been a boundary or mark-tree, and like the famous Chertsey oak probably was marked with a X.

The forest of Norwood must at one time have been of vast extent. Even within the memory of living men the whole of Norwood Hill, including the ground on which the Crystal Palace now stands, was a wood, until Norwood, joined Dulwich Wood and Gipsy Hill, the whole forming one immense irregular plantation of pollard oak, scrubs and furze; with the exception of a cottage here and there, "The Woodman" public-house on the top of the hill was the only structure visible. The gardens of this old "Woodman" used to be a favourite resort in summer of the cockneys, whose fortunes were told by a numerous gang of gipsies. Formerly it was no uncommon sight to see from thirty to forty gipsies' tents pitched on that open down, the site of which still retains the name of Gipsy Hill. About forty years ago the tea-gardens of the old "Jolly Sailor" at South Norwood, also were a noted rendezvous for Londoners bent on pleasure, and at South

Norwood too, numbers of gipsies used to consort. Rogers's farm is old; and excepting some wooden huts about, it was the only habitation between the "Jolly Sailor" and Selhurst.

The mineral spring afterwards known as Beulah Spa, had long been held in great repute; a little green sward extended by the well, and there used to be a thatched open summer-house adjoining. The charge was sixpence a glass. When John Cator, Esq., sold the manor of Whitehorse to John Davidson Smith, Esq., the latter gentleman made the road over Beulah Hill, now called the Grange Road, and also laid out the Beulah Spa. The spring once so famed for its medicinal virtues is however utterly neglected, and the lovely Spa grounds, cut up, now consist of villa residences.

CHAPTER XIV

MISCELLANEOUS.

SEVENTY years ago two large elm-trees grew by the roadway of Crown Hill; and adjoining, still remains an old house, described in its title-deeds as "The Rookery." The large block of tenements abutting on Bell Hill, the pointed gables of which are visible from High Street, looking like some old farm-house, as, indeed, some say it once was, must be at least 300 years old. A handsome old house formerly stood where the premises Nos. 7 and 8 Surrey Street now are; the house referred to was at one time the Judges' lodgings; it had oak-panelled walls, and in the hall, a pavement of white and black marble. Afterwards it became the British School, but eventually it was pulled down. Under No. 20, Surrey Street is a curious old cellar, with pointed stone arches, and a stone ribbed roof; it is a vestige, perhaps, of cellarage, which at some remote former period, belonged to a tenement connected with the old Archiepiscopal Palace. A picturesque timbered residence, overhanging the top of where Oak Alley joins Middle Street, remains to attest the former importance of that now faded locality.

Old Families.—The Court Rolls of the manor show that the family of Farley has held land in this parish for upwards of 300 years; the family of Covell is also one of the oldest in Croydon. With respect to the Blake family, we read in the parish register that "Wyllm Blake" was married on Oct. 8th, 1582, and that on Sept. 9th, 1583, Thomas Blake was buried; there is another entry, to the effect that on the 27th of June, 1585, "Wyllm

Blake" was married, and John Blake was buried Nov. 27th, 1588: the name "Wyllm Blake" occurs again as having been married on the 4th June, 1592, and James Blake was buried July 1, 1602. From the repeated mention, at so early a date, of the name of Blake, it may be inferred that this is an old Croydon family. Meager and Bennington also were old Croydonians; connected with the latter were the Gilpins. Under date 1612, we read that "Luke Gylpin" was christened the 26th day of September; "John Gilpin" was buried the first day of June, 1621. An ancient chalice, in the old parish church, bears an inscription to the effect that it was "the gift of Mr. John Gilpin of Croyden." Of this family is said to have been that John Gilpin whom the poet Cowper has immortalized; he bought the estate of Collier's Water in this parish. The name Mathew occurs in the burial register, no less than nine times between July 14th and August 17th in the year 1625; they all died of the pest.

Inns.—The old inns of some of our English towns are replete with interest, not only on account of their picturesque appearance, but also because they serve as memorials of past proprietorship, and furnish us with a clue to the habits and manners of former times. There are not many pretty hostelries in this parish, nevertheless, some of the inns of Croydon are ancient. "The Greyhound" Hotel, in High Street, justly ranks as an old and first-class establishment, mention being made of "the good wyfe of the grewond" in our parish register, under date 1563. Next comes "The Crown," named, in a letter from the Rev. Mr. Finche, dated 19th Feb. 1596; next "The Swan," referred to in a paper written by Archbishop Whitgift about the year 1599. The above-named three hostelries still flourish. Some of the other inns of Croydon may be equally ancient or older even than these, although evidence to that effect is wanting; and some hostels that were old, such as " The George," which stood at the corner of George Street, opposite Whitgift's Hospital, no longer serve the purposes of an inn, but have been converted into shops or private dwellings. Where Katherine Street runs used to be merely a yard, like the Greyhound yard: the yard in question was the old " King's Arms" stable-yard, which reached from High Street to Park Lane. Entwistle's wine and spirit establishment, in High Street, occupies the exact site of the old " King's Arms." The present " King's Arms," in Katherine Street, is reared upon the site of the tap of the former " King's Arms;" and a grocer's shop, afterwards converted into an upholsterer's, faced High Street, where now is the open roadway of Katherine Street. George the Fourth used to change horses on his way to Brighton at the old " King's Arms," the change was effected in about a minute. But one day, near the time of the trial of Queen Caroline, a rude fellow, poking his head through the open window into the carriage in which the King was sitting, inquired, "why did'nt you bring your wife, George?" After that George IV. was never known to drive through Croydon.

Of the " Three Tuns," in Surrey Street, there are extant more than one very perfect tradesman's token of the year 1667. The " Green Dragon," in High Street, was a great coaching house in days of yore. Land adjoining the " Half Moon" tavern, London Road, is named on the map of the year 1800, " Half Moon Fields." The old " Gun" orchard was at the back of the Little Almshouses; the sign of " The Gun," in Church Street, used to contain a representation of an artilleryman, standing with lighted match applied to the touch-hole, and the motto,—" Hit or miss, luck's all."

The variety of figures and devices on the signboards of inns have frequently engaged the attention of the curious. These signs, in short, are one of the surviving relics of those happy days when, instead of carefully painted names affixed to the corner of every street, and denoting numbers on each door, the banker or trader suspended from his lintel the sign under which he hoped to gain an independence, and by that distinguishing badge his house and business became known. Inn signs, such as the "Greyhound," the "Hare and Hounds," the "Horse and Groom," the "Fox and Hounds," and the "Horse Shoe," all of which are to be found in this parish, imply that Croydon was the centre of a fine sporting country; whilst signs like those of "The Crown," and the "King's Arms," have a smack of loyalty and good old Toryism. The "Rose and Crown" was the badge of the house of Tudor; the "Royal Oak" dates back to the days of the Stuarts. "The George" probably refers to that accompaniment of the Garter. Concerning the sign of the "Three Tuns," three was a favourite number. Those of the "Green Dragon," "Red Deer," "Half Moon," and "Star," evidently had an heraldic origin. From the sign of the "Canterbury Arms," as from names of various streets in our parish, may be inferred the status of the Archbishop in the manor. The signs of the "Gun," the "Cannon," and the "Volunteer," recall to mind their former proximity to the old barracks.

Respecting the "George Inn," of which mention has been made, it stood exactly where Mr. Miller, the draper's, and adjoining houses on either side, now are. A capacious tenement, therefore, was the old "George," and notwithstanding many mutations, the gigantic chestnut beams of its basement, banqueting room, and long gallery, still remain, to attest its former grandeur. Ugly stories at one time, however, got afloat concerning the management of this wayfaring establishment, for it was alleged that travellers who put up at the old "George" never were seen afterwards; the tradition being, that their remains were boiled in a huge cauldron, by the landlady. Accordingly, mine hostess acquired her nickname of "old mother hotwater," by which sobriquet the landlady of the "George," in former times, was known and dreaded far and wide.

But seventy or eighty years ago this same tenement had been converted into a school, kept by Mr. Bissett. Bissett, said my informant, was a stout jolly old fellow, who after his tuition labours were over, used to saunter down to the old "Ship" and have his glass.

Smuggling.—A great deal of smuggling was carried on formerly in the neighbourhood of Croydon. Mounted gangs of armed smugglers might often be seen in the neighbourhood of Addington and Sanderstead, or crossing over, as if from the coast, towards their hiding-places in the Norwood. These strange-looking horsemen rode along in the dusk with a small barrel of Hollands or brandy in front, and another behind; or laden with sacks, in which were secreted a number of smaller kegs, which they would stow away in rabbit holes.

Town Hall and Jail.—Situated towards the middle of High Street, and on its west side, stands the substantial structure known as the Town Hall of Croydon. This stone fabric occupies the site of a more ancient Town Hall, which was constructed chiefly of wood. An inscription on the front of the older Hall informed the inquirer that it was built in 1609, and repaired in 1781. This old Town Hall was surmounted by a belfry or cupola, and from the front of the building a clock projected over the heads of the passing-by Croydonians. To judge from a rude sketch of the old Town Hall, in the writer's possession, the ground floor of this building was railed in, and devoted to the purposes of a market. This must have been the same as that old Market House which Franc Tirrell, "citizen and grocer of London" is said to have built at Croydon in the year 1566; for, when it was pulled down in 1807, the inscription quoted on page 54 was discovered. The lines, referred to, are now affixed to an interior wall on the north side of the lower Court of the present Town Hall, and over them is another inscription, recording that the existing structure was "rebuilt by Act of Parliament of the XLVI. of King Geo. III. with monies arising from the sale of part of the waste lands of this parish, A.D. 1808." The heavy blocks of stone, with which the present Town Hall was built, were brought from the quarries of Messrs. Jolliffe & Banks, at Merstham. The original cost of the building was about £8000.

Croydon Town Hall is an ordinary classical design; it was built from a plan of the late Samuel Pepys Cockerell. Above is the clock tower, surmounted by a belfry and weather vane. Formerly the Town Hall bell used to sound the alarm in cases of fire, but this use of it has been discontinued. The Town Hall of Croydon contains courts, and the necessary offices for holding the Summer Assizes for the County of Surrey, which are held alternately at Croydon and Guildford. In the basement of the Town Hall are a number of strongly formed cells, and these, during assize time, serve the purposes of a Town Jail. Previously, however, to the year 1861, Croydon Jail occupied a portion of what is now Mr. Smith's corn warehouse, on the other side of Surrey Street.

Pillory, Stocks, Whipping Post, and Gibbet.—About the year 1811, the moveable pillory at Croydon was temporarily stationed at the back of the Town Hall. It stood, said one who had seen it, high out in the thoroughfare, revolving, with the wretch's head, hands, and feet in a vice. The Stocks were fixed nearly in front of the "Three Tuns," but on the opposite side of Surrey Street. The Whipping Post, with iron loops to fasten the criminal to, was planted by the south-west corner of our Town Hall. Mr. Clive informed me that he had seen a lad tied to the cart-tail, and flogged by Jack Ketch through Surrey Street, from the Jail to the corner of Church Street, and back. In the works of John Taylor, the water poet, printed at London in 1630, is a long account of a murder committed by John Rowse on two of his children, for which he was executed at Croydon, on June 2nd, 1612. A gibbet stood at "Gibbet Green," near the entrance into Sanderstead Lane; and two headless skeletons were dug up opposite to it, at Nancy Cock Shaw, within a short distance of Brighton Road. The terrible fact has been already mentioned, that six men were executed at Thornton Heath on one day, in the year 1722.* The late Mr. T. Farley said his father could remember one of the gibbets at Thornton Heath standing just where the kitchen garden now is at the back of Dovercourt. When digging in his paddock, a little to the north-east of his house, adjoining Waddon Marsh Lane, Mr. Appleton found human bones. He told me of a tradition, that once when a man was hung on the gibbet fixed at this spot, the rope broke, and the man taking to his heels ran into the wood which formerly adjoined on the south-east, and escaped. After robbing passengers on the London Road, by Norbury, the highwaymen used to run through the wood, in the direction of Norwood.

Cannon Balls.—An iron cannon ball, along with bones of a horse, was found in the gravel when relaying the floor in the cellar under Mr. Pelton's premises, No 130, High Street. Another cannon ball was discovered in digging up the roots of a large tree which grew on the Blount House estate, near St. Peter's Church, and along with it was the cord as of an epaulette. A smaller cannon ball was dug up when making the sewer in the London Road, opposite Dunheved Road.

Barracks were erected near the town on the south side of Mitcham Road in 1794. Originally they were intended as a temporary station for cavalry, during the preparation of troops for foreign service. Afterwards they formed the depôt and head-quarters of the Royal Waggon Train. During the Russian war the barracks at Croydon served

* See page 66.

as a station for drilling, &c., recruits for the Grenadier, Coldstream, and Fusilier Guards.

The band of the Royal Waggon Train was a very fine one, and used, by its splendid performances, to contribute much to the happiness of the Croydonians. Three or four blacks with cymbals, &c., were attached to this band.

Croydon Old Bank was established by the late Mr. Miller, in his drapery shop, adjoining the "Greyhound Hotel," and the site of this, the first bank in Croydon, is now occupied by the ironmongery establishment of Messrs. Hammond and Hussey. Mr. Miller conducted the banking in his counting-house, and kept no clerk; but regular bank-notes were issued. For about ten years this was the only bank in Croydon. Then came Messrs. Smith, Moore, and Watney's bank, held where Page the fishmonger's shop now is; afterwards a Corndealer's Bank, Russell's, next door to the "Ship," on the south side; and then Harman and Tait's, situated on the spot where Messrs. Fuller and Moon's office now is. Eventually the business of Miller's bank was transferred to Crafton, the chemist, who carried it on for a short time on the premises still occupied by Mr. Crafton, but simultaneously with the starting of the London and County Bank this banking concern was handed over to them.

Post Office.—In 1816 the General Post Office for Croydon was situated at the "Hare and Hounds Inn," Waddon. Afterwards it was removed to the corner of Church Street, to the house in which Pine, the printer, lives, adjoining which is a yard still called Post-office Yard. Croydon Post Office was next moved to where the "Castle" Coffee Tavern now stands, in High Street, thence to Crown Hill, underneath Mr. Newton's shop, and finally to where it remains, in High Street.

Coaching in the Olden Time.—Prior to the opening of the railway some fifty regularly appointed stage coaches rattled every week-day through the good old town of Croydon—that is to say, twenty-five coaches a-day passed each way, making in all fifty, and this without counting His Majesty's Mail, which, every morning, drove along High Street to London and returned to Brighton at night. Of the aforesaid fifty-two vehicles, eighteen or nineteen passed daily to Brighton, and the same number back again to London every day; there was one stage coach to Lewes and back, one to East Grinstead, and another to Reigate and back every day; besides a coach three times a week to Eastbourne. Some of these stagers had three horses, but the most were four-horse coaches. The "Sovereign" the "Dart," "Vivid," the "Item," and the four "Times" were all driven from London to Brighton and back by the same drivers every day; the "Age" was likewise a first-rate turn-out.

From the town of Croydon itself there were six four-horse coaches, and five or six one pair-horse coaches daily to London and back. There were the White coaches and the Red; they belonged to opposition companies.

The fare to London from Brighton by the regular conveyances, which ran all the year round, was a guinea inside, and twelve shillings outside; but with what were styled the "Butterflies," or coaches put on merely for the summer season, the fare used to be somewhat lower. It cost another one pound one, of course, to get back to Brighton. From Croydon to London, fifty years since, the regular fare was three shillings inside and two shillings outside, for the single journey; but this was afterwards lowered to two shillings and sixpence in, and one and sixpence out.

The Mail had scarlet-coated driver and guard, the latter having charge of the bags, which were stowed away under his feet or in the box on the top of the coach. The guard blew his horn.

Their favourite place for pulling up was the "Green Dragon;" for the local service between Croydon and London, however, passengers booked at the "Crown." The late

Mr. Southgate, who drove between Croydon and London for over thirty years, told me that accidents were rare. A friend of Mr. Clive's father, on being asked to return to London by Matthew's coach, replied, "No! I'm in a hurry:" it was old Matthew's practice to make his passengers get out and walk up Brixton Hill.

In those days there was no direct service between Croydon and Epsom, or Dorking, nor yet betwixt Croydon and Bromley, or Wimbledon; to reach such cross-road places one had to hire.

Hunting.—The country round Croydon used to be famous for yielding abundance of sport to lovers of the chase, and several noted packs of hounds were kept either in the parish or in this immediate neighbourhood. A famous pack of foxhounds was kept at Shirley, by Colonel Maberly; and Mr. Thomas Meager had a pack of harriers at Croham. Three miles off the town, at the Oaks, the Earl of Derby maintained his celebrated pack of staghounds; then eight miles distant, at Merstham, Mr. Jolliffe kept a pack of foxhounds; and there were packs of harriers also at Beddington and Sanderstead. The old Sanderstead "Blue Mottle," a particular breed of harriers, were so called on account of the manner in which they were marked. And, besides all these, two or three little packs of beagles likewise scoured the neighbourhood.

> "The hounds, and horn
> Cheerly rouse the slumbering morn."

The great horse-race called "The Derby" was founded, and indeed named, after that Earl of Derby who resided on the borders of this parish; as, in like manner, was the race for mares, known as "The Oaks," so called from the name of this residence of the same noble sportsman.

For the convenience of the numerous scarlet-coated gentry who used to attend the meet, Croydon could boast of several excellent hunting stables. An old hunting stable was situated in George Street, where Waters, the coachmaker, now is; it was Morton's. Another hunting stable stood in the long yard at the south side of Hussey's the ironmonger; McArty was the last who kept it. Both Morton and McArty had other stables in Croydon besides these, such as the Derby Arms Livery Stables, which at one time was occupied by Morton, and afterwards by Bignell. Here, for forty years, the late Sir Francis Goldsmid, M.P., kept all his hunters and hacks under the charge of Mr. Bignell, father and son.

The hunting season at Croydon, in the olden time, lasted from October to Easter Monday, during which there might be a couple of hundred good hunters lodged in the Croydon stables. But railways and building speculations are not conducive to fox-hunting, and sly reynard has retreated from our town to more secluded haunts. Still we have in this neighbourhood the Surrey Staghounds, and also the old Surrey Foxhounds, kept by Edmund Byron, J.P., lord of the manor of Coulsdon; these last have been hunted by the Hill family for quite seventy years.

The *Sporting Magazine* of January, 1793, gives the following account of an economical sportsman, then or lately before, resident at Croydon. This was Mr. Osbaldeston, who was the youngest son of a gentleman of good family but small fortune in the North of England, who having imprudently married one of his father's servants, was turned out of doors with no other fortune than a favourite hound, big with pup, whose offspring afterwards became a source of profit and amusement to him. " This Mr. Osbaldeston went to London, where he officiated as an attorney's clerk, and in spite of popular prejudices against the profession, is said to have been an honest man. This honest limb of the law being married, has at least half a dozen children, whom, with as many couples of hounds, and a brace of hunters, he maintains . . . . . out of what? To support himself, a wife, six children, twelve dogs, and two horses, he has not a penny more than sixty pounds per annum; and, if possible, to increase the miracle, he did this in London for many years, paying everybody their own, and keeping a tight coat for Sundays and holidays. But, to explain this seeming paradox, after the expiration of the time which Mr. Osbaldeston owed his master, he acted as an accountant for the butchers in Clare Market, who paid him in offal; the choicest morsels of this he selected for himself and family, and with the rest he fed his hounds; his horses were lodged in his cellar, and fed with grains which he had from a neighbouring brewhouse, and on damaged corn, with which he was supplied by a corn chandler whose books he kept in order. Once or twice a week he hunted during the season, and by giving a hare now and then to the farmers over whose grounds he sported, secured their good will and permission: besides which, several gentlemen, struck with his extraordinary economy, winked at his going over their manors with his moderate pack. Accident, however, removed this uncommon character to Lewes, in Sussex, where on the same stipend, he maintained the same family: 'Curiosity,' says a gentleman who paid him a visit there, 'led me to visit this extraordinary party; about their dinner time the two-legged part of it were clean, though not superfluously clothed, and seemed to live like brothers with the surrounding animals—it looked in short like the golden age: Mr. Osbaldeston seemed and acted like the father of the quadrupeds as well as of the bipeds, and as such decided with the utmost impartiality—for Master Jackey having taken a bone from Jowler, he commanded instant restitution—and on the other hand, Doxy, having snatched a piece of liver from Miss Dorothea, was obliged, on the spot, to restore it to the young lady.'

"The family afterwards removed to Croydon, Surrey. His residence at Croydon, was in Pound-Street (now George Street) next to the chapel, where he still continued to keep his hounds in his garret, and to hunt with them as before. He had a small stable for his two horses, which he used to drive in a phaeton. He continued in this situation till he died. One of his daughters is still living in the town, supporting herself by her own industry. He is well remembered, by several persons now living in Croydon, for his singularity; was much reduced before his death, and entirely supported by his charitable friends."

George III.—His Majesty, old King George III., on horseback, has been seen to whip round the corner of Whitgift's Hospital, with groom behind, on his way to Lord Liverpool's, at Addiscombe.

Trade, Old and New.—An old indenture relating to Messrs. Crowley's Brewery commences as follows:—" This indenture made the seven and twentieth daw of October Anno dm. 1637 and in the thirteenth yere of the Raigne of o[r] Sovraigne Lord Charles by the Grace of God of England Scotland France and Ireland King defendor of the Faith etc. Betwene John Roffey of Chipsted in the County of Surrey, Blacksmith of the one parte and William Mullen the Elder of Croydon in the said county of Surrey Maltman of the other parte witnesseth that the said John Roffey for and in consideration of the sume of Three hundred Thirty Eight pounds of lawfull money of England to him in hand paid by the said William Mullen before ther sealing and delivery hereof whereof hee acknowledgeth the receipt and there of and of every parte and parcell thereof doth clerely acquite exonate and discharge the said William Mullen his heires executo[rs] and administrato[rs] for ever by theis p[r]sents Hath graunted bargayned sold aliened enfeoffed and confirmed and by these p[r]nts doth fully clerely and absolutly graunt bargayne sell alien enfeoffe and confirme unto the said William Mullen his heires and assignes for ever all those three messuags or tenenm[ts] w[th] all ediffices buildings *malthouses* barnes stables orchards," &c. The indenture refers to premises on the present site of Crowley's brewery.

Corney's tobacco-pipe manufactory is more than one hundred and fifty years old.

The blacksmith's business, near the S.W. corner of Upper Coombe Street, has been in existence for at least a hundred years: it was Butt's Smithy. Another blacksmith's, namely, Collier's, or as it is now called Davis's, at the corner of Southbridge Row, is probably even older. Pidgeon, the farrier's, was at the corner of Scarbrook Hill, which, indeed, often used to be called Pidgeon's Hill. Pidgeon's fine business is now represented by Mr. Peter Thrale, whose mother was Pidgeon's daughter. Sturt's shop (now Lee, the farrier's) was older still, perhaps; the name is preserved in "Sturt's Yard." These represented the old blacksmiths' trade of Croydon, and the stroke of business which each did establishes the fact that hereabouts hunting and coaching formerly prevailed.

About twenty years ago a large business was carried on at Croydon in the manufacture of what were called "basket-carriages." So great, indeed, was the demand for this description of vehicle, that one maker, the late Mr. Lenny, of North End, employed over two hundred men; and there is scarcely a corner of the globe to which a basket carriage of some description has not been forwarded from Croydon.

The large brewing concern of Messrs. Nalder and Collyer is an old foundation.

Overton's brewery was established by the enterprising father of the present proprietor.

The business now carried on by George Price and Son, wine merchants, was originally a distillery and wine and spirit business, established by Mr. Chatfield in the year 1745.

From time immemorial there has been a barber's shop where Pointer, the hairdresser, carries on his business at No. 4, King Street.

The grocery concern now conducted by Mr. Pelton, the business of Mr. Crafton, the chemist, and Stapleton the clothier's, all of which are in High Street, represent sound ancient callings.

Some of the above belong not only to the old, but also to the modern trade of Croydon; and, amid numerous other and worthy representatives of the latter, may be mentioned the boot and shoe manufactory of Messrs. Cooper and Son; the optical and mathematical instrument making works of Mr. W. F. Stanley; the steam joinery works and sawing mills of Mr. J. W. Hobbs; and Messrs. Hammond and Hussey's general ironmongery business.

Our townsman, Mr. Alfred C. Ebbutt, exhibited at the Paris International Exhibition of 1878, the "Croydon Cabinet." In reference to this piece of furniture, the *Art Journal* has observed that, "it is a most elaborate work of the very highest class, a complete triumph of the cabinet-maker, and confers the utmost credit on all who have been engaged in its production."

At the clock and bell founding establishment of Messrs. Gillett, Bland, and Co., of Croydon, were designed and manufactured the great clock and carillon machine of the Town Hall of Manchester, the works of which, in the aggregate, constitute, certainly, a splendid example of mechanism. Here also, at Croydon, and by the same firm, were cast those two fine bells which, now suspended aloft in the new Eddystone Lighthouse, are destined, we trust, by their sharp ringing notes, resounding amidst storms, oft-times to warn mariners to avoid the dangers of that rock. The Eddystone Lighthouse bells are a little over two tons weight each, and are made of a mixture of copper and tin; their diameter at lip is 5 ft. $1\frac{1}{4}$ in.

Croydon Theatre.—In the year 1800 a theatre was built, and neatly fitted up, on Crown Hill. At this old theatre the renowned Edmund Kean played Sir Giles Overreach, and acted Richard III.

Croydon General Hospital.—The following is an Extract from the Minute book of the Select Vestry :—" 11th August 1829. Mr. Inkpen reported that the old Messuage or Tenement situate on Croydon Common and used by the Parish as a Pesthouse had been sold pursuant to a Resolution of the General Vestry for the sum of one hundred pounds, and requesting the directions of the Vestry in what manner the money was to be expended."

" Resolved that the money so received be laid out in building an Hospital or Infirmary at the present workhouse at Duppa's Hill, and that Mr. Daniel Thompson Brooke be requested to obtain an estimate from some surveyor upon the costs of the building," etc.

(Signed) WILLIAM INKPEN, *Chairman.*

Such was the small beginning of what unquestionably is one of the most important and beneficent institutions in the parish. Croydon General Hospital is situate in the London Road, and was opened on the 27th of September, 1873, by his Grace the Archbishop of Canterbury. From the foregoing extracts it will have been surmised that for many years previously an Infirmary formed part of the Old Workhouse at Duppa's Hill; but, strictly speaking, the establishment of Croydon Hospital dates from the year 1867, when, after the removal of the Union Workhouse to Queen's Road, the premises of the Old Workhouse were adapted for the purposes of affording to the poor of the neighbourhood the advantages of medical and surgical skill in cases of disease and accident. The Old Workhouse being again required by the Guardians, eventually Oakfield Lodge was purchased for £10,000, raised by voluntary subscription, and converted into what may be described as a large Cottage Hospital, where the inmates enjoy all the comforts of a well-regulated home, and receive the utmost possible attention from a staff of skilful medical officers and experienced nurses. The wards of Croydon Hospital, well-lighted and ventilated, contain all the improvements science has brought to bear on the alleviation of disease; whilst the beautiful plantations that environ the fabric present a surrounding so cheerful, that Nature is found to accelerate the convalescence of those who unfortunately, either from disease or accident, are compelled to seek a cure at this establishment.

The "Goat House" Inn, S. Norwood, was so named on account of its proximity to that ancient goat or deer-house, belonging to the archiepiscopal lord of this manor, which stood amid what was once the forest.

The fine Newfoundland dog that served as a model to Edwin Landseer, when he was painting his well-known picture of "A distinguished Member of the Humane Society," belonged to Newman Smith, Esq., when he lived at Birdhurst, Croydon. The dog's name was "Leo."

Earthquake.—Very early in the morning of the first Tuesday in October, 1863, a slight shock of an earthquake was felt at Croydon.

The last *Perambulation of the boundaries* of this Parish was made in the month of May, 1876.

Worthies of Croydon.—To the list of distinguished persons, whose names already enrich my chronicle, may be added that of Sir Francis B. Head, K.C.H. He saw some active service in Spain, and was present at Quatre Bras, and Waterloo. In 1825 he went out to South America, and on his return home published a narrative of his adventures, under the title of "Rough Notes taken during some rapid journeys across the Pampas and among the Andes." This lively and graphic narrative was read with much interest, and the rapidity of his journeys gained for him the sobriquet of "Galloping Head." In 1830, Capt. Head gave to the world "The Life of Bruce, the Abyssinian Traveller;" and this he followed up by an amusing volume entitled "Bubbles from the Brunnen of Nassau." In 1835 he became Lieut.-Governor of Canada; and when, in 1837, an insurrection broke out in Upper Canada, it was soon quelled by the local militia under the command of Sir Francis Head. In 1850 appeared his "Stokers and Pokers," and in the same year his pamphlet on "The Defenceless State of Great Britain." Besides these, Sir Francis was the author of many other books and pamphlets.

Conversing with Sir Francis Head, on the 22nd of April, 1871, he told me that he had been more or less connected with Croydon for forty-five years. He was very fond of riding; riding and writing, he said, were his two favourite occupations; and when he came to inquire what country was capable of affording scope for his favourite exercise, he was advised to settle down at Croydon, in the neighbourhood of which were fine open downs. He resided in the house called Duppa's Hall, on Duppa's Hill; where he breathed his last on July 20, 1875; and was buried at Sanderstead.

Concerning John Unwin, Esq., who died at Croydon on the 21st of September, 1789, we read in the *Gentleman's Magazine*" that he "was of Doctors' Commons, and, for many years past, employed as an agent for buying and selling livings, by which he was supposed to have acquired a good fortune, which, as he died a bachelor, he has bequeathed to the widow and children of his nephew, who now reside in his house at Croydon." The widow and children here alluded to, were those of the Rev. Wm. Cawthorn Unwin, of Stock, Essex, whose interest in the affection of the poet Cowper is well known.

Sir Arthur Helps lived for a time at the corner of North Park, in the residence known as Argyll House, St. James'

Road. He was Clerk to the Privy Council: with him Her Majesty lost a faithful servant, English literature an ornament, and humanity a friend.

Cuthbert W. Johnson, F.R.S., born in Kent in 1799, was by profession a barrister, but, devoting himself to the science and practice of agriculture, he became an authority on that subject. In 1820 he published an "Essay on the Uses of Salt for Agricultural Purposes," and this was followed by "The Advantages of Railways to Agriculture," in 1837; "On Liquid Manures," 1837; "On Fertilisers," 1839; "The Objects and History of the Thames Improvement Company," 1839; "On Gypsum as a Fertiliser," 1840; "On Saltpetre and Nitrate of Soda as Fertilisers," 1840; and "On Increasing the Depths of Soils," in 1840. In 1841, conjointly with Mr. Shaw, he began "The Farmers' Almanack," which has existed uninterruptedly up to the present time. In 1842 he undertook "The Farmer's Encyclopædia," an extensive work of 1,320 pages. Then followed "The Farmers' Medical Dictionary," 1845; "The English Rural Spelling Book," 1846; "Our House and Garden," 1867; besides "A Calendar for Young Farmers," "The Modern Dairyman," and other minor publications.

Mr. Johnson advocated the passing of the "Public Health Act," and no sooner was it passed than, aided by a few other gentlemen, he succeeded in establishing a Local Board of Health in Croydon. For some time previously he had been experimenting and writing on the important subject of the disposal of the sewage of towns. He early pointed to irrigation as the best mode of turning evil into good, and his views were ultimately sanctioned as correct by the Report of a Government Commission. Mr. Johnson was the first chairman of the Croydon Local Board; and, with only a short interval, he occupied that post from the appointment of the Board in 1849, till his retirement in 1877, when he was presented with a piece of plate, bearing the following inscription :—" Presented to Cuthbert William Johnson, Esq., F.R.S., by his fellow members of the Croydon Local Board of Health, in testimony of the valuable assistance in Law and Science rendered by him for upwards of a quarter of a century as their Chairman, and in memory of their high esteem and affectionate regard. 1877."

Mr. Johnson published an edition of the " Public Health Act," with notes. He was buried in St. Peter's Churchyard.

Colonel Maberly, who lived at Shirley House, was a sportsman as well as a shrewd man of business. A characteristic story of him is current in regard to the alteration of the roadway in front of Shirley House. The old roadway, a narrow inconvenient way, passing close by the mansion, the Colonel applied at Quarter Sessions to have it widened and diverted, so as to run further off his house; but the application was unsuccessful. Adopting a more indirect method to obtain his end, he next invited the county magnates to a grand banquet at Shirley House. Meanwhile, apprising the neighbouring farmers of his design, he induced them to block up the narrow path with their dung carts and waggons, just about his dinner hour. Consequently, it was only after much uproar, and the greatest exertions, that the dons at length succeeded in reaching their destination; but not until the dinner-hour had passed. Very soon afterwards Colonel Maberly obtained permission to divert the course of the old road as he had wished.

John Christian Schetky, who resided at the corner of George Street, Croydon, was, for many years, Professor of Drawing at the Hon. E. I. Company's College at Addiscombe, where he closed his public career by retirement, in 1855. When a boy, Robert Burns, his father's friend, begged young Schetky off a flogging for playing truant to sail toy ships at Leith. " Christopher North" mentions him more than once in " Noctes Ambrosianæ;" and Sir Walter Scott and Schetky were intimate friends. Schetky was marine painter successively to George IV., William IV. (" the Sailor-King)," and her present Majesty. He painted with the left hand; was tall, and generally wore a sailor's jacket. If he wanted to hail any one, he would out with a whistle, which he always carried with him, and pipe " all-hands." A most agreeable companion and vocalist, as well as an accomplished player on the guitar, Mr. Schetky's society was much courted. He published some works illustrated by engravings and chromo-lithographs; his marine sketches are in various collections. He died on the 29th of January, 1874, at the great age of ninety-five.

Rev. Jonathan Cape.—Opposite to where Mr. Schetky lived, in the house known as " Whitgift House," George Street, resided the Rev. Jonathan Cape, M.A., F.R.S., formerly Professor of Classics and Mathematics at the E. I. College, Addiscombe. He was born February 9, 1793, and died September 9, 1868.

Next door to Mr. Cape lived the Rev. R. C. Fell, who wrote the life of Alderman Kelly.

John Wickham Flower, F.G.S., for many years resided in the old mansion at Park Hill, which he adorned with a choice library, and a large collection of antiquarian and geological objects of interest. Archæology, natural history, and geology were his delight. "The particular problem," writes that eminent geologist, Mr. Prestwich, "which he set himself to work out, on his settling at Croydon some twenty-five years ago, was to ascertain whether the immense pebble-beds of Addington, belonging to the Lower Tertiary series, were not formed of flints derived from the destruction of higher beds of chalk than any which now remain in the neighbourhood of London." In pursuance of this object he carried on, for years, an examination of the flint pebbles forming the Addington Hills, and broke up many thousands of them in search of the small fossils they occasionally contain. As an antiquary Mr. Flower was zealous and liberal, his collection of stone implements, both of the Palæolithic and Neolithic periods, was almost unrivalled. Dying at Park Hill on the 11th of April, 1873, he sleeps in the pretty churchyard at Shirley.

Robert Fitzroy, the famous meteorologist, died in this parish, by his own hand, at his residence near to the Queen's Hotel, Upper Norwood, on May 1, 1865. He was the youngest son of the late General Lord Charles Fitzroy, by his second marriage with Lady Frances Anne Stuart, eldest daughter of Robert, first Marquis of Londonderry. He was born on the 5th of July, 1805, and entering the navy at an early age, eventually became Vice-Admiral. In 1843 he was appointed Governor of New Zealand. When, in 1854, the meteorological department of the Board of Trade was established, Captain Fitzroy was placed at its head, and to him are owing the storm signals and other modes of warning that are now in use for the benefit of seamen. His own life was unfortunately the price of his too intense devotion to his duties. He published — "Narrative of the Surveying Voyages of H.M.S. *Adventurer* and *Beagle;* "Remarks on New Zealand;" and "Sailing Directions for South America." Admiral Fitzroy was interred in the churchyard of All Saints, in this parish.

Sir Stephen Lushington, G.C.B., was the second son of Sir Henry Lushington, Bart. He was born in 1803, and entered the Navy in 1816. During the years 1823-4-5, he was employed in the suppression of piracy in the Archipelago, and became Lieutenant in 1824. He commanded the *Ætna* bomb in the operations against Morea Castle in 1828, and for his services there received the Order of St. Louis of France, and the Greek Order of the Redeemer. In 1829 he became Captain. Superintendent of the Indian Navy from 1848 to 1852, Captain Lushington served with distinction during the Crimean War, and commanded the Naval Brigade, on shore, at the siege and capture of Sebastopol. For his services against the Russians, in 1855, he was appointed a K.C.B., and Officer of the Legion of Honour; he was promoted to be Commander of the Legion of Honour in 1857; and received the second class of the Medjidie, 1858. He was made Rear-Admiral of the Red in 1858, Vice-Admiral in 1865, and, the same year, an Admiral on the reserved list. He was Lieut.-Governor of Greenwich Hospital during 1862–5. He married Henrietta, daughter of Admiral Sir H. Prescott, G.C.B.. After a long illness, which he bore with exemplary patience, Admiral Lushington died at his residence, Oak Lodge, Thornton Heath, on the 28th of May, 1877. He rests in our Cemetery.

Edward Foss, for the last five years of his life, resided at Croydon. His chief publication was "The Judges of England," a work distinguished for laborious research, acuteness, and impartial judgment, and the reputation of which, as an historical authority, is established. Mr. Foss was a Fellow of the Society of Antiquaries, Deputy-Lieutenant for Kent, and a magistrate for Surrey. He died at Frensham House, Addiscombe, on July 27, 1870, and was interred at Shirley. At Frensham House remains a valuable collection of MS. notes in Mr. Foss' handwriting.

Joseph Nash, who delineated the Mansions of England in the Olden Time, and gave to the world another grand series relating to Windsor Castle, was born at the Rectory Manor House, in North End, and spent his youthful years at Croydon.

Sir John William Kaye may be mentioned among other distinguished men who received their military education at Addiscombe. He wrote the "History of the War in Afghanistan," "a work," says the *Quarterly Review*, "as awful, as simply artistic, and as clear and lofty in its moral as an Æschylean trilogy." Selected by the Court of Directors of the Hon. East India Company to be Secretary in their Political and Secret Department, he held that post for nearly nineteen years. His "Lives of Indian Officers" has become a textbook for every Anglo-Indian. He was made, without application, a Fellow of the Royal Society; in 1871 he was created a Knight Commander of the Star of India.

Henry Thomas Riley, M.A., of Corpus Christi College, Cambridge, and Exeter College, Oxford, died at Hainault House, the Crescent, Selhurst, on April 14, 1878, of an illness which had been brought on by hard mental work. In him English history, and especially the history of English Corporations, lost a zealous and learned student. He translated Ingulph's "Chronicle of the Abbey of Croyland," and several other works for Bohn's "Classical" and "Antiquarian" Libraries; and he was a valued contributor to the *Gentleman's Magazine*, and the *Athenæum*. Early in 1858 Mr. Riley was appointed to edit the "Liber Custumarum" and the "Liber Albus," and henceforth he was regularly engaged as one of the editors of the series of important historical publications issued under the direction of the Master of the Rolls. Mr. Riley was also employed by the Corporation to edit "Memorials of London in the Thirteenth, Fourteenth, and Fifteenth Centuries," which was printed in 1868. In 1869, Mr. Riley was appointed one of the Inspectors of Manuscripts under the Historical MSS. Commission, and was chiefly occupied in the examination of the records of Corporations, ecclesiastical as well as lay. He was in his sixtieth year; and of the Inner Temple, Barrister-at-law.

Augustus Applegath, known as the originator of some important improvements in the art of printing, was the inventor of the composition-ball and composition-roller, and afterwards of the steam printing-press, &c. The establishment for his experiments in Bank notes that could not be forged was at Croydon: he received from the Bank authorities £18,000 for the invention.

Hablot Browne, better known by the name of "Phiz" attached to those inimitable comic etchings and drawings on wood with which he adorned the earlier pages of Dickens and *Punch*, used to live on Duppa's Hill.

Saxe Bannister, M.A., of Lincoln's Inn, Barrister, was born at Steyning, Sussex, on June 27, 1791. He was some time Attorney-General of New South Wales, to which office he had been appointed in 1823. He was author of many tracts and papers on Schools, British History, Philanthropy in the Colonies, &c. Mr. Bannister died at Thornton Heath on September 16, 1877.

Thomas Lockyer, the celebrated Surrey cricketer, was born at Croydon. His original avocation was that of a bricklayer, but this he early forsook for the cricket-field, where he became a good general, a hard hitter, an excellent bowler; but his name stood highest of all as a wicket-keeper, and the certainty with which he took the fastest bowling, both with right hand and left, was unsurpassed. For his astonishing wicket-keeping, Tom was often applauded; "and such at times," to quote Lillywhite, "was the effect of his performances upon the spectators, it was not believed, by many, that the ball had ever been delivered and returned to the bowler again." Lockyer was one of the English Cricketers who in 1859 visited Canada and the United States, where they won all matches. He afterwards took part in the first cricketing expedition to Australia, from whence he returned to die of consumption, at Croydon, in the prime of his life.

Sir John W. H. Anson, who occupied Shirley House for some years during the minority of the present Lord Eldon, was one of the victims of that dreadful railway accident which occurred at Wigan on the 22nd of August, 1873. The remains of this unfortunate gentleman are interred in Shirley Churchyard.

A parishioner of Croydon, Mr. Scovell, lost his life in that sea of flame which resulted from the Irish mail train near Abergele running into some waggons laden with barrels of petroleum, when thirty-three persons, unable to get out of the carriages, were burnt alive, their bodies being reduced to cinders.

When H.M.S. *Captain*, iron-clad, foundered off Cape

Finisterre, on September 7, 1870, young West, of Alexandra Road, Croydon, went down in her. His name is recorded on the commemorative brass tablet in St. Paul's Cathedral.

Genealogical.—Of the freeholders of this parish there are some who may justly claim to be well descended. To these belong Septimus Richard Scott, Esq., of Crown Hill, Lower Norwood, a scion of the Kentish family of Scott, of Scot's Hall. The Scotts, of Scot's Hall, claim to derive their surname through the family of John le Scot, last Palatine Earl of Chester and Earl of Huntingdon; and they likewise claim an uninterrupted descent from William Baliol le Scot, brother of John Baliol, King of Scotland, and of Alexander Baliol, Lord of the Honour and Castle of Chilham in Kent.*

In respect to Arthur Henry Nicholas Kemmis, Esq., J.P., of Croham Hurst, he is the only son of the late Thomas Arthur Kemmis, Esq., M.P., who was a magistrate for Surrey, and formerly in the Grenadier Guards, by Henrietta Anne, fourth daughter of Charles Kemeys Kemeys-Tynte, Esq., of Halswell House, near Bridgewater, Co. Somerset, and Cefn Mably, near Cardiff, Co. Glamorgan, who was declared by a Committee for Privileges of the House of Lords, in 1845, senior co-heir of the whole blood to the Barony of Wharton.

The genealogy of Joseph Leete, Esq., F.S.S., of South Norwood Park, Co. Surrey, was traced by the late Charles Bridger, Esq., of the Heralds' College, in a direct line up to John Leete, of Eversden, Co. Cambridge, Farmer of the parsonage there in 1544, under the Abbot of St. Albans.† Mr. Leete is a *Chevalier de la Légion d'honneur*.

* See page 243 of "Memorials of the family of Scott, of Scot's Hall, in the County of Kent. With an Appendix of Illustrative Documents." By James Renat Scott, F.S.A. London: Simmons and Botten, Shoe Lane, E.C. 1876."

† "The Family of Leete," &c. MDCCCLXXXI. Printed for private circulation.

Admiral the Honourable Plantagenet Pierrepont Cary, who has long resided at S. Norwood, and is a landowner of this parish, is brother to the 10th Viscount Falkland, and heir presumptive to that title. The 2nd Viscount was the celebrated adherent of the Royal cause, who fell at the battle of Newbury.

Veterans.—Near to the N.E. corner of St. James', Croydon, is buried William Truncheon, who was in the action on the 1st of June, 1794, when Lord Howe gained a signal victory over the French fleet at Ushant.

Robert Brick, long resident at Croydon, entered the army about 1803, in the 57th Regiment, in which he remained. In 1805 he formed one of the garrison at Gibraltar. Just before the battle of Trafalgar some of the British men-of-war put in to Gibraltar to get fresh ammunition, &c., when Brick assisted to carry the ammunition on handbarrows to the boats of the British fleet. He told me that he heard the reverberation of the distant booming of the cannon, as the combined Spanish and French fleets were fighting against the British, on the ever-memorable 21st of October, 1805. After the victory some of the shattered ships returned to Gibraltar, and our townsman could distinctly remember Admiral Collingwood, who so gloriously had led the lee column of the British fleet first into action, walking on shore at Gibraltar, and also seeing many of the wounded, with their bandages on, carried on shore to the Hospital. In 1810 this same Robert Brick fought under Wellington at the heights of Busaco, in Portugal, and came out of the heat of battle unscathed. He fought likewise in the Peninsula at Albuera, where a gun-shot went, in a slanting direction, through the bony part of the palm of his right hand, just as he was biting off the end of his cartridge, and at the same moment a fragment of a shell lodged in his right temple. The 57th Regiment was nearly cut to pieces in the bloody battle of Albuera, fought 16 May, 1811. This old Chelsea out-pensioner attained the age of ninety-three years : he was buried at Mitcham Croydon Cemetery in February, 1879.

Michael Mitchell, when he was about nineteen years of age, entered the Connaught Rangers, and had not enlisted more than six months ere he was called out. In the Peninsula, he was in the retreat, and at the battle of Corunna, where he had a brother killed, but he himself was not wounded. He followed Sir John Moore to his grave. They literally, he said, dug Sir John Moore's grave with their bayonets at dead of night, and it was done in a hurry. Subsequently Mitchell took part in the hard-fought battle of Talavera. He also was present at the siege of Badajos, and likewise at the battle of Salamanca. Michael Mitchell, after having long resided here, died at the Croydon Infirmary on March 13, 1881.

James Lloyd was born in Surrey Street, Croydon, in 1796. Enlisting in the 7th Hussars, in 1814, he fought at Waterloo. The 7th Hussars, he told me, covered the retreat on the 17th of June, 1815, but on that same evening they were ordered to charge. In this charge the 7th Hussars lost many men, and Lloyd had his horse killed, under him, when, to avoid being trampled down and sabred by the French cuirassiers, he jumped into a ditch, up to his neck. He was a prisoner for an hour or two, but afterwards managed to escape, on a desperately wounded French horse, back to the British lines. Owing to there being no horse for him to ride on, he did not fight on the 18th. He had the Waterloo medal.

Thomas Stagg, a native of Croydon, fought at Waterloo, and came out unscathed: he was wont, in joke, to say, "the French didn't aim straight enough to hit me." He lies in our Cemetery. Of the soldiers between whom he fought, one was killed; the other was

William Constable, born at Croydon Old Town, and him a cannon-ball deprived of his left arm, at Waterloo.

In memory of Charles Goodwin, formerly a private in the Royal Artillery, and afterwards Verger at St.

Matthew's Church, Croydon. He fought at Inkermann, and served throughout the Crimean campaign; he rests in our Cemetery.

William Patterson, one of the gallant troop who made the charge at Balaclava, was, on the 17th of September, 1873, buried at the Cemetery, Croydon. Another of the heroes of the Balaclava charge was unfortunately killed through the breaking of a spoke of the ladder on which he was standing, whilst at work in Addiscombe; and he also received Christian sepulture in Croydon Cemetery.

The charge of the Light Brigade at Balaclava took place on October 25, 1854. I have heard the memorable event described by one of the survivors, Joseph Gammage, of this town. He says that, from the spot where the order was brought from the Earl of Lucan to Lord Cardigan by Capt. Nolan, up to the Russian battery in front, which the Light Brigade were ordered to silence, was over a mile. To reach that battery the English had to traverse an open grassy plain, about a half a mile wide, and on either side of this were heights also crowned by Russian batteries, and swarming with riflemen. The English charged in three lines. On the right of the first rode the 13th Light Dragoons, along with the famous "Death or glory" boys, the 17th Lancers. The second line was composed of the 11th Hussars, and on their left rode the 4th Light Dragoons. The 8th Hussars formed the rear, a space of from 100 to 150 yards intervening between each line. Our townsman rode in front with the 13th Light Dragoons; for to the two squadrons of dragoons were attached four trumpeters, and Gammage was one of the four. The morning was fine, and the mist clearing off it became sunny and bright.

> "Into the valley of Death
> Rode the six hundred."

First "trot" was trumpeted, then "gallop," for them to quicken their pace through that flood of smoke and flame which now belched forth on the British from the entire line of the enemy; and finally, Gammage sounded "charge" as, with fearfully diminished ranks, our heroic countrymen plunged into the smoke of the battery, to cut down the Russians at their guns. Exposed as they were to an oblique fire from the batteries on the hills on both sides, as well as to a terrific fire from the front, and from volleys of musketry and rifles, the course of the Light Brigade was marked by instant and ever-increasing gaps in its ranks, by dead men and horses, and by riderless steeds flying wounded over the plain.

> " Cannon to right of them,
> Cannon to left of them,
> Cannon in front of them
>   Volley'd and thunder'd;
> Storm'd at with shot and shell,
> Boldly they rode and well,
> Into the Jaws of Death,
> Into the mouth of Hell
>   Rode the six hundred."

The first line had approached to within fifty yards of the battery in front, and the Russians were pouring in their deadly volleys of grape and canister, when, just at this instant, our trumpeter's steed suddenly sprang up in the air, and then dropped down dead, Gammage meanwhile flying over the poor animal's head, to be stunned for a moment by his fall. Recovering, he looked up, and saw the Russian gunners creeping under their limbers, where the Lancers were piercing them through. At length Gammage worked his way back, amid a murderous storm of grape, through dead and dying men and shrieking horses, to where he had started from—unwounded!

Sun never shone on a more glorious or desperate exhibition of valour. From the first giving of the order to charge till all was over, scarce forty minutes elapsed; yet, in this short space of time, out of six hundred British, who went into the charge, only one hundred and ninety or two hundred returned, some on foot, part on horseback; while of the eighteen men quartered in Gammage's tent, only five remained that night, all the rest being either killed, wounded, or taken prisoners.

After the Crimean war our hero volunteered into the 17th Lancers, to proceed to quell the Indian Mutiny, and he was present at the execution of the notorious Tantia Topee at Sepree. But, after being twenty-eight years in the British army, Gammage was compelled to undergo an operation, which incapacitated him from further military service; and so he lost his full pension. He is in the possession of four medals, one of them being for meritorious conduct.

CHAPTER XV.

MODERN DEVELOPMENT.

THE parish of Croydon is situated in the Eastern Division of the County of Surrey. It is about thirty-six miles in circumference, and its area, including the detached portion, called Selsdon or Croydon Crook,* according to the Ordnance Survey, is a fraction over 9,901 acres. The town itself lies due south of London, on the Brighton Road; the distance between Croydon Town Hall and the Royal Exchange being a little over ten miles. On the north, Croydon is bounded by the parishes of Streatham, Lambeth, Camberwell, and the hamlet of Penge, the latter being a detached portion of Battersea parish; on the east, by Beckenham and Addington; on the south, by Sanderstead and Coulsdon; and on the west, by Beddington and Mitcham. Croydon is an assize town, sharing with Guildford the honour of alternately having the assizes for the County of Surrey held in it. Petty sessions are held at Croydon every Saturday, and a police court daily. Croydon Petty Sessional Division contains a population, according to last census, of 121,523. The Croydon Bench numbers eleven or twelve magistrates; the Court has a clerk and an assistant. Although outside the district, prisoners are occasionally committed to the Central Criminal Court. The amount contributed by this parish in 1881 towards the Metropolitan Police was upwards of £10,500.

* Croydon Crook, consisting of nearly 889 acres, with a population of about forty inhabitants only, lies at a distance of some 300 yards from the main area of the parish, from which it is cut off by Addington and Sanderstead.

Croydon is a place of election for the Eastern Division of the County; and it has both a cattle and corn market. The County Court of Surrey, for the Croydon district, is also held in the Town Hall twice a month.

According to Ducarel, in 1783, Croydon contained between 700 and 800 houses. In 1801 there were 1,800 houses, and a population of about 6,000; in 1831 there were 2,600 houses, and a population of about 12,500. The number of houses in the town and parish of Croydon, at the present time, including empties, is over 15,250. There are about 13,780 inhabitant householders. The total number of inhabitants of Croydon is estimated to have been, in the year 1783, about 4,000; the population of Croydon in 1841 was 16,712; in 1851 it was 20,355; in 1861, 30,240; in 1871, 55,652; and according to the census of 1881 it was 78,947. This rapid and continuously extraordinary rate in the increase of the population of Croydon is due, partly to the salubrity of its position, mainly on a substratum of gravel and chalk, at the foot of the north downs; partly on account of the beauty of the neighbourhood; much to a constant supply of water unsurpassed in purity, and good drainage; but chiefly because of its proximity to the metropolis, ready access to every part of which from Croydon, in all directions, by means of train, rendering this parish a desirable place of residence for merchants and others, whose engagements necessitate their daily attendance in London. Croydon is a place convenient of access also from different parts of the country. There are no less than eleven railway stations within the parish.* There is also an omnibus

---

* Namely:—West Croydon Station, the oldest, situate in the London Road: it is the principal station for the passenger traffic with London, and serves for the Epsom and Wimbledon branches of the London, Brighton and South-Coast Railway; East Croydon Station and New Croydon Station, situated side by side, in Upper Addiscombe Road, the former of which serves for the main Brighton and South-Coast, and South-Eastern Companies, and the latter

Modern Development. 229

service from Croydon to London *viâ* Streatham and Brixton. And to these advantages of communication must be added the local tramway.

In 1849, the rateable value of the parish was £80,000. The valuation, according to the list settled by the Assessment Committee, was in March, 1872, £323,899; in March, 1881, it had risen to £481,247.

The parish of Croydon is an Urban Authority, acting under the Public Health Act and its amendments, and it has a Local Board of Health, consisting of eighteen members. The Public Health Act was applied to Croydon by Provisional Order, dated August 1, 1849, which was subsequently confirmed by an Act of Parliament, 12 & 13 Vict. c. 94. At the time of the issue of the Provisional Order the following authorities were in existance in the parish: 1. The Vestry; 2. The Board of Highways; 3. The Waste Lands Trustees as to markets, burial-grounds, gravel-pits, and Town Hall; 4. The Improvement Commissioners, with jurisdiction over lighting the streets, and providing judges' lodgings, accommodation for prisoners, fire engines, &c. Croydon was one of fifteen towns included in the first Provisional Order. The election of members for the Board took place in the same month as the passing of the Act; and on the

for the local traffic, and the trains of the London and North-Western Railway Company; South Croydon Station, the terminus of the local line which passes through New Croydon Station; Waddon Station, on the Epsom line, at the foot of Duppa's Hill; Selhurst Station, midway between the town of Croydon and Norwood; Thornton Heath Station, the next station on the same line; Norbury Station, nearer Streatham, on the London Road; Norwood Junction, a large station, contiguous to High Street, South Norwood; Addiscombe Station, situate in Lower Addiscombe Road, the terminus of a branch of the South-Eastern line; and Woodside Station, nearer London on the same line. Besides these eleven, there is also Central Croydon Station, near the Town Hall, but this is closed at present for passenger traffic: and soon will be opened stations for the new Railway, now being cut between Woodside, *viâ* Croham, to East Grinstead.

3rd of September, 1849, the Board commenced those various public duties, which they have since continued to perform. The Local Board have to deal with all the important questions coming before them as an Urban Sanitary Authority, and they have two Sewage Farms to manage; they are the Highway Board, with, at the present moment, the supervision of seventy-five miles of roadway; they are ex-officio members of the Burial Board; they have the management of the public water supply of the town or district; and in addition they have the regulation of three public recreation grounds. The Provisional Order directed twelve to be the number of members of the Croydon Board of Health; but in 1862 the Norwood Ward was created, and three members were allowed to Norwood, making a total of fifteen; again, in 1868, the number of members at the Local Board was increased to their present number of eighteen, of whom twelve were allotted to the Croydon, and six to the Norwood Ward. The acreage of the Croydon Ward is 7,200; that of the Norwood Ward, 2,600.

Croydon has been a pioneer in the course of sanitary science, and many other towns have profited, and will continue to profit, by its experience. The following extracts will enable the reader to judge of the almost incredible state of things that existed at Croydon before the adoption of the Public Health Act: the first is a quotation from the Report of the Superintending Inspector to the General Board of Health, dated 12th of April, 1849:—

"The town itself is situated in the county of Surrey, on the east and west sides of a valley, with the river Wandle somewhat distorted from its course in the bottom, whose tributary streams flow from the eastern side of the Brighton Road, either in open or closed channels, to the east side of the old town of Croydon, forming Bog Island, which is occupied by numerous houses; from thence it passes through the Palace bleaching-grounds, fringed by a series of privies, and supplying in its course several ditches, it passes close by the side of the southern and western walls of the new burial-ground, a recent addition to the churchyard; and from thence towards Waddon, in its course to which place it is pent back for the purpose of supplying a mill situated within about sixty yards of the church, and it is again pent back at Waddon to form the mill-head of another mill there. The dam already alluded to near the church, with that of the Waddon mill dam, both having been increased in height, throw the waters back upon the lower parts of the town, so that when the water of the Bourne, at certain irregular periods, flows with increased volume, some of the streets are covered with water."

Referring to the sanitary condition of Croydon before the formation of the Board, Dr. Westall observes:—

"In the lower parts of the town dense fogs prevail, and hang upon the surface in the vicinity of Southbridge and Bog Island; whilst at or near Waddon there are marshes with stagnant ditches, from twelve to fifteen feet wide, charged with animal and vegetable matter, from which noxious exhalations are conveyed by the prevailing winds to the town. Moreover, the town itself is entirely devoid of under drainage, and therefore dependent on a surface drainage, which is a source of unhealthy exhalations, giving rise to epidemics which have of late years increased."

Mr. Penfold thus describes some of the nuisances that formerly prevailed in the parish:—

"Those enormous reservoirs for the reception of filth, called Laud's and Scarbrook Ponds, have been used from time immemorial to receive the sullage of the town, as well as that from slaughter-houses and private dwellings. Laud's Pond is not only an abominable nuisance at all times, but must be the means of creating fevers and other diseases. The stench from it is very bad, and in the summer unbearable. . . . . Scarbrook is an able seconder of Laud's Pond, in their joint occupation of spreading fever and death among the inhabitants."

And again:—

"Though the town is furnished by Nature with an inexhaustible supply of water, that which is intended for our good we convert into evil. The springs are nearly all contaminated, the water tainted, privies erected close to wells, into which the soil percolates, and the water rendered impure, the sufferer having no remedy."

In 1849, out of 1,550 houses, it was found that 755 were not supplied with water at all; 275 complained that the water was not good, and that the supply was insufficient; the occupants of 14 houses were obliged to buy beer in order to get water from the landlord's pump; whilst in the old town, out of 213 houses, 143 were deficient in supply, and in 24 cases the water was unfit for use. It was likewise shown in evidence that the inhabitants of Croydon generally had no other means of obtaining supplies of water except by pumping or fetching from a distant source. Such being the condition of affairs previous to the commencement of its operations by the Board of Health, it will excite no surprise to learn that this town was the most unhealthy in the county, the death-rate here being higher than in any other district.

One of the first cares of the Board, acting in their capacity as guardians of the public health, was to secure a supply of pure water to the town, and this they accomplished by sinking Artesian wells into the upper chalk. The Board's water-works adjoin Surrey Street, and here are four wells, connected together by means of syphons. Their borings are: two to the depth of 75 feet, one to a depth of 150 feet, and one, the last bored, to the depth of 214 feet. By means of three Cornish pumping-engines, and one grand compound differential engine of 150 horse-power, the quantity of pure water pumped up from these wells, in one day, has reached the enormous total of 2,996,663 gallons. Two rising mains, one of 12, and the other 18-inch diameter, are laid from the engine-house, in Surrey Street, to the covered reservoir at Park Hill. This reservoir consists of a domed chamber, 74 feet in diameter by 35 feet in depth, and is capable of containing 900,000 gallons of water. Adjoining the reservoir stands a Norman brick water-tower, two engines and engine-house, with a distinct set of mains attached, for the water service of the higher parts of the parish. At present, about 11,500 houses are supplied from the Board's water-works, the Lambeth Water Company supplying most of the remainder.

Soon after the Croydon water-works were formed, a serious litigation arose with the mill-owners on the river Wandle, who claimed compensation for the lessening of their mill-stream in consequence of the pumping of the Board's well, and a writ was issued against the Board of Health in an action to try the right of the Board to the water-supply from their well. A trial of great importance, "Dickenson v. The Grand Junction Canal Company," had just taken place, and in it the plaintiff Dickenson had obtained a verdict against the Canal Company for abstracting underground water by pumping, to the diminishment of his neighbouring mill-stream. In this emergency, the Board entrusted their difficulties to the late Mr. John Drummond, who laid the whole case carefully before counsel, Mr. George Miller of this town ; when he, with singular prescience, gave it as his opinion that, the judgments of all the four judges who had decided the dispute between Dickenson and the Canal Company were wrong, and that, if the Croydon Board of Health were to try their case, and carry it to the House of Lords, they would reverse that judgment. Our Board accordingly defended the action, gained a verdict in the Exchequer, a confirmation in the Exchequer Chamber, and subsequently a victory in the House of Lords. This memorable action cost our Local Board over five thousand pounds ; it deserves to be recorded, determining, as it did, a great principle as to the rights of owners of the soil to the water percolating through it.

The superior purity of the chalk-derived water supplied to this parish has been attested by a repeated searching analysis.

The evils of retaining decaying animal and vegetable substances near our dwellings, and the abominations that poison every undrained locality, constrained Parliament, in order to secure the public health of the country, to pass the measure known as the Public Health Act. No sooner had this beneficial measure become law than many towns, including Croydon, hastened to avail themselves of its advantages, and commenced with ardour to remove their sewage, by pouring it as speedily as possible into the nearest river, under an idea that the stream would bear it harmlessly away. Very different, however, was the result, and large sums of money have been expended in the vain attempt to purify sewage by chemical and mechanical agencies, before turning it into the streams of the country. Upon the ground now occupied by the public slaughter-houses at Pitlake, our Board constructed works for dealing with the sewage of this town, by means of filtration and deodorization, but allowing the sewage water afterwards to flow into the Wandle. It was soon found that these works did not prevent the river becoming polluted to a fearful extent; nausea and sickness were the result of its feculent scum, and numerous actions and injunctions against the Board arose from those who had property in the drainage valley below the town. Fortunately, by the passing of the Local Government Act of 1858, empowering Local Boards to carry sewers out of their district, and to take land for the purpose of sewage irrigation, our Board was enabled to surmount the obstacles which presented themselves in consequence of their fouling of the river Wandle, and henceforth avoiding the evil practice of turning their sewage into the river, by an easy and natural process they succeeded, not only in effecting the purification of the sewage, but in applying it by irrigation to agricultural purposes. The extension of the town in the direction of Waddon, rendered it then expedient to remove the site of the filter-works to a greater distance, and accordingly land was purchased, and works were erected beyond Waddon, at Brimstone Barn. Here the crude sewage, as it comes from the town, is conveyed in its natural state, by means of two four-feet culverts to the extractor, which, acting as a revolving sieve, removes all the lumps of solid excrement, paper, rags, sticks, &c., and then passes the liquid sewage, without further treatment, first through a culvert, and then an open cutting, on to the lands of the Irrigation Farm at Beddington. Two of "Latham's Patent Solid Sewage Extractors" are in use at Brimstone Barn; the solid matter is carted away to be used as ordinary manure. It is calculated that the sewage of about 45,000 persons comes on to the farm by this channel, and 18,000 by the Norwood sewers, which are lower down. The amount of sewage passing through the outfalls varies much, in consequence of the rainfall of the district being admitted into the sewers. According to Mr. Latham, the volume of sewage passing through the Brimstone Barn outfall was as follows:—

Date.	Total Volume.	Rainfall.
July 28, 1880	2,827,800 gallons	·115
Feb. 18, 1881	8,736,470 gallons	{ The Bourne was flowing, but no rain.
Feb. 24, 1881	10,406,070 gallons	·53

The Beddington Sewage Farm has been recently purchased by the Croydon Local Board of Health at a total cost of about £142,000. Its area is 540 acres, of which 470 acres are now available for sewage irrigation. By means of carriers, made in concrete, in order that they may be more easily cleared, the crude sewage is sent on to the land for 12 or 24 hours at a time, irrigating the whole of it by turns. After going on to a second, and sometimes even over a third field, before it leaves the farm, finally, cleansed and purified of its noxious ingredients, the effluent passes by two outfalls on the northwest into the river Wandle. In addition to the Local Board's farm at Beddington, an irrigation area has been laid out on the stiff clay soil at South Norwood, which also answers the end for which it was intended—namely, the purification of the sewage of this parish.

Although considerable sums have been annually realized by the Local Board on account of the sale of milk, cattle, and vegetables of various kinds, the produce of their sewage farms, it cannot be affirmed that these have proved a financial success; yet this is not due to any want of productiveness, but rather to other and perhaps avoidable causes. Certainly the evidence afforded to sanitary science through the experiment of the utilization of the sewage of Croydon by surface irrigation is most important. Sewage irrigation has been continuous on the Beddington farm for upwards of twenty years; and, tested either by the vital statistics of its neighbourhood, or scrutinized in any other way, the result demonstrates that the sewage of a town passing over, and through land, undergoes a change, whereby it becomes chemically and physically so altered, that neither disease nor any other mischief can afterwards arise from it.

In addition to their work of sewering this district, the Board has removed the mill-dam near the old church, which, if suffered to remain, would have rendered abortive every attempt to drain the lowermost parts of the town. "My Lord's" and other stinking ponds have been filled in; and by the construction of an extensive brick culvert, laid with open joints, through the southern and lowest part of the town, the intermittent waters of the Bourne that used, in days of yore, to flood the area of the old town, are now conducted, without inconvenience, into the Wandle.

One of the gravest mistakes committed at Croydon in the earlier days of its sanitary experience was the total absence of any system of ventilation of the sewers, a grievous error, that led to an outbreak of fever. A more perfect system of ventilation was, however, devised, and is now carried out.

The utility and value of sanitary science is shown by the altered death-rate of Croydon, for whereas in 1848, the year previous to the adoption of the Public Health Act by the parish, the mortality had risen to 28·16 per thousand; since then it has steadily declined, the death-rate of Croydon parish for the year 1881 being only 16·13 per thousand. In short, from an undrained district, surrounded by every kind of filth tending to generate disease of the worst description, Croydon has been transformed into one of the dryest, cleanest, and healthiest towns in England.

That the battle of science against disease and death is not waged without cost, and that the road-making, and lighting, water-service, and sewage of an extensive parish cannot be attended to without a large expenditure, the following figures will show. The amount raised for Local Board of Health rates in the year 1849–50 was £3,476. According to the last published "Abstract of Receipt and Expenditure for the year ending Lady-day, 1881," of the Croydon Local Board of Health, the sum realized by rates levied by the said Board during the year was £58,136 19s. 4d.; and this is exclusive of the sum of £14,444 19s. 10d., received by the Local Board for water during the same period. The sum of £268,154 1s. was passed in cheques by the Finance Committee of the Board during three years ending March, 1881. The total balance of loans due from the Board on the 25th of March, 1881, was £343,336 2s.

The facility with which the governing bodies of towns can pile up figures against not only the existing but future generations of ratepayers, ought indeed to rouse the Legislature to consider as to the best means of checking a practice fraught with serious injury to the community; it is but fair, however, to our own Local Board of Health to add that, in the possession of their freehold water-works, and lands purchased for sewage-farming, recreation, and other purposes, the ratepayers of Croydon possess much valuable property. The public recreation ground on Duppa's Hill consists of 36 acres of land; that on Addington Hills of 85 acres. The excellent Croydon Public Baths, in Scarbrook Road, were opened on the 30th of June, 1866; the Public Baths at South

Norwood, which also belong to the Local Board, were formally opened in 1881.

For the administration of the laws for the relief of the poor, on the 21st of May, 1836, Croydon was united with the hamlets of Penge and Wallington, and the parishes of Addington, Beddington, Coulsdon, Merton, Mitcham, Morden, Sanderstead, and Woodmansterne, by the name of the Croydon Union. The average annual amount contributed by the parish of Croydon for the relief of the poor during the three years ending Lady-day, 1839, did not exceed £3,088; for the year ending Lady-day, 1859, the sum contributed was £8,738; for that ending Lady-day, 1869, £21,586; but during the year ending Lady-day, 1881, it amounted to £31,145; this includes County Rates, £4,236 11s. 3d.; but neither the Police, nor Burial Board, nor School Board rates. The sum is more than half that total of £52,149 received by the Union from the eleven united parishes.

It would be too curious to inquire how much of the sum annually levied from the Croydon ratepayers under the name of Poor-rate actually reaches the down-stricken objects on whose behalf it is ostensibly levied. Yet if, after eliminating all the fees and salaries, and jobs and charges of every description to which the fund is liable, it could be ascertained how much of this huge rate remains to be expended, not on the professional pauper or idle vagrant, but on the really deserving poor, such an analysis would prove neither uninstructive nor uninteresting!

The voting power of Croydon at the Board of the Croydon Union does not fairly represent its contribution, since only seven out of twenty-two guardians are allotted to this parish. Notwithstanding the enormous relative increase, both of the population and rateable value of this particular parish of Croydon, since the establishment of the Union in 1836, its ratepayers continue to return just the same number of guardians as they always did. A redistribution of seats at the board of the Croydon Union, somewhat more in accordance with the present population and rateable value of the respective parishes constituting the Union, seems therefore imperative.

The Croydon Union or workhouse, with master's residence, and all convenient offices, and garden attached, is situate in Queen's Road. The site occupies about 10 acres of land; the total cost of ground and erection was £48,935. Close by, the new infirmary of the Croydon Union is now being reared on a site occupying 8 acres of ground abutting on May-day Road. Independently of the sums paid for the site, and walling and fencing thereof, the first contract for the building of this pauper infirmary amounts to £59,695.

In treating of the Old Church, it has been already mentioned that, previously to the year 1827, St. John the Baptist's remained the only episcopal church in Croydon; but, owing to the vast increase of its population since that date, it has been found necessary to subdivide the ancient parish into no less than sixteen ecclesiastical districts—namely, that of the previously referred to Old Church; St. James', constituted in the year 1827; All Saints', Upper Norwood, also in 1827; St. John the Evangelist, Shirley, in 1835; St. Peter's, 1851; Christchurch, 1852; St. Mark's, South Norwood, 1852; St. Andrew's, 1857; St. Matthew's, 1865; St. Saviour's, 1867; Holy Trinity, Selhurst, 1867; St. Michael and All Angels, 1871; St. Mary Magdalene, Addiscombe, 1871; St. Luke's, Woodside, 1872; St. Paul's, Thornton Heath, 1872; and St. John the Evangelist, Norwood, in 1876. Each of these districts or sub-parishes contains its own proper ecclesiastical edifice. The interior of the new church of St. John the Baptist is an imposing example of the Early Perpendicular style; this church was rebuilt after the designs of G. Gilbert Scott, R.A. St. Peter's, and the present church at Shirley, both good specimens of Early Decorated, were also designed by that eminent architect. St. Matthew's was the work of A. W. Blomfield, M.A. The church of St. Michael and All Angels, as well as that of St. John the Evangelist, Norwood, are the conceptions of J. L. Pearson, A.R.A. In St. Saviour's, over the communion table is Theed's sculpture of the Last Supper.

Besides the above-named places of worship, there are about twenty chapels in the parish, belonging to various denominations; some of these are handsome and commodious edifices; and there are sundry mission-houses.

Croydon Cemetery adjoins the Union grounds in Queen's Road; it comprises 22 acres, ten of which are reserved for Dissenters. There are two neat chapels. The total cost of land and building was about £16,000. The members of the Board of Health constitute the Burial Board. The first interment took place on July 26th, 1861; but in this cemetery now sleep a great multitude, of whom, some perhaps were dear to the reader, as one was very dear to me; they rest in the mighty keeping of God until the morning of the Resurrection!

The schools of a town are not the least important of its adjuncts, and in this respect Croydon is not behindhand. In North End stands the Whitgift Grammar School, a noble foundation, which the parishioners owe to the benevolence of Archbishop Whitgift. It was a *free* grammar school that Whitgift founded and attached to his hospital; the original fabric, with schoolmaster's house adjoining, still remaining in George Street. In 1856 a decree of the Court of Chancery authorized the erection of this school at North End, and accordingly it was built, out of proceeds arising from the sale of lands belonging to Whitgift's Charity. The capitation fee for the education of sons of parishioners of Croydon in this North End School was limited by the Court of Chancery to £4 per annum; but by a recent new scheme of the Charity Commissioners the entrance and tuition fees here are to be paid in advance, "such entrance fees being not less than

£1 nor more than £2 for any boy, and such tuition fees being at the rate of not less than £10 nor more than £20 a year for any boy," whether or not he belongs to Croydon. The handsome school in North End was designed by A. W. Blomfield, M.A.; it was opened on the 4th of May, 1871. Besides this grand seminary there is another school attached to the foundation, called the Whitgift Middle School. In Wellesley Road is the capital structure of the "Girls' Public Day School Company;" and scattered throughout the parish are various good private seminaries. Independently of those elementary denominational and Sunday Schools connected with most of our places of worship, Croydon possesses an admirable British School; and it has also a School Board. The first election for the Board took place in March, 1871. At a cost of nearly £60,000, it has planted large groups of schools in Beulah Road, Brighton Road, the Oval Road, Princess Road, South Norwood, Mitcham Road, Sydenham Road, and at Upper Norwood. The gross cost incurred by the Croydon School Board for the year ending 29th September, 1880, was £10,099 14s.; of which the net cost from the rates was £7,452 0s. 11d. Treating of schools in this parish, we must not forget to mention "The Royal Normal College and Academy of Music for the Blind," at Upper Norwood; which was officially opened by her Royal Highness, Princess Louise, Marchioness of Lorne, on July 12th, 1877: and concerning which the Duke of Westminster then said that "he regarded this as the most perfect institution in the world." On the 29th of July, 1879, this College had the honour to be visited by their Royal Highnesses the Prince and Princess of Wales. In respect to Schools of Art at Croydon, there are two, in connection with the Department of Science and Art, South Kensington. The original Art classes in Croydon were proposed and established in 1868, by Mr. Montague Wigzell, and successfully conducted by him for eleven years, the works of six of

R

his pupils being exhibited in the Royal Academy in one year, with three on the line.

One of the most conspicuous objects in the centre of Croydon is that Hospital of the Holy Trinity, founded by Archbishop Whitgift, of which mention has already been made. To this hospital it was that Queen Elizabeth's favourite prelate attached his free Grammar School. Over the main entrance to the ancient quadrangle is inscribed QUI DAT PAVPERI NON INDIGEBIT—*He that giveth to the poor shall not lack.* And as if to forewarn plunderers of the helpless of that fate which, according to Holy Writ, eventually shall overtake all such, the prelate selected as the device for the corporate seal of his endowment a scene from the parable of the Rich Man and Lazarus. The lands and tenements that Whitgift gave to the warden and poor of the Hospital of the Holy Trinity have become very valuable. The decree of the Court of Chancery transferred the management of the estate from the poor brethren to governors; and the Whitgift foundation and its endowment is at present administered according to a scheme framed by the Charity Commissioners and approved by Her Majesty in Council in 1881. Besides that of Whitgift, Croydon is rich in other charities, of which the more important are Elye Davy's, Smith's Deptford and Stockenden, Archbishop Laud's, and Tenison's, the Church Tenements, Inkpen's, &c. The Freemasons' Asylum belonging to "The Royal Benevolent Institution for Aged Freemasons and their Widows," was consecrated and opened by the craft in 1850. Built in the Tudor style, it stands not far off Lower Addiscombe Road, facing the London and Brighton Railway.

There are two Fire Brigades in the parish.

We have no Public Reference Library or Museum as yet, but, instead thereof, a Literary and Scientific Institution. One of the best organizations in the place is the Microscopical Club.

Seven or eight newspapers are published here.

With regard to the lighting of the town: Croydon was formerly supplied with gas by Mr. Overton, at from 12s. to 13s. per thousand square feet; but, in 1847, the Croydon Gas Company bought up Mr. Overton's interest, and, under their Act, the Company now supplies the whole parish, with the exception of that portion which is supplied by the Crystal Palace Company. The handsome office of the Croydon Gas Company is in Katharine Street; their works are outside the town, by Brimstone Barn.

In July, 1874, the Bath and West of England Society held their Agricultural Show at Waddon. During the 9th, 10th, 11th, and 12th of October, 1877, the Church Congress held its 17th Annual Meeting at Croydon.

When using the expression of the town of Croydon we refer to that larger and more ancient nucleus of habitations clustering around the Town Hall; but indeed the whole area of this parish is being rapidly built over, and even now Upper as well as South Norwood, Thornton Heath and Selhurst, from the number of their resident populations may justly claim to be considered as important suburbs of Croydon.

Croydon is not a Parliamentary borough. An effort has just been made to procure a municipal charter of incorporation to this town and parish, and a petition in favour of making Croydon a borough, signed by 7,634 inhabitant householders of the parish, was presented to Her Majesty in Council. A petition against incorporation, signed by 2,300 householders was, however, lodged; and a public inquiry on the subject commenced at the Town Hall, Croydon, on October 31, 1881, which occupied eight days. For the moment the question as to the expediency of converting Croydon into a borough is in suspense.

The general appearance of Croydon is of a residential character, with numerous rows of clean modern streets, churches and chapels, and rows of villas in all directions. A healthy feature in our town is the abundant foliage which has been preserved in large trees studding it here and there, or in the shrubbery of gardens, pleasantly serving to break the monotony that otherwise might weary the eye by a constant contemplation merely of bricks and mortar. Through the middle of the town extends one long roadway, the central and narrower portion of which is called High Street, and this is intersected at right angles by another principal thoroughfare, declining westward, down Crown Hill, towards the Old Church; whilst branching off, on either side of these two more important thoroughfares, are other streets. Croydon, however, still derives a certain old-fashioned air from its Hospital, and the relics of its old Palace, its gables here and there, and the swinging Inn sign of its principal hostelry, which, as in the days of the Stuarts, is suspended right across the High Street. But these vestiges of antiquity are, year by year, diminishing, and shops with showy plate-glass windows and joint-stock banks, in the latest architectural mode, are occupying all the available sites in the leading thoroughfares.

Fain would my pen linger to describe the glorious natural scenery of the neighbourhood of Croydon, the sylvan charms of Croham Hurst, the wolds of Duppa's Hill, or, still wilder, the heather-clad mountain range on Addington Hills; but want of space forbids. Yet let not any scribe conclude even a mere outline of the history of this town without remembering to invoke, "*Continued prosperity to the good old town and trade of Croydon.*"

ARTHUR B. EBBUTT,

CARPET, FLOORCLOTH, LINOLEUM,

AND

COMPLETE FURNISHING WAREHOUSES,

13 & 94, NORTH END, CROYDON.

Agent for the West of England Fire and Life Insurance, and Norwich Union Life Assurance Society.

R. & W. AMOS,

WHOLESALE AND RETAIL GROCERS AND PROVISION MERCHANTS,

82 & 17, CHURCH STREET, CROYDON.

Hotels, Schools, and Large Purchasers served at Special Low Prices for Cash.

GILLETT, BLAND & CO.,

CHURCH, TURRET-HOUSE, AND MUSICAL CLOCK MANUFACTURERS TO THE QUEEN.

CHURCH & CARILLON BELL-FOUNDERS.

Specially appointed Contractors to Her Majesty's Government, the Post-Office, War Office, and several Colonial Governments.

STEAM CLOCK FACTORY AND CHURCH BELL FOUNDRY,

WHITEHORSE ROAD, CROYDON.

T. J. YEOMANS,

BOOKSELLER AND STATIONER,

72, GEORGE STREET, CROYDON,

(Opposite the School of Art and Public Hall).

Established 1818.

W. H. CAMPART,

HATTER,

31, HIGH STREET, CROYDON.

A choice selection of Christy's and Foreign Hats always in Stock.

Large assortment best Town-made Umbrellas.

THE CROYDON CENTRAL MONUMENTAL WORKS,

WHITGIFT STREET, HIGH STREET.

CHARLES GULY

(Late T. Williams).

Monuments and Grave Stones in Marble, Granite, or Stone. Architectural Designs carried out.

Established 1856. Estimates furnished.

E. WHITTAKER, Parish Clerk,

5, ST. JOHN'S GROVE, CROYDON,

Where applications for Banns and Marriages are to be made.

J. HANSMANN,

FAMILY TAILOR AND HABIT MAKER,

6, OAKFIELD TERRACE, LONDON ROAD, WEST CROYDON.

THE "KING'S ARMS" HOTEL,

KATHARINE STREET, CROYDON,

(OPPOSITE THE TOWN HALL).

B. JOHNSTON, Proprietor.

Wedding Breakfasts and Dinners provided. Apartments en Suite. Handsome Billiard and Dining Saloons. Spacious Coffee Rooms.

J. RIDGE & SON,

CABINET MAKERS AND UPHOLSTERERS,

BEDDING MANUFACTURERS,

CARPET WAREHOUSEMEN, AND

UNDERTAKERS,

60, NORTH END, CROYDON.

a

EAST SURREY STEAM MASONRY WORKS.

J. STEPHENS,
MARBLE, STONE, MONUMENTAL, & GENERAL MASON.

SOUTH END, CROYDON, S.

W. BENNETT,
WINE, SPIRIT, & BEER MERCHANT
(Importer and Bonder),
OLD "GUN" TAVERN, 37, CHURCH STREET,
CROYDON.

Agent for Bass's Burton Ales and Barclay's celebrated Stout and Porter in Cask or Bottle.
FAMILIES SUPPLIED.

D. HOGBEN,
ART CABINET MANUFACTURER,
UPHOLSTERER,
DECORATOR, HOUSE & ESTATE AGENT.

FUNERALS CONDUCTED ON MODERATE
AND
FIXED CHARGES.

AUCTIONEER & LAND SURVEYOR.

47, GEORGE STREET, CROYDON.

F. HUMPHREY,
FAMILY TEA DEALER, GROCER, AND
PROVISION MERCHANT,
8, BROAD GREEN, CROYDON.
Huntley and Palmer's Reading Biscuits.
Agent for W. & A. Gilbey, Wine and Spirit Importers.

D. TILLING,
PLUMBER, PAINTER, GLAZIER,
WRITER, GRAINER, GILDER, AND PAPERHANGER,
20, HANDCROFT ROAD, CROYDON.
Gasfitting in all its branches.

RICHARD TAYLOR,
FAMILY BUTCHER,
68, ST. JAMES ROAD,
CROYDON.

J. JOHNSON,
SADDLE & HARNESS MAKER,
121, HIGH STREET
(*Next door to London and County Bank*),
CROYDON.
Saddlery and Harness for Exportation. Horses carefully fitted.

W. J. ALLBRIGHT,
VENTILATING & SANITARY ENGINEER,
GAS FITTER, BELLHANGER,
BROAD GREEN, WEST CROYDON.
Rooms and Public Buildings Lighted and Ventilated on an improved system.
Fire and Burglar Alarms. Electric Bells and Speaking Tubes fitted under Personal Supervision.

Established 1824.

HENRY GATES,
FANCY BREAD AND BISCUIT BAKER,
100, OLD TOWN, CROYDON.

Pure Home-made and Whole Meal Bread.

School and other Cakes made to order.

R. LANDON,
LINENDRAPER AND SILK MERCER,
140, HIGH STREET, CROYDON
(Next door to Post Office).

DEPARTMENTS:

Silks and Velvets.	Prints.	Lace.	Hosiery.
Mantles.	Calicoes.	Ribbons.	Gloves.
Dresses.	Flannels.	Flowers.	Corsets.
Skirts.	Linens.	Feathers.	Furs.

MILLINERY & DRESSMAKING.
A orders by post, or otherwise, receive personal and immediate attention.

BY APPOINTMENT TO HIS GRACE THE ARCHBISHOP OF CANTERBURY.

STOVELL BROS.,
POULTERERS AND PORKMEN,
LICENSED DEALERS IN GAME, &c.,
112, HIGH STREET, CROYDON.
Established 1810.

FREDERIC M. PAGE,
TAILOR AND HABIT MAKER,
(Ladies' Jackets, Ulsters, &c., to order),
HOSIER AND SHIRT MAKER, &c.
30, HIGH STREET, CROYDON.
N.B.—Special attention given to the Shirt Department.
Agent to the Phœnix Fire Office.

S. ATKINSON,
SLATER.

SLATE, BRICK, LIME, CEMENT,
AND
GENERAL BUILDERS' MERCHANT.

DINGWALL ROAD,
EAST CROYDON
(Close to East Croydon Railway Station).

Established 1854.
JANNAR BROS.,
DYERS AND CLEANERS,
51, HIGH STREET, AND 23, SURREY STREET,
CROYDON.

H. VINCENT MOSS,
FAMILY GROCER & PROVISION DEALER,
LOWER ADDISCOMBE ROAD,
ADDISCOMBE.
No Wines or Spirits.

H. LONG,
PLUMBER, PAINTER, AND GLAZIER, GASFITTER,
Paperhanger and House Decorator,
11, SYDENHAM ROAD, CROYDON.
Baths and Hot Water Apparatus provided and Fixed on reasonable terms.
WRITING, GRAINING, GILDING.
Estimates given for general Repairs.

T. WALLIS,
TRICYCLE AND BICYCLE WORKS,
37, NORTH END, CROYDON.
Machines Repaired and Painted.

W. OVERALL,
FAMILY MILLER, BAKER,
Corn and Seed Merchant, &c.,
8, OAKFIELD TERRACE, LONDON ROAD, CROYDON.

J. R. LEE
(Eleven years with Messrs. MARSHALL & SNELGROVE)
REGENT HOUSE,
115, HIGH STREET, CROYDON,
SILK MERCER, LACEMAN, HOSIER, AND DRAPER.
Mantles, Costumes, Dressmaking, and Millinery.
FAMILY MOURNING OF EVERY DESCRIPTION.

F. T. MULLETT,
ARCHITECT AND SURVEYOR.
LAND AND ENGINEERING SURVEYING. BUILDING SURVEYING.
(Quantities, Extras and Omissions, and Dilapidations)
Sanitary Engineering and Ventilation.
56, GEORGE STREET, CROYDON,
And UNITY BUILDINGS, TEMPLE STREET, BIRMINGHAM.

Messrs. EDWIN WILLIAMS & SONS,
SURGEON-DENTISTS,
3, WELLESLEY VILLAS, WELLESLEY ROAD, CROYDON, S.

Also at 65, CHARLOTTE STREET, PORTLAND PLACE, LONDON, W., any day by appointment.

Late Member of the College of Dentists of England; Member of the Odontological Society of Great Britain, &c.

ESTABLISHED 1845.

J. DAVIES,
HOT WATER ENGINEER,

WHOLESALE & RETAIL FURNISHING & BUILDERS' IRONMONGER,

GAS FITTER,

STOVE AND RANGE MANUFACTURER,

LOCKSMITH AND BELLHANGER,

26, 27, & 48A, SOUTH END, CROYDON.

Plumbing in all its Branches.

J. E. COSNETT
(Late C. W. BREWIN),

BERLIN WOOL & ART NEEDLEWORK ESTABLISHMENT,

99, GEORGE STREET, CROYDON.

Scotch Yarns, Silks and Crewels.

Fancy Goods from Vienna of Newest Design in Brass, Nickel Silver, Morocco and Russia Leather.

All Materials for Needlework.

Ladies' Work Finished and Mounted.

LESSONS GIVEN.

Birthday and Christmas Cards.

ORDERS BY POST PUNCTUALLY EXECUTED.

C. A. BLOGG,
SANITARY PLUMBER,

ZINC AND IRON WORKS,

CISTERN AND TANK MANUFACTURER,

54, CHURCH STREET, CROYDON.

First Prize awarded to E. COSTAR, 1872, *for Decorative Art, by the Worshipful Company of Painters, London.*

E. COSTAR,
GENERAL HOUSE DECORATOR,

129, CHURCH STREET, CROYDON.

W. P. WENHAM,
GAS, HOT WATER, & SANITARY ENGINEER,

81, CHURCH STREET, CROYDON.

Factory at Waddon.

ESTABLISHED 1852.

F. J. BURTON,
BLIND MANUFACTURER.

Spring Blinds of every description for Conservatories, Balconies, and Shop Fronts.

MANUFACTORY:—71, NORTH END, CROYDON.

MRS. CLARK,
Old Established

CHINA AND GLASS WAREHOUSE,

22, CHURCH STREET, CROYDON.

Brooms, Mats, Ironmongery, Tinware, Knives, Forks and Electro-plated Goods.

China and Glass Rivetted. Goods Lent on Hire.

JOHN HORROCKS,
BUILDER AND CONTRACTOR,

STEAM SAWING AND MOULDING MILLS,

THE OVAL, EAST CROYDON.

JOSEPH MOORE,
GENERAL ENGINEER AND MACHINIST,

Maker of Two to Four-horse power Vertical Engines and Boilers. Water Engines for Organ Blowing. Brick-making Plant; Force and Lift Pumps, &c. &c.

Planing, Shaping, Screw Cutting, Smith's Work, and Repairs of all kinds.

WORKS :—OVERTON'S YARD, SURREY STREET, CROYDON.

ESTABLISHED 1870.

GREEN,
"CROWN HOTEL," CROYDON.

Dinners, Ball Suppers, Wedding Breakfasts, &c. Provided.

WINE & SPIRIT MERCHANT.

RICHARD WALTON,
GROCER AND CHEESEMONGER,

6 & 93, HIGH STREET,

CROYDON.

ALBION HOUSE.

D. B. MILLER,
MERCER AND GENERAL DRAPER,

1, HIGH STREET, AND 102 & 103, GEORGE STREET, CROYDON.

Departments:

Fancy Dresses.	Millinery and Underclothing.	Trimmings and Haberdashery.
Silks and Velvets.	Ribbons and Laces.	Calicoes and Linens.
Mantles and Costumes.	Hosiery and Gloves.	Blankets and Flannels.
Skirts and Corsets.	Sunshades and Umbrellas.	Damasks and Cretonnes.

Dressmaking in all its Branches.

FAMILY MOURNING OF EVERY DESCRIPTION.

Established upwards of 80 years.	A. ALLEN,
ALEXR. LOWE,	GLASS, CHINA, AND EARTHENWARE DEALER,
Practical Locksmith & Bellhanger,	35, ST. JAMES'S ROAD, CROYDON.
41, HIGH STREET, CROYDON.	*Toilet Sets, Breakfast, Dinner, Dessert, and Tea Services.*
Only First-class Work done.	Choice assortment of Tin, Iron, Baskets, Brooms. Tea and Coffee Urns. Goods lent on Hire.
J. MATTHEW,	
WAGGON, DRAY CART, AND VAN BUILDER,	ALEXR. SHAPCOTT,
Tyre and General Smith,	*Plumber, Gas, and Hot Water Engineer,*
SOUTHBRIDGE ROAD, CROYDON,	
Contractor to the Croydon Board of Health.	PUMP PAIL ROAD, CROYDON.

ROBT. W. FULLER & MOON,
AUCTIONEERS AND ESTATE AGENTS,

CROYDON & REIGATE.

AGENTS FOR THE ROYAL EXCHANGE LIFE AND FIRE ASSURANCE CORPORATION.

PURE WHOLE WHEAT MEAL BREAD.

W. BROWN,
Family Baker, Pastrycook, and Confectioner,

7, BROAD GREEN, CROYDON.

AGENT FOR THE TEA PLANTERS' ASSOCIATION.

Vienna Bread Daily.   Hot Rolls every Morning.   Families waited on Daily.
Wedding Breakfasts and Ball Suppers supplied.

ESTABLISHED 1859.

W. SHARP & CO.,

MINERAL WATER & GINGER BEER MANUFACTURERS,

SUMNER ROAD, CROYDON.

ALFRED SMITH
(LATE T. WELLER),
MANUFACTURING AND RETAIL JEWELLER,
GOLD AND SILVERSMITH,
WATCH AND CLOCKMAKER,
2, HIGH STREET, CROYDON.

Every Description of Clocks attended to by Yearly Contract.

THE ONLY MANUFACTURING CUTLERS IN CROYDON.

J. ALLDIS & SON,

MANUFACTURING AND WORKING CUTLERS,

30, SURREY STREET, CROYDON,

5, MARKET SQUARE, BROMLEY, KENT; & 27, GRAY'S INN ROAD, LONDON.

All kinds of Table and other Cutlery of the best quality and finish at the same prices as our London Establishment.
Carefully Assorted Stock of Knives and Scissors of every kind.
CUTLERY GROUND, REPAIRED AND POLISHED.

THRALE BROS.,

VETERINARY SURGEONS,

GEORGE STREET, CROYDON.

ESTABLISHED 1869.

F. A. EGLETON,

FURNISHING, AND BUILDERS' IRONMONGER,

LEAD, GLASS, OIL AND COLOUR MERCHANT,

2 & 3, LONDON ROAD

(Opposite West Croydon Railway Station).

Every description of Glass—Plate, Sheet, Coloured and Ornamental.
Paper Hangings in great variety; 100,000 pieces to select from.

MESSRS. PODMORE AND MARTIN,

AUCTIONEERS, SURVEYORS AND VALUERS,

AND

VALUERS FOR PROBATE AND LEGACY DUTY,

145, HIGH STREET, CROYDON,

AND

45, WEST STREET, HORSHAM.

ALFRED C. EBBUTT,
ART FURNITURE MANUFACTURER,
CARPET WAREHOUSEMAN AND
COMPLETE HOUSE FURNISHER.
CARVER & GILDER.
FACTORY AND SHOW ROOMS OPPOSITE TOWN HALL,
CROYDON.

PEARSON BROS.,
GROCERS AND PROVISION DEALERS,
5 & 6, DUPPA'S HILL PLACE,
CROYDON.

ESTABLISHED 1860.
A. E. THORNTON & CO.,
GENERAL HOUSE FURNISHERS.

UNDERTAKERS.

2, RAILWAY BUILDINGS, AND
8, PORTLAND ROAD, } NORWOOD JUNCTION.

J. PRINGLE,
GENERAL AND FURNISHING IRONMONGER,
GAS AND HOT WATER ENGINEER,
WESTOW STREET, UPPER NORWOOD, S.E.

JOHN OLDFIELD,	R. MORGAN,
LAND AND ESTATE AGENT—SURVEYOR,	
Valuer for Probate, Mortgages, &c.,	**PRINTER,**
80, NORTH END, CROYDON.	WESTOW STREET, UPPER NORWOOD, S.E.

R. H. JENKIN,
BUILDER AND CONTRACTOR,
FIRST-CLASS INTERIOR DECORATOR,
HOUSE AND ESTATE AGENT,
WESTOW STREET, UPPER NORWOOD, S.E.

Established for the sale of First-Class Produce.

C. AKERS,
TEA, WINE, SPIRIT, AND PROVISION MERCHANT,
NORWOOD HOUSE, AND 11, WESTOW HILL TERRACE,
UPPER NORWOOD, S.E.

KEEN & SON,

FIRST-CLASS INTERIOR DECORATORS,

CHURCH STREET, CROYDON.

W. WALKER,
GENERAL AND FURNISHING IRONMONGER, &c.,
36, HIGH STREET, SOUTH NORWOOD.

Dealer in Fenders, Fireirons, Cutlery, Electro Plate, China, Glass, Earthenware, Brooms, Brushes, Baths, Atkins' Lipscombe's and Doulton's Filters, &c.

per cent. allowed on all parcels of Furnishing Goods of 10s. and upwards, paid on or before delivery.

MESSRS. NEWBERRY & CO.,
AUCTIONEERS, VALUERS, AND ESTATE AGENTS,
3, STATION ROAD, SOUTH NORWOOD.

Printed List containing particulars of 1,000 properties to let or sell may be had on application.

ESTABLISHED 1854.
S. ASH,
FAMILY BAKER AND CONFECTIONER,
PORTLAND ROAD, SOUTH NORWOOD.

The only house in the neighbourhood for the celebrated Welsh Bread, made three times a week.

CARTS TO ALL PARTS DAILY.

N.B.—Bride, School, and other Cakes made to Order.

THE NORWOOD REVIEW	W. H. CHAPMAN,
AND CRYSTAL PALACE REPORTER.	*FIRST-CLASS PRACTICAL PAPERHANGER,*
First-Class Local Paper, circulating over a wide district.	GILDER & GENERAL DECORATOR.
Office for Advertisements, &c.,	PAPERHANGING WAREHOUSE,
WESTOW STREET, UPPER NORWOOD.	STATION ROAD, WEST CROYDON.

GAS AND HOT WATER ENGINEERS, PLUMBERS, &c.
S. & J. SQUIRRELL,
UPPER STATION ROAD, AND PORTLAND ROAD,
SOUTH NORWOOD.

IRON AND SMITH'S WORKS, PORTLAND ROAD.

Estimates given for General Repairs.

THOS. PASCALL & SONS,
MANUFACTURERS OF
BRICKS, TILES, DRAIN PIPES,
GARDEN POTS, CHIMNEY POTS, &C.

LIME, SAND, CEMENT, PLASTER, AND SANITARY GOODS MERCHANTS,

27, HIGH STREET, AND HARRINGTON ROAD,
SOUTH NORWOOD, SURREY, S.E.

Sole Manufacturers of Pascall's Patent Expanding Ridge Tiles.

BENJAMIN BUCKWORTH,

GENERAL DRAPERY WAREHOUSE,

12, NORTH END, CROYDON.

Always on hand a Large Assortment, at lowest possible Cash Price.

MILLINERY, MANTLE, AND COSTUME WAREHOUSE,

95 & 96, NORTH END

(Opposite).

DRESSMAKING ON THE PREMISES.   CHARGES MODERATE.

NOTE ADDRESS—BENJAMIN BUCKWORTH,

THE DRAPER,

CROYDON.

NORTH END IRONWORKS,

R. E. POWELL,

IRONMONGER, STOVE AND RANGE MAKER,

BELLHANGER, LOCKSMITH, TINMAN, AND BRAZIER,

PLUMBER,

GAS, HOT AND COLD WATER, AND SANITARY ENGINEER,

25, NORTH END, CROYDON.

OFFICE AND WORKS—100, TAMWORTH ROAD, CROYDON.

FIRST-CLASS

BUILDER AND DECORATOR.

F. R. DOCKING,

CARPENTER AND PLUMBER.

All work done under CONSTANT PERSONAL SUPERVISION.

JOHN WALTON,	JOHN WALTON'S
Corn, Seed, and Flour Merchant,	*ANIMAL MEDICINES.*
38, ST. JAMES'S ROAD, CROYDON.	LABORATORY—
Meals, &c., Wholesale and Retail.	ST. JAMES'S ROAD, CROYDON.
POULTRY, GAME, AND PIGEON FOOD.	Roup Pills and Tonic Paste for Poultry, Pigeons, &c.

G. KING & CO.,

COAL AND COKE MERCHANTS,

3, STATION ROAD, WEST CROYDON,

Desire to intimate to the Inhabitants of Croydon and neighbourhood, that all Orders, by Post or otherwise, with which they may be entrusted, will meet with immediate and careful attention.

BEST WALLSEND,   SILKSTONE,   KITCHEN,
,,   NEWCASTLE,   DERBY BRIGHTS,   BAKERS',
ANTHRACITE, STEAM, NUTS,

And all other kinds of Coal always on hand, and supplied at the Lowest Prices for Cash.

ESTABLISHED UPWARDS OF SIXTY YEARS.

G. J. BANCE & CO.,
UPHOLSTERERS,
CABINET MAKERS, BEDDING MANUFACTURERS,
AND
UNDERTAKERS,
117, HIGH STREET, CROYDON.
VALUATIONS MADE.

JOSEPH RIDLEY,

HOSIER, GLOVER,
AND
PRACTICAL SHIRT MAKER,

12, HIGH STREET, CROYDON.

WALTER HOPEKIRK,
ARTIST IN HAIR,
THE HAIR-DRESSING SALOONS,
CRYSTAL PALACE.

No. 8, WESTOW HILL TERRACE, UPPER NORWOOD.	No. 238, WESTMINSTER BRIDGE ROAD, LONDON.

Tailor and Habit Maker. *Servants' Liveries, &c.*	THE NOTED AND WELL-KNOWN LONDON TAILOR. **E. GREENBOAM,**	*Naval and Military Uniforms.*

32, CHURCH STREET, CROYDON.
65, 66 & 67, GRACECHURCH STREET, } LONDON.
43 & 44, LOMBARD STREET,
Gentlemen can be waited upon by an Experienced London Man.

G. WATERS, *FAMILY BAKER AND CONFECTIONER,* ELYS DAVY'S ROAD, CROYDON. Wedding and School Cakes. Pastry made to Order. Families waited on Daily.	ALFRED J. POPE, *GENERAL PRINTER,* 40, ST. JAMES'S ROAD, WEST CROYDON. Established 1870.

GILLINGHAM & SON,
M.R.C.V.S.L.
VETERINARY SURGEONS,
LOWER CHURCH STREET, CROYDON.
SHOEING ESTABLISHMENTS.
HOSPITAL FOR HORSES.   HORSES EXAMINED.

ESTABLISHED 1849.
RUSSEN & SONS,
LONDON AND SUBURBAN CARRIERS.

London Depôt—WESTON STREET, TOOLEY STREET, LONDON BRIDGE.
Croydon Depôt—OLD PALACE YARD, CHURCH STREET.
OMNIBUSES, BREAKS, AND VANS.
Furniture, Luggage, Pictures, Glasses, and Pianos Removed and Warehoused.
ESTIMATES FREE.

ESTABLISHED 1859.

C. STAGG & SON,

CARPENTERS, BUILDERS, CONTRACTORS, AND GENERAL HOUSE DECORATORS,

CHURCH ROAD, CROYDON.

ESTIMATES GIVEN FOR EVERY DESCRIPTION OF WORK.

Greenhouses built and fitted up on the most improved principles. All kinds of Sanitary Work promptly attended to. Venetian Blinds made and repaired. Orders by post promptly attended to.

B. ROBERSON,

COACH, VAN, AND CART BUILDER,

In all its branches,

14, PARSON'S MEAD, WEST CROYDON,

Two Minutes' Walk from West Croydon Station.

THE CROYDON AND SURREY SCHOOL OF ART,	ART EXHIBITION ROOMS,
GEORGE STREET, CROYDON.	GEORGE STREET, CROYDON.
Head Master,	Secretary and Manager,
Mr. MONTAGUE WIGZELL.	Mr. MONTAGUE WIGZELL.

Established upwards of a Century.	*Established* 1798.
W. PLOWMAN,	**BUTT AND PEERLESS,**
WHOLESALE AND RETAIL BASKET, SIEVE, AND HAMPER MANUFACTURER,	SHOEING SMITHS, &c., PRACTICAL SMITHS IN GENERAL,
12, *SURREY STREET, CROYDON.*	11, SOUTH END, AND COOMBE STREET,
Cane and Fancy Chairs Re-Seated. Basket Carriages Re-Wickered. Coopering, &c.	CROYDON.

RIDGE & BROUGHTON,

ART DECORATORS,

CROYDON.

Old Established Coal Depôt, THORNTON HEATH RAILWAY STATION.	Established upwards of 50 Years.
J. WRATTEN,	**A. GROSSMITH,**
COAL AND COKE MERCHANT,	GLOVE AND GAITER MAKER,
FURZE ROAD,	13, *SURREY STREET, CROYDON.*
THORNTON HEATH.	All kinds of Leggings kept in Stock. Washleather, Housemaids' Gloves, Gardening Gloves, Satchels, Straps, &c. Braces and Leather Purses.
Orders by post or otherwise promptly attended to for Cash.	Noted House for Driving Gloves. Waterproof Coats Repaired, &c.

MESSRS. COLE & SON,

EAGLE BREWERY,

SOUTH END, CROYDON

Guarantee that their Ales are brewed from Malt and Hops *only*.

PRICE LIST ON APPLICATION.

PARK HILL NURSERY,
And at East Croydon Station.
C. CHAFF,
NURSERYMAN, SEEDSMAN, AND FLORIST.

Balls and Evening Parties furnished with Plants, &c.

CHOICE CUT FLOWERS, WEDDING AND OTHER BOUQUETS TO ORDER.

Estimates for laying out and planting Gardens.

GARDENS KEPT BY CONTRACT OR PER DAY.

CONTRACTOR TO THE ROYAL PALACES.

J. MORLEY,
WOOD BROKER AND CHARCOAL MANUFACTURER,

BROAD GREEN, CROYDON.

S. PROBERT,
2, NORTH END, CROYDON, AND 35, BOROUGH HIGH STREET,

FAMILY HOSIER AND OUTFITTER,

Spécialité:—PERFECT FITTING SHIRTS.

A SAMPLE MADE TO MEASURE FOR APPROVAL.

ALL THE BEST MAKES IN GLOVES AND HOSIERY.

N.B.—Gentlemen Waited on at Office or Residence.

E. AYLING,
PORTRAIT, LANDSCAPE, AND ARCHITECTURAL PHOTOGRAPHER,

172, HANDCROFT ROAD, CROYDON.

Estimates given to Estate Agents, Builders, Masons, &c. Photographs of all the Churches and Public Buildings in Croydon and Neighbourhood.

HOLLY HOUSE.	C. W. COOPER,
WILLIAM SNELL,	GAS, HOT WATER, & SANITARY ENGINEER,
BREAD AND BISCUIT BAKER,	SOLE AGENT FOR THE ALBO-CARBON LIGHT
1, SOUTHBRIDGE PLACE, CROYDON	IN CROYDON.
(*Near the Waldron's*).	
ilies waited on daily. School Cakes made to order.	5, LOWER ADDISCOMBE ROAD, CROYDON.

TURRELL & SONS,
HORTICULTURAL BUILDERS AND RUSTIC WORKERS,

SOUTH NORWOOD RUSTIC WORKS,

ADJOINING SELHURST STATION, } CROYDON.
AND AT STEAM WORKS, PAWSON'S ROAD,

(The Tramway passes the Works at Selhurst.)

mmer Houses and Conservatories made to any Design. Dealer in all kinds of Building Materials. A large Stock of Rustic Work to select from. Goods delivered Free to any distance.

JAMES HOOKER,
LEAD, WINDOW GLASS, PAPER-HANGINGS,

OIL AND COLOUR MERCHANT,

REMOVED FROM 101, NORTH END, TO

OPPOSITE PUBLIC HALL, GEORGE STREET,

CROYDON.

Established 1842.

J. B. SHAKESPEARE,
UNDERTAKER,
FUNERALS CONDUCTED TO ALL PARTS.
The Trade Supplied.
PRIVATE ADDRESS:—10, SCARBROOK ROAD,} CROYDON.
OFFICE & WORKSHOPS:—CHURCH ROAD,

A. BOULDEN,
TALLOW CHANDLER, MELTER, AND WHOLESALE OILMAN,
28, *SURREY STREET, CROYDON,*
AND AT 160 & 358, OLD KENT ROAD, AND 18, WESTMORELAND ROAD, WALWORTH.
Lamps of every Description; and Oils of the finest quality.

JAMES HAYWARD,
LIME MERCHANT,
HALING LIME WORKS,
BRIGHTON ROAD; AND AT THE WINDSOR CASTLE, CROYDON.
Stone, Chalk and Ground Lime. Sand and Flints.

J. R. BEX,	THOMAS WHITE,
CARPENTER, JOINER, AND UNDERTAKER,	CAB AND FLY PROPRIETOR,
1, *DERING ROAD.*	"*GEORGE THE FOURTH*" *YARD,*
SOUTHBRIDGE ROAD, CROYDON.	GEORGE STREET, CROYDON.
Whitewashing, Painting, Paper-Hanging, &c.	Office:—61, George St., near St. Matthew's Church.
Estimates given.	*All Orders punctually attended to.*

A. T. BURT,
CARVER, GILDER, AND PICTURE FRAME MAKER,
14, *SURREY STREET, CROYDON.*
Old Frames Regilt. Old Paintings and Prints Cleaned and Restored. Importer of Window, Coloured and Ornamental Glass.
GLASS SHADES OF EVERY DESCRIPTION.
Birds and Animals Preserved and Mounted. The Trade supplied with all kinds of Moulding.

OLD CURIOSITY SHOP.
E. REEVES,
COOPER AND BROKER,
DEALER IN ALL KINDS OF NEW AND SECOND-HAND FURNITURE,
WEST STREET, NEXT DOOR TO THE CHAPEL,
AND 69, PARSON'S MEAD, CROYDON.
Casks Bought, Sold, and Repaired. Water Butts of every size, from 30 to 200 Gallons.
Every description of Coopering Work done.

Established 1851.
T. HILL,
STONE AND MARBLE MASON,
QUEEN'S ROAD, CROYDON
(Opposite the Cemetery).
Estimates given for every description of Stone, Marble, and Granite Work.
Designs of Monuments, Head Stones, &c., sent on application.
MONUMENTS REPAIRED. INSCRIPTIONS ENGRAVED. LETTERS IN LEAD.

By Appointment to His Grace the Archbishop of Canterbury and the Right Rev. the Lord Bishop of Rochester.

HANSCOMB & CO.,
UMBRELLA MANUFACTURERS,
7, CROWN HILL, CROYDON,
ESTABLISHED UPWARDS OF HALF A CENTURY.

Umbrellas Repaired and Re-covered with dispatch. A good Assortment of Walking Sticks always in Stock.

ALF^D. BULLOCK,
CONTRACTOR,
FURNITURE, &c., REMOVED BY SPRING VANS,
SOUTHBRIDGE PLACE, AND TANFIELD ROAD,
CROYDON.

Carting in all its branches. Orders by Post punctually attended to. Estimates given.

EDWIN J. COLLINS,
PURVEYOR OF PURE MILK AND CREAM,
BEDFORD DAIRY,
GLOUCESTER ROAD, CROYDON.

Cows kept for Infants and Invalids.
FAMILIES REGULARLY SUPPLIED WITH GENUINE MILK AND CREAM.
All Orders shall meet with prompt attention.

ALFRED KNIGHT,	H. PINYON,
FURNISHING UPHOLSTERER,	COAL MERCHANT,
67, *GEORGE STREET, CROYDON*,	GRANT ROAD, ADDISCOMBE,
Opposite the Public Hall.	(Adjoining Addiscombe Road, Station.)
Linoleum, Staines' Make only in Stock, at London Prices.	Orders by Post, or otherwise, promptly attended to.

GEO. FINDLAY,

MASON AND CONTRACTOR,

GLOUCESTER ROAD, CROYDON.

JOHN BRADFORD,	S. WEBB,
ENGLISH & FOREIGN TIMBER MERCHANT,	PORK BUTCHER,
STEAM SAW MILLS.	36, *SURREY STREET, CROYDON.*
KNIGHT'S YARD, MITCHAM ROAD, CROYDON.	Pure Lard, Pork, and German Sausages.
Contractor for Railway, Park, and other Fencing.	Smoked Sausage and Saveloys, Wholesale and Retail, all made on the Premises and guaranteed genuine.

Established upwards of 100 Years.

CHARLES RUSSELL
(Successor to H. CORNFIELD),
FAMILY BAKER, &c.,
2, *CROSS ROAD, CROYDON.*

FAMILIES WAITED UPON DAILY.

T. DEAN,

EAST SURREY FOUNDRY,

PITLAKE BRIDGE,

CROYDON, S.

ARNOLD AND COLDWELLS,

HATTERS, TAILORS, AND MILITARY OUTFITTERS,

78 & 79, NORTH END, CROYDON.

GRANT BROS.

(From Marshall & Snelgrove),

GENERAL AND FANCY DRAPERS,

SILK MERCERS AND MILLINERS,

8 & 9, HIGH STREET,

CROYDON.

Specialities in all Departments.

Show Rooms for Mantles, Jackets, &c.

FAMILY MOURNING OF EVERY DESCRIPTION.

H. HATCH,

BUTCHER,

111, HIGH STREET, CROYDON.

FAMILIES WAITED UPON DAILY FOR ORDERS.

(*No Connection with any other House.*)

PICKLED TONGUES. SOUTH DOWN MUTTON.

D. H. WESTON,

WINE, SPIRIT, ALE AND STOUT MERCHANT,

25A, NORTH END, CROYDON.

AGENT FOR

MAX GREGER'S CARLOWITZ IN FLAGONS AND BOTTLES,

BEER AND CO.'S PRIZE MEDAL CANTERBURY ALES.

Mark.	4½ jars.	9 gallon casks.	18 gallon casks.
A B		7s. 6d. nett	15s. nett.
A A	4s. 6d. nett	9s. nett	17s. nett

In Imperial Pint Bottles, 2s. 6d. per Dozen.

WILLIAM STEVENSON,

Grocer, Tea Dealer, and Provision Merchant,

123 & 124, HIGH STREET, CROYDON.

WINE & SPIRIT MERCHANT.

B. CULPECK,

COACH AND HARNESS MAKER,

6, 7 & 8, LONDON ROAD, CROYDON.

J. A. SMITH,

WATCH AND CLOCK MAKER,

31, CHURCH STREET, CROYDON.

A large assortment of Clocks, Gold and Silver Watches and Jewellery, Jet Brooches and Earrings, Spectacles, &c.
All kinds of Watches and Clocks Cleaned and Repaired.
ENGRAVING, GILDING, AND PLATING. HAIR DEVICES TASTEFULLY MADE UP.
N.B.—J. A. S. guarantees a Personal Superintendence of all Repairs entrusted to him.

BARRITT & DIX,	J. E. CHAPMAN,
DISPENSING CHEMISTS,	COOK AND CONFECTIONER,
36, HIGH STREET, CROYDON.	3, HIGH STREET, CROYDON.
Physicians' Prescriptions and Family Recipes carefully dispensed.—Genuine Drugs.	Soups, Jellies, Creams, Ices, Bride Cakes, &c. Families supplied with Pure Bread.
J. ROGERS,	BENNETT & SON,
FAMILY OILMAN,	*PLUMBERS, GASFITTERS & DECORATORS,*
BROAD GREEN,	107, HIGH STREET, CROYDON.
For Genuine Soap and Pure Oils.	

CHARLES THORPE

(Late of Crystal Palace),
NATURALIST,
16, SOUTH END, CROYDON.

Birds, Animals, &c., Modelled to Nature. Skins of every description Dressed and made into Rugs. Plumes and Humming Birds mounted for Ladies' Hats.
ENTOMOLOGICAL APPARATUS.
A Large Collection of British Insects always in Stock.

ARTIFICIAL TEETH.

HIGH-CLASS DENTISTRY AT MODERATE CHARGES.

MR. W. G. FENN,

SURGEON-DENTIST,

100, GEORGE STREET,
CROYDON.

www.ingramcontent.com/pod-product-compliance
Lightning Source LLC
Chambersburg PA
CBHW032142230426
43672CB00011B/2419